THE
INTERNATIONAL
LIVING
GUIDE TO
RETIRING
OVERSEAS
on a Budget

THE
INTERNATIONAL
LIVING

GUIDE TO

RETIRING
OVERSEAS
on a *Budget*

How to Live Well on $25,000 a Year

SUZAN HASKINS
DAN PRESCHER

WILEY

Library of Congress Cataloging-in-Publication Data:

Haskins, Suzan.
The international living guide to retiring overseas on a budget : how to live well on $25,000 a year /
  Suzan Haskins, Dan Prescher.
      pages cm
    ISBN 978-1-118-75859-5 (cloth); ISBN 978-1-118-86316-9 (ebk); ISBN 978-1-118-86315-2 (ebk)
        1. Retirees—Finance, Personal.   2. Investments.   3. Retirement, Places of—Foreign countries.
  4. Retirement income.   I. Precher, Dan.   II. Title.
  HG179.H3197   2014
  332.024'014—dc23

                                                                                    2013045012

Printed in the United States of America
10 9 8 7 6 5 4 3 2 1

CONTENTS

PART THREE
Once You Get There: Adjusting to Your New Life

CHAPTER 19
Changes in Latitudes, Changes in Attitude: Maintaining the Bridge between Your Past and Present Lives

CHAPTER 20
When the Hammock Gets Boring: What to Do after You Retire and Move Overseas

CHAPTER 21
Moving On: This Is Not a One-Way Highway

EPILOGUE
If We Knew Then What We Know Now

INDEX

FOREWORD

IN 1979, I STARTED A LITTLE NEWSLETTER called *International Living*. It explored a fairly contrarian idea at the time: the idea that you could move abroad and save money as well as living a happier, richer, and even healthier life.

International Living grew out of a love of international travel and a belief that the world is alive with opportunities—for fun, personal growth, adventure, and profit. And those opportunities are closer at hand than you might imagine. Everybody says the world is getting smaller, but it is actually getting larger. New air routes are opening all the time. Exotic island paradises and bustling metropolitan centers on the other side of the world are easily accessible. Huge countries that were off limits only a few years ago are now open for business as well as travel.

When *International Living* started, we hoped to open up new possibilities for its readers. To give them new ideas about places to visit . . . and live. To show them ways to make their international lifestyle profitable, or at least self-supporting. To help them adjust to a rapidly changing world.

Today, some 30-odd years later, the idea of living a happier, healthier life overseas for a fraction of what the same lifestyle would cost in the United States isn't quite as contrarian as it used to be. But it's still a little out of the box. The vast majority of U.S. citizens will never obtain a passport, much less seriously consider moving to Panama or Uruguay or Italy.

But as the economic ride in the United States gets bumpier, more people than ever are realizing that looking beyond their own shores is not just a viable option—it's often the smartest move they can make. And this realization isn't limited to retirees. Young people, families with children, business entrepreneurs, investors, and many others are finding better opportunities, lower startup costs, less regulation, improved health care, greater freedom, and generally lower costs of living abroad.

Two early adopters of this international lifestyle were Suzan Haskins and Dan Prescher, who made their move overseas in 2001 and have been living the expat life ever since. They've been writing and reporting on their travels, trials, and triumphs in Latin America for more than a decade now. Their experience is unmatched when it comes to identifying the best locations and strategies for a successful move abroad.

In this book, Suzan and Dan distill their years of experience into a well-researched manual that not only gives the reader the best potential locations to consider, but also a detailed blueprint showing how to approach, plan, and follow through on the journey.

Whatever your reason for considering a move overseas, you'll find this book invaluable. Suzan and Dan know the road and show you the best way to reach your own destination—a happier, healthier, and more prosperous life abroad.

It's a great journey, but there are traps and pitfalls to avoid. This book can serve as your trusty guide.

—Bill Bonner
Founder, *International Living*

INTRODUCTION

What if you could retire better, more affordably, and *even earlier* than you expected?

WHEN WE LEFT OMAHA IN 2001 to work as editors for *International Living* magazine in Quito, Ecuador, this idea—that you could live better for less in an overseas locale that closely matched your idea of paradise—was relatively novel. We could pretty much count all the "gringos" living in Ecuador at the time on one hand. Two or three in Cuenca, a handful in Vilcabamba, another handful in Otavalo. Most of the expats in Ecuador lived in Quito and were associated with the petroleum industry. Only a few were baby boomer "retirees."

But over the years, we've met more and more people who've done what we have.

They've left the rat race of the workaday world behind and relocated to places like Ecuador, Panama, Costa Rica, Mexico, Spain, Malaysia, and more . . . with warmer weather, a better quality of life, less crime, more cultural activities, healthier and less expensive food, better and less expensive health care . . . and they're enjoying every bit of it for about $2,000 a month or less, *all in*. Many of them aren't even of "official" retirement age.

Ron and Terresa Moore, for example, have been retired in Ecuador since 2009—long enough for Ron's ponytail to grow all the way down his back. In 2008, though, when Ron was 54 and Terresa was 50, they were struggling. They'd lost a third of their nest egg and were so close to losing their home that all they could do was walk away.

Today they own two homes in Ecuador outright: one in an always-perfect-weather mountain climate and another front and center on a gorgeous stretch of beach where, from their balcony, they watch pelicans bob and dolphins frolic in the surf—not to mention amazing sunsets. (Both homes are just a fraction of a degree from the equator, by the way.)

Believe it or not, to maintain both homes and pay all their utility bills, medical insurance, health care expenses, prescriptions, food, entertainment—everything—*Ron and Terresa's monthly expenses average just $1,000 a month!*

Gary DeRose, on the other hand, lives with his girlfriend, Kate, in a beautiful, historic Mexican city where he plays in a blues band and acts in local theater productions. He takes in symphony concerts and goes to gallery openings, and, being a gourmet cook, he loves the fresh produce available in the local markets.

Like Ron and Terresa, Gary owns his home outright. It has a swimming pool and a pretty, walled courtyard with a fountain. He's only about 45 minutes from the beach and the weather allows him to swim there or in his pool year-round. By moving overseas, Gary, too, was able to retire at a younger-than-normal age—at just 53. Of course it helps that, as he reports, *Gary and Kate's expenses average about $3,000 a month.*

In another Pacific Coast beach community in Panama with year-round perfect weather, Ellen Cook and her husband, John, enjoy a golf course, an equestrian center, loads of great restaurants, three shopping centers with several upscale 24-hour supermarkets, and a modern medical clinic.

But the best thing, says Ellen, is the low price tag of it all. A cancer survivor, she pays $1 to see an oncologist for regular checkups at a public hospital. She paid just $1.50 at such a hospital for physical therapy treatments she needed for a knee injury.

Ellen and John's total monthly living expenses amount to about $1,500. They don't have rental costs since they own their home, but their monthly expenses include utilities, insurance, property taxes, Internet, gas for the car, medical bills . . . even food, "which is a big part of our spending," Ellen admits. "We mostly eat at home but we go out to dinner once a week."

These stories are not unique. In case after case, would-be retirees are discovering that by expanding their focus to include options outside the United States and Canada, they're finding a dizzying array of solutions to their financial and lifestyle challenges.

In the following pages, we'll take a detailed look at the steps involved in successfully living and retiring abroad. We'll introduce you to the countries that we think make the most sense for retirees looking for better weather and a lower cost of living without sacrificing safety or modern amenities.

We'll include examples and stories of expats who have already made the move. We'll learn from their triumphs *and* their mistakes, including our own . . . and rest assured, since we moved abroad in 2001, we've had plenty of both as we've lived in seven locations in four countries!

We'll give you the knowledge you need and outline the actions you can take to make your own successful move to the place of your dreams. We'll take you step-by-step through the process . . . from beginning your research to getting organized and actually making the move.

Importantly, with this information, you'll know better whether or not you even want to move overseas in the first place. The international lifestyle is not for everybody; it's not even for most people. It takes a huge appetite for novelty, adventure, problem solving, and stepping out of your comfort zone. We've found these to be exactly the things that keep us engaged, active, and feeling young each day. But not everyone feels the same way about the challenges of living abroad.

The truth is, back in 2001 when we made our move, there wasn't a lot of guidance about retiring overseas—at least not readily available on the Internet. (And much of the information you'll find on the Internet today is either outdated or just plain wrong.) So our decision to make the move was based primarily on gut reaction and our personal penchant never to have any regrets in life.

We didn't want to look back sometime in the future and wonder, "What if?" And after all, if we could retire to a place with better weather . . . where we could have a better quality of life but for a greatly reduced cost of living . . . why wouldn't we?

Note: All prices quoted in this book are in U.S. dollars.

PART ONE

Contemplating an Exciting Move . . .

FOR YEARS, WE'D KNOWN IT WAS COMING: More than 10,000 of us—*in the United States alone*—are turning 65 every day. That's 79 million people drawing Social Security benefits and at the mercy of Medicare. And, by the way, we're now living longer than ever.

We have a lot of time left . . . but not so much that we don't want to enjoy every minute of it. So just like we did way back when, in the 1960s and 1970s, some members of our generation are challenging conventional ideas and seeking alternatives. We're taking matters into our own hands and carving out a revolutionary retirement experience.

If you think about it, people have long sought greener pastures for their retirement years. Our grandparents retired from the farm to town. Our parents retired to Florida and Arizona. And us . . . well, we're rebels at heart. Dreamers. Adventurers. Inclined to march to the beat of a different drummer—no matter how exotic or offbeat.

As the late John Lennon said about our generation in the 1960s, "We were all on this ship . . . going to discover a New World." While it's not the '60s any longer, the journey never ended. Now, with so many of us in our fifties, sixties, and seventies, we look a little different, for sure, but we're still all about seeking new experiences and exploring New Worlds.

And why should retirement be any different?

1

Can You Afford to Retire Where You Live?

WE EXITED THE TERMINAL with our 90-pound chocolate Lab trotting at our side. He was delighted to have been liberated from his travel crate after the short four-hour flight from Miami. A smiling porter followed along, carting our two large suitcases and four huge cardboard boxes. (This was back when airlines allowed three pieces of luggage each—and a dog—at no extra charge.)

It was November 1, 2001, and we had jettisoned our previous lives to begin anew in Quito, Ecuador. Just as the thick fog that wrapped its arms around us that night, the future felt fresh and full of possibility.

The Ecuadorian friends we had met on a previous visit greeted us with cheers and hugs and loaded us up for the short ride to the home we'd rented for the coming year. Located in one of the city's most charming neighborhoods, it had four bedrooms, two bathrooms, a guesthouse, and a gorgeous walled garden. The rent was just $600 a month.

As we walked into the house, the fireplace was roaring . . . more for ambience than anything else. November evenings in Quito are warm compared to our home state of Nebraska. The comforting fire and the kindness of new friends melted any hesitations we'd had about reversing the course of our lives in our mid-forties.

Why had we sold everything and run away from our lucrative marketing business? We were tired of the rat race. Tired of chasing the almighty dollar. Plain and simple, we were tired. And this was "our time." With kids grown and parents still in great health, this was our chance to strike out on our much-anticipated adventure.

Why Ecuador? If you've ever been there, you know the answer to that. It has miles of unspoiled beaches. Rich rainforest. The amazing Galápagos Islands. Historic colonial cities, and clean and healthy rural villages. . .

For us, the mountains beckoned. There's something about the Andes that steadies the soul. Llamas grazing the green slopes of snow-capped volcanoes . . . open-air markets overflowing with the biggest, brightest fruits and vegetables you've ever seen . . . the quick smiles and gentle nature of the people. . .

It doesn't hurt that Ecuador boasts extraordinary weather. No down parkas or snow shovels needed here. In its cities, you'll find great restaurants and shopping—a truly first-class infrastructure (and yes, high-speed Internet and excellent hospitals).

And then, of course, there's Ecuador's famous affordability. Although some prices have risen since our initial touchdown in 2001, you can still take a taxi just about anywhere in Quito for $1 to $5 and find a *menu del día*—usually a full-course meal of soup, salad, meat/rice/vegetables, dessert, and beverage—for $3 or less.

But back to our story. We left Ecuador at the end of 2002 because we wanted to experience more of Latin America. And since then, we've certainly done that. We've lived in seven different towns and cities in four countries—Ecuador, Mexico, Panama, and Nicaragua—researching and reporting about each of them as well as traveling extensively elsewhere in the world on behalf of *International Living*, which was founded in 1979 expressly to provide information to retirees looking for more satisfying and more affordable overseas lifestyles.

The Five Most Common Questions Asked about Moving Overseas

Q. Must I give up my citizenship if I move overseas?

A. No way! You can if you want, of course, but most expats don't. Instead, they get a residence visa in the country they move to. In some countries you can even live indefinitely on a tourist visa.

Q. Can I still collect my Social Security if I move overseas?

A. Yes, absolutely! In most cases, you can even have it direct-deposited into your new foreign bank account.

Q. What about Medicare? Will it cover me overseas?

A. Unfortunately not. But in many countries, you'll find better, lower-cost options for health care. We know expats paying as little as $50 a month for a full-coverage health plan.

Q. Must I still pay U.S. or Canadian income taxes if I move overseas?

A. Maybe and maybe not. You certainly have to continue to file your annual tax return, but moving overseas can reduce your tax burden to the point where you may not owe much.

Q. Is it safe to live overseas?

A. We wouldn't suggest countries that aren't politically stable or don't have good public safety records. That said, you should exercise caution everywhere these days . . . including in the United States and Canada.

We've uprooted and moved so often that we joke that we've become "serial relocators." There's something about the romance of exploring new places and the honeymoon of making them your home. You could say that "Love the One You're With" has become our motto.

Four years ago, though, we came back to the Andes for a visit and now here we are, living in Ecuador once again—this time in the small mountain village of Cotacachi in the northern province of Imbabura. That doesn't mean, of course, that we'll be here for-ever. But when we add up all that Ecuador has to offer, *right now* and *at this point in time for us*, no other place matches up.

From the terrace of our condo (which we bought for $52,000 in 2010) we can watch the sun and clouds play across the mountains, the cows and horses grazing in the fields below. We can walk to the local *mercado* and purchase a tote bag full of fresh-from-the-farm fruits and veggies for $10 or less that will last us the entire week. (If the bag is too heavy, a taxi home costs just $1.)

For $5 we can select four dozen long-stemmed roses so fresh they last the entire month. For $10, we can hire someone to clean our home once a week. We don't pay rent or have a mortgage. We can easily live in Ecuador on a budget of $1,500 a month.

So how did we get so lucky? How did we manage to get out from under the plague of bad weather, bad debt, and rampant consumerism that so many Americans succumb to?

It was actually pretty easy. We thought about the direction our lives would go if we didn't take this opportunity. We had a lot of tedious "work years" ahead of us. A lot of snowstorms to dig out from. We did the math and figured that, on our savings (and we're not by any means wealthy), we could live very well on very little money. Anything we could earn to supplement that would be icing on the cake.

More and more of our fellow baby boomers, it appears, are cal-culating similar equations and looking for a way to rescue their retirement dreams. Today, interest in retiring overseas is growing by leaps and bounds. Every week we get more and more requests for interviews from the mainstream media and more inquiries from people who are in the same shoes we were in more than a decade ago.

Fortunately, the baby boomer generation is one that has always embraced change and new experiences. Typically, they're not afraid to take chances and they understand the potential gain is at least worth the consideration of a grand retirement adventure.

And because today's technology makes a move overseas almost as easy as a move across a state or the country, it's not hard to understand the appeal.

WHY ARE MILLIONS OF BABY BOOMERS RETIRING OVERSEAS?

It doesn't help that, as our friend, Gloria Yeatman, says, "Most of us can't afford to retire in the U.S. anymore. Besides, there's just a lack of civility in general in the U.S. these days, especially when it comes to how older people are treated."

Paul and Gloria's story may be similar to yours or that of someone you know.

Paul is 10 years older than Gloria; they met and married later in life. In 2008, when Paul started thinking about retiring, he didn't want Gloria to have to wait until she reached official retirement age.

But they were worried they didn't have enough money saved. They were afraid that the home they owned in Baltimore, which they hoped to rent out, wouldn't hold its value. They wondered if their IRAs would ever rebound.

Most of all, they worried about how they would be able to afford health care if they stopped working. (They'd be facing health insurance premiums of at least $1,000 a month.) What could they do, they wondered, and where could they go where their money might go further? Sound familiar?

So Paul and Gloria carefully considered their options.

Sure, they could downsize. Sell the house and everything else. They thought about moving to the southeastern United States. But what would they do about health insurance? Paying high premiums and out-of-pocket expenses for medications and doctor's visits was *not* an option.

It would be several years before Gloria was eligible for Social Security and both were too young for Medicare. If there was no money coming in, they'd burn through their retirement savings in no time. And then what would they do?

So they chose another option. They chose to do what millions of Americans and Canadians are doing. They retired overseas—to Costa Rica, where the weather is better and the cost of living is lower. And a top-notch and efficient health plan ensures that all citizens and legal residents—including foreign residents—have dependable and low-cost access to health care.

Yes, You Can Have Your Social Security Checks Sent to Your Overseas Bank or Address

The U.S. Social Security Administration says it sends about 550,000 payments overseas. The top 10 countries where these payments are sent are:

- Canada (108,200)
- Mexico (50,800)
- Japan (45,700)
- Germany (38,500)
- United Kingdom (33,300)
- Italy (32,600)
- Philippines (24,500)
- Greece (23,700)
- France (13,200)
- Portugal (12,500)

"We wanted to live in another culture, a Latin culture, and to speak Spanish . . . to broaden our perspective, to experience the fact that the rest of the world does not necessarily think, live, or make the same choices as we do in the United States," Gloria says. "We wanted to live less expensively, and that definitely includes affordable health care. We could afford to stop working full time and create a new life for ourselves and have more time to enjoy being together while we are both healthy."

So Paul and Gloria packed up and moved to Costa Rica where, as legal residents, they've joined and made use of the national health care system. Instead of spending $1,000 a month for health insurance with a high deductible, they pay just $55 a month (total for the both of them) for a full-coverage health plan with no deductible at all, through Costa Rica's national health system. *They're saving $11,340 per year in health insurance costs alone.*

"There is an incredible freedom knowing that you have affordable health care coverage and that you don't have to fear losing everything if you get sick," Paul says. "We had high hopes for the health care here in Costa Rica and we haven't been disappointed. We are saving money, yes, but we have also found the quality of health care here more than adequate, and in some areas, excellent."

Best of all, they say, it never snows in Costa Rica. In fact, the climate is so perfect that they don't need heat or air conditioning.

"That keeps costs low. Our goal was to retire on $2,000 a month or less," Gloria says, "and we're doing exactly that."

And you can easily do the same.

In fact, millions of American, Canadian, and European retirees have learned what Paul and Gloria have. Moving just a few hours by plane from where you live now can save you tens of thousands of dollars every year, and may mean you can finally afford and/or greatly reduce your health care costs. And living in a more welcoming climate may not only improve your overall quality of life, but also can actually improve your health.

In many cases, retiring overseas may mean the difference between working for another 10 years or more or retiring *now*.

The truth is, this idea of retiring overseas is no longer a radical one. While the U.S. Census doesn't track Americans living abroad, the State Department estimates close to 7 million Americans live outside the country—about 550,000 of these are military personnel and their families, and some of the others are employed by multinational companies. Others are those with dual citizenship. But many of the balance are retirees.

It's important to note that this number of 7 million only accounts for those who voluntarily report their status to U.S. embassies, and therefore even the State Department admits this is a soft estimate. Many of those living overseas never bother to check in with the State Department at all. We suspect the number of retirees relocating overseas—a number that has grown by more than 500 percent in the past 40 years—will continue to increase greatly going forward.

How Much Does It Cost to Retire Overseas?

Your cost of living will depend on your lifestyle, of course. In the countries you read about in this book, however, you should be able to reduce your living expenses by as much as 30 to 50 percent over what you may be spending in the United States or Canada . . . maybe more, depending where you choose to live.

Like Paul and Gloria Yeatman in Costa Rica, our friends, Edd and Cynthia Staton, say they're living very comfortably in Cuenca, Ecuador, on a budget of less than $2,000 a month. In fact, they report that they spend just $1,800 a month, and that includes rent.

"We live in a gorgeous two-story penthouse apartment," Edd says. "It's about 3,000 square feet, and we have four bedrooms, four-and-a-half baths, and expansive windows with a beautiful 270-degree view.

"Our budget includes all the regular expenses and more—fresh flowers, gym membership, massages, manicures and pedicures, and hair care for Cynthia."

Plus, Edd says, this includes doctor visits. "You usually get an appointment the same day you call, and they generally cost $25—and follow-ups are free!"

WHAT IF YOU COULD RETIRE EVEN EARLIER THAN EXPECTED?

Paul and Gloria Yeatman weren't expecting to retire when he was just 62 and she just 52.

"We weren't running away from family, debt, or jobs we hated," Gloria says. "We had jobs we liked, a great house with a fixed mortgage that we were able to pay, savings in the bank, and zero credit card debt."

But they also wanted to "enjoy." They wanted fun and adventure.

So they took a serious look at their financial situation and started thinking outside the box about what they could do to be able to retire early.

They made a checklist of everything they were looking for in a retirement destination. One thing they knew for sure, says Gloria, was that they wanted to live in a place where it never snowed. "Those heating and air conditioning bills in Baltimore were awful."

So they started doing some research about Costa Rica. They took an exploratory trip to see if everything they'd read about the friendly people, the temperate climate, the low cost of living, and the affordable health care was really true.

"We fell in love with Costa Rica on our first visit," Paul and Gloria write on their blog (RetireForLessinCostaRica.com). "Everyplace we went, we just kept saying, 'wow'—there is so much natural beauty in such a small country!"

At elevations from 3,000 to 5,000 feet, they found the weather in Costa Rica's Central Valley suited them perfectly. "Temperatures ranged about 65 to 80 degrees," Gloria says, "the air was clean and fresh, and our bedroom windows opened to the outdoors . . . no screens needed. There were lush, green tropical plants, and vivid flowers everywhere you looked. The people were kind and help-ful, making us feel welcome."

They went back home to "think about it," they write in their blog, "but all we could think about was going back, living, and retiring there."

Today, Paul and Gloria live in a comfortable three-bedroom home on a lush mountainside in Costa Rica's Central Valley—just 45 minutes from the beach—near what they call a "real *Tico* [Costa Rican] town." It's close to San José and the international airport, but not too close. And it has a good hospital and a univer-sity that offers many free cultural activities.

They spend a lot of time outdoors, they say. "Our porch is like a private getaway just outside our front door, overlooking the green all around us. Almost every evening, we turn on some jazz and have dinner by candlelight there. Sometimes we have guests, sometimes it's just us, but there's always candlelight and music."

They calculate that they've reduced their living expenses by 65 percent. That's not to say that some goods and services don't cost more in Costa Rica and there aren't occasional frustrations, but as expats anywhere in the world will tell you, learning to "live like a local" is part of the learning curve.

"There have been challenges, for sure," Paul says, "but we wouldn't change a thing."

Moving to Costa Rica allowed them not just to retire early but with the confidence that they wouldn't outlive their retirement savings.

"We've benefited far more than just financially," Gloria says. "We have wonderful friends here and have had so many enriching experiences. We absolutely love our lives."

We know hundreds of stories like Paul and Gloria's. Our friend, Gary DeRose, who we mentioned in the introduction to this book, retired to Mérida, the capital of Mexico's Yucatán state, at age 53. Ron and Terresa Moore retired to Ecuador when they were 55 and 51, respectively. Scores of others have stories just like these.

And yes, all of them had a retirement nest egg . . . but they knew if they stayed in the States it would soon be cracked beyond repair. So they put pencil to paper and did the calculations. How long could they live on their savings if they stayed at home? How many more years would they have to work before they could retire? How much would they save by retiring overseas *now*?

You can guess how the numbers worked out. And only you know if retiring early is the right move for you. But if you could retire early, and all it would take was a move to a safe and welcoming place with better weather, better scenery, and a lower cost of living, why wouldn't you?

▬▬▬

TECHNOLOGY MAKES IT ALL POSSIBLE

Like many baby boomers, we were both born smack dab in the middle of the post–World War II years—the Eisenhower era, when families moved in droves to affordable new homes in safe, tidy suburbs.

You could "see the USA in your Chevrolet" because the price of gasoline was about the same as a hamburger at the A&W. (We both clearly remember gas selling for 19 cents a gallon—and it was pumped for you by a smiling attendant.) Every summer we took a family vacation to a neighboring state or maybe even went as far as California to visit Disneyland.

Unlike our parents, we came of age with television instead of radio. Family Christmas cards were of us kids and the dog, proudly posed in front of our console TV/stereo combo—the most expensive piece of furniture we owned.

Times were prosperous then. Families could afford those big, new televisions . . . and electric washing machines and refrigerators (as well as the electricity to power them).

We played with Barbie dolls, Erector sets, board games, hula hoops. . . The most dangerous fad was a new thing called "rock 'n' roll," and it was served up on big, platter-sized disks called LPs.

Wow, have times changed. As you probably have, we've been big adopters of new technology. We're happy to report that smartphones and other gadgets—as well as high-speed Internet and satellite TV with all your favorite English-language channels—can pretty much be had anywhere in the world these days.

For those of us living overseas, the Internet has been a complete game changer. Not only can we instantly communicate with friends, family, colleagues, and others around the world; we can keep up with current events in any remote corner of the planet, we can source and buy anything and everything with a single mouse click. . . In fact, we can monitor and control every aspect of our lives, from our bank accounts to our blood pressure (which, sadly, aren't always independent of each other.) We can even have a real-time video chat with our friends and family back home, anytime we want.

Travel, too, has evolved to the point where you needn't put much thought into it. When we were kids, flying on an airplane was a big deal, a real event. Today, no one thinks much of it. It's nothing to board a plane on a cold, dark winter morning and a few hours later be digging into a lunch of fresh seafood on a sun-drenched beach in the Caribbean.

And of course, arranging for travel is easier than ever. From your kitchen table, you can access a myriad of websites that will help you compare and contrast itineraries and costs of travel by train, plane, automobile, motorcycle, bicycle, horseback, or any other mode of transportation that strikes your fancy. You can instantly find recommendations for hotels, restaurants, local attractions, individual tour guides, and more.

Thanks to today's technology, being an expat is pretty easy. Craving a craft beer? Looking for a dog groomer? Need a plumber? Solar panels? Organic chard? These are just a few things we've seen our expat neighbors searching for on local forums in recent months. Within minutes in most cases, they got the answers they were looking for. Nothing, it seems, is out of reach.

The point is, it's never been easier to be a citizen of the world. You truly can travel and live just about anywhere your heart desires without sacrificing much at all. And when you choose to live outside the United States or Canada, your cost of living will most likely drop dramatically.

2

Can You Really Live (*Well*) Overseas on $25,000 a Year?

ALTHOUGH IT WASN'T THE *ONLY*—OR EVEN the *primary*—reason, we moved overseas, the lure of a more affordable lifestyle was certainly a strong motivator. And it's one that's attracting more and more baby boomers to far-flung corners of the world.

After all, the opportunity to halve your cost of living and still enjoy better weather, healthier food, quality medical care, and a truly relaxed, "off the treadmill" pace of life is hard to pass up.

So what does it cost to live in one of those exotic locations you've been dreaming of? Well . . . how much does it cost to live where you live now? How much does it cost to live in Philadelphia or Phoenix, in Wichita or tiny Augusta, Arkansas?

IT'S PERSONAL . . . AND COMPLETELY SUBJECTIVE

The answer, of course, is completely subjective. It all depends on your personal needs, wants, and—most importantly—your comfort zone.

This is probably where we should share all those stories of people we know who are living a caviar lifestyle on a hot dog budget. And believe me, we have stories to tell. In fact, we've told many of those stories many times during our tenure as writers for *International Living*.

But a funny thing happens when we share someone else's budget . . .

Remember the old adage that if you don't want to end up in an argument, you should never talk about religion, politics, sex, or money? Probing into people's budgets and financial situations is intrusive. And there's always something they forget or choose to leave out (pet food, cigarettes, booze, guitar strings, travel), so answers are often not as accurate as they might be. And no fault implied. If we really knew how much we spent on our pets, hobbies, and vices, what fun would that be?

So instead of regaling you with other people's budgets, we'll share our own . . .

Make no mistake: We live well. We go out to lunch and dinner at least once a week. At home, we like to cook and we don't scrimp on ingredients. We enjoy the occasional martini or scotch, and every evening with dinner, we polish off a bottle of wine.

Dan and Suzan's Monthly Budget, Living in Cotacachi, Ecuador:

Homeowners' association dues:	$100
Electricity:	$25
Gas:	$5
Water and trash collection:	$2
Transportation (bus/taxis):	$5
Phone (land line) and Internet:	$55
Phone (cell phones):	$10
Satellite television:	$45
Medications:	$80
Groceries/alcohol	$675
Dining out	$250
Housecleaning	$45
Miscellaneous (clothes, music, guitar strings . . .)	$100
TOTAL:	$1,397

Unfortunately, wine and spirits are highly taxed in Ecuador (as are most imported items), so a good bottle of wine doesn't come cheap. But life is too short to drink cheap wine, so we consider its expense our most pleasurable splurge. If we were to give it up, our grocery bill would probably be more like $300 a month . . . maybe even less.

What's not included? Obviously, there is no line item for rent or house payment. We own our condo outright and have no expenses in that regard. The average rental property in the countries most popular with expats starts at about $300 a month. And that's for something very basic, often (but not always) unfurnished. In the small town in Ecuador where we live, you might expect to pay $600 a month for a nice, fully furnished, two- or three-bedroom rental . . . possibly even with utilities and Internet included. By the way, our annual property taxes are $52 and change.

You may also notice there's nothing listed for travel or health care. We occasionally treat ourselves to a night or two in Quito, and our costs for that vary greatly, depending if we stay at a hostel ($30 a night), a mid-range hotel ($80 a night) or a four-star hotel ($150 a night). In Quito we're usually on the prowl for ethnic food we can't get in our little town, and those costs can range anywhere from $4 or $5 per person for Indian food at a spartan hole-in-the-wall to $45 per person for a five-course tasting menu at an upscale Peruvian seafood or Argentine steak restaurant.

We travel back to the States to visit family at least once a year. Airfare seems to be always on the rise, so we budget $1,000 each for that. Once we get back to Arkansas or South Dakota, our expenses can vary greatly, depending on whether we're staying with family and friends or off on our own.

As for health care, because we travel extensively for our work, we've opted for a private international policy that covers us anywhere in the world we travel. We have a $5,000 deductible and the policy costs a bit more than $5,800 a year. Most expats, however, opt for a local-coverage health plan, which costs far less. (Read about health care options in Chapter 5.)

Add it all up and you can see that our annual expenses hover right at $25,000. And that's with no sacrifice or frugality on our parts. We could certainly spend less. And we know plenty of people who do. We also have friends who spend far more than we do. They live in spacious city apartments or large beach homes and have all the boats, cars, bells, and whistles.

Your cost of living is a personal issue. We've no doubt you can live on $25,000 a year, as we do, in many of the world's most popular retirement destinations. But we stress: Reducing your cost of living should not be your only reason for retiring overseas. This has to be something you *want* to do, not something you feel *forced* to do.

Don't Forget about Startup Costs and Unexpected Expenses

In your first months of living overseas, we'd suggest you have a financial cushion of at least $3,000 if you're single and double that for a couple, because you'll spend that much or more on visas, rental deposits, household items, and other startup expenses. And be sure to budget for unexpected expenses that will always occur, no matter where you live, such as medical and dental bills or new eyeglasses, replacing a broken computer or appliance, and so on. And put a little aside for an emergency fund and/or for trips back home.

STRATEGIES FOR REDUCING YOUR RETIREMENT COSTS OVERSEAS

Choose Your "Place" Wisely

Some countries can be more affordable than others. The best advice we can give is to do your due diligence before you bust a move overseas.

And just as at home, some cities and towns can be more affordable than others. It's pretty much a given that it costs more to live in a city than in the countryside. There are just far more temptations in cities . . . more places to spend money in and more things to spend it on—cultural activities, restaurants, shopping, transportation costs, and so on. That's not to say you should avoid city living. If that's the lifestyle you're after, don't deny yourself. But do choose wisely.

Same thing goes for weather. It's unlikely you're looking to move to a place with colder, drearier weather, where a good chunk of your monthly bill will go to heating costs. But keep in mind that in some warm-weather climates, your air conditioning bills may be hefty.

In Latin America and Asia, for example, electricity costs may be higher than you're used to at home. That's why hotels often give you key cards to slip into a wall slot for power. Remove the key card, leave the room, and the power goes off. It's also why most homes in these regions utilize mini-split air conditioning units rather than central or whole-house air cooling. If you cool just the rooms you use, you can save greatly.

If you have your heart set on living at the beach, you'll figure out how to save on the air conditioning that you'll no doubt want in your bedroom on a hot summer night. And of course, what you save on other line items in Latin America or Asia—like health care or rent—may offset your air conditioning costs.

Our advice: If cost of living is of critical importance to you, consider mountain and higher-elevation locales in the tropics—Lake Chapala or San Miguel de Allende in Mexico, Costa Rica's Central Valley, Panama's mountain communities of Boquete or Volcán, and the Andes Mountains of Ecuador or Colombia. Freshly grown local produce is abundant and affordable, and you'll rarely need heat or air conditioning. For our small two-bedroom condo in Ecuador, our monthly utility expenses rarely exceed $25 for electricity, $2 for water, and $5 for propane for hot water and cooking.

Consider Travel and Transportation Costs

This goes hand in hand with choosing the right place to live. But it's so important it deserves its own category. You may think that you'll rarely need to go back to your country of origin, but as they say, "Life is what happens while you're busy making other plans."

Certainly, you'll want to go back to visit children and grandchildren, parents, and other family members—especially for special occasions like weddings, graduations, and the birth of a new baby.

And when you least expect it, the 3 *F*s could come calling: Family emergencies, friends in need, and financial issues may require a quick trip back home.

Be sure you budget for these events or that you consider your options. It may make sense to live somewhere with access to an international airport with frequent, low-cost flights to the States and Canada. Mexico and Central America offer many good options in this regard.

One of the best things about moving overseas is that you may not need a car. Coming from a city like Omaha where it is essential to have a car (or two), we were happy car owners when we lived in Mexico, Panama, and Nicaragua. But did we *need* a car in those places? Not really. And when we moved to Ecuador we decided that car ownership was no longer a justifiable expense.

In Ecuador, the cost of gasoline is just $1.50 a gallon, and public transportation is ridiculously affordable. A taxi ride anywhere within Cotacachi, where we live, is just a dollar or two. It costs us 25 cents for the 20-minute bus ride to the larger town of Otavalo, where we can catch a bus onward to Quito for $2. A driver with a

---

Living "Outside the Expat Zone" Can Be a Big Money-Saver . . .

Even in First-World Europe

In response to a blog post we wrote for the Huffington Post about how to save money overseas was this comment:

"I moved to rural Europe a few years ago. Unemployed in the U.S. for a couple of years and had to move to find work. Seems to have worked out as a perfect fit. Slow pace of life, healthy living, inexpensive food and housing, beautiful women, great wine and neighbors that watch out for one another. Not to mention unbelievable art, museums, castles and some of the best preserved ancient ruins in Europe.

"I'm still working for another 3–4 years but living pretty well on $1300+/- USD/mo. That's even taking a couple of trips on the

---

motorcycle a month for 2–4 days. Healthcare is first class and quite affordable.

"One of the best things is I'm the only American for over 100 miles. The more Americans, the more expensive. The more American amenities, the more expensive. The more knowing about the place, the more expensive.

"The trick is not in going to places listed in magazines and blogs. The trick is finding someplace that others haven't discovered yet with local customs, food and culture intact. There's literally millions of towns like that and those are the real jewels in the world."

---

private car to take us anywhere we want to go locally costs about $10 an hour. So who needs to spend money on a car . . . or to pay for maintenance, gas, and insurance? Not us.

Live Like a Local

This can take a little doing, especially if you're used to convenience foods and/or not yet ready to give up those favorite recipes you enjoyed back home that require lots of prepackaged or exotic ingredients.

But if instead, you eat locally sourced produce and prepare your meals with local ingredients, flavors, and seasonings, you'll not only be eating healthier, but you'll make a healthy impact on your pocketbook. Plain and simply: imported items cost more. Those Cheerios and Cheez-Its you love may cost more than twice as much in some overseas destinations. And sure, it's okay to splurge once in a while when you need a quick fix from home, but you'll be better off in every way to just say no.

The same goes for cleaning products, cosmetics, clothes, and prescription medications you may take. If it's imported it will undoubtedly cost more. But you'll find local equivalents of all these things, and if you convert to their use, you'll be dollars ahead.

As we mentioned earlier, following the lead of locals who don't own cars can also save you money. Even foregoing taxis in favor of shared vans (called *colectivos* or *combis* in Latin America) can put money in your pocket. In our former hometown of Mérida, Mexico, a taxi might cost you 30 pesos (or $2.50) while you can travel even farther—anywhere in town—via *colectivo* for 6 pesos—less than 50 cents. Again, it comes down to personal choice and the lifestyle you're comfortable with.

Most locals also don't spend money on expensive electronics . . . even things we take for granted, like microwave ovens, bread makers, fancy coffee makers, deluxe barbecue grills, dishwashers, and clothes washers and dryers. And you may be surprised to learn that you won't need these things, either. In fact, learning to live a simpler lifestyle will not only save you money, it can be very cathartic and make you happier overall.

Our advice: Downsize—both the size of your home and the stuff you fill it with. (Why buy an expensive washer/dryer when you can get a load of laundry washed, dried, and folded for $3?) When we first moved overseas, we thought we'd need a home with several bedrooms for all the family and friends who promised to visit. Well, guess what? With a few exceptions, most have never come. We now live in a small two-bedroom condo. And on the occasion we have more guests than we can accommodate, we can rent an apartment or put them up at a local hotel for $25 or $30 a night—a win-win situation for us all.

3

What's Your Deal Breaker?

TO GET TO THE POINT WHERE you shut the door on your current life and embrace a new, very different culture and language takes a little doing. You need to weigh the pros and cons and make some wise decisions about where you'll go and what you'll do once you get there. For some people, this is a piece of cake. For others, it can be a nerve-racking experience.

There are so many decisions to be made that it's easy to go into information overload. It's kind of the way we feel when we go into a restaurant with a five-page menu. Too many choices.

So what can you do to narrow down those choices and identify the best place for you? It's pretty simple: *Profile yourself ruthlessly*.

This sounds easier than it is, of course. We know more than a few people who moved to the beach, for instance, only to find out that they're not beach people. It's a great place to go on vacation, but living there is something else. If you're not keen on heat, humidity, pesky insects, and sand in every crevice, it may not be for you.

Likewise, if you can't live without the sounds of the waves lulling you to sleep at night, a mountain town may not be your cup of tea. And city people may not do well at all in a small village that lacks the cultural opportunities they're accustomed to.

The more effort you put into knowing exactly what it is you need to make yourself comfortable, the more successful you will be.

———

CONSIDER THESE EIGHT FACTORS

Here, then, and in no particular order, are eight factors to consider when choosing your overseas retirement destination:

1. *Affordability.* How does the cost of living stack up with your income and budget?

2. *Health care.* Will you be comfortable with health care options, are good health insurance or hospital plans available to you, and will costs be in line with what you can afford?

3. *Ease of transition.* Are you comfortable with language and currency issues? Are there some familiar items in the grocery stores and pharmacies? (If not, can you live without them?) How easy is it to get a resident visa and to import your household items?

4. *Accessibility.* How close is it to your friends and family back home? Is there an international airport, and are other amenities you'll need, such as good hospitals, nearby?

5. *Community.* Is there an expat group? Are you comfortable with the locals and their culture?

6. *Housing prospects.* Are homes for rent or sale at a reasonable price? If you buy a property and later change your mind, will you be able to sell it easily enough?

7. *Climate.* Are you hoping for four seasons or year-round warm weather? It's best to plan your exploratory visit during the worst weather season so you'll know exactly what to expect.

8. *Things to do.* What are your hobbies and will you be able to continue to enjoy those? If you like good restaurants or artistic events, will there be enough of these to keep you busy?

Prioritize these in order of importance to you. Assign some weight to each factor and add in any others that concern you. Maybe you'll be taking children on this journey and you need good, accredited schools close by. (Find this information at the website of the Council of International Schools: www.cois.org.) Maybe you'll want to find work or start a business. The place you move to should be conducive to your needs.

Make a "Healthy" Decision Based on Your Personal Fitness

While it's true that moving to a warmer climate can often improve your health, as you'll spend more time outside and will probably get more exercise, please consider a move of this magnitude carefully if you have any chronic health issues. Yes, you'll find top-quality health care nearly everywhere in the world, but some of the approaches, procedures, and medications may be different than you're used to, or even unavailable. If you have any health issues of critical concern, be sure to do an overabundance of research about the options available to you. You may find that moving overseas is not your best choice.

And here's the best advice: You *must* spend time in a place before you even think about moving there. Most importantly, *don't settle for less*. If the locale you have your heart set on doesn't match with your personal wish list, keep looking. Your paradise is out there and the more ruthlessly you profile yourself and stick to your guns, the easier it will be to find it and the happier your experience will be.

Let's go a bit further now. Dig deep and ask yourself . . .

CAN YOU *REALLY* ADAPT TO A FOREIGN CULTURE?

One thing you can count on when you move to a foreign country is that things will change for you. And often in ways you can't antici-pate. You'll find some challenges, for sure, and if you can learn to manage your expectations and go with the flow, the better off you will be. So here goes . . .

The *Mañana* Syndrome

You may know that the word *mañana* literally means "tomorrow." But in Latin America, when someone tells you they will do something for you "*mañana*," it typically means "sometime in the future" and not necessarily "tomorrow." Get used to it.

As for the Latin tradition of being late for meetings and appointments, well, yes, it happens. Just like at home, you may find yourself in a waiting room for a good length of time. But you, on the other hand, should always arrive promptly. Unless of course, it's a party. Parties rarely start on time and if you arrive at the appointed hour, you may find your host still in prep mode.

But don't worry. Over time, you'll learn to deal with these idiosyncrasies and they'll become second nature.

Noise: Most of us these days don't live next to roosters, but there are many places around the world where you are more likely than not to have at least several in your neighborhood. (And believe us, roosters don't just crow in the morning.) If that bothers you, you may think about your ability to adapt. Enforceable zoning laws involving chickens and other livestock—involving almost anything, in fact—are rare outside most First-World countries.

(One of the biggest challenges we see expats struggle with, especially in Latin America and Asia, is the treatment of animals. Local governments just don't have the personnel for animal rescue efforts or the funding for animal shelters such as we're accustomed to in the States and Canada. Homeless street dogs, especially, can tug at the heartstrings, and animal rescue is one area where expats commonly focus their volunteer activities.)

By the way, speaking of roosters . . . as compared to the United States and Canada, the rest of the world lives life loud—very loud. Crowing roosters, barking dogs, car alarms, deafening fireworks, ear-splitting church bells, vendors trolling the streets with loudspeakers, and raucous celebrations can happen any time, day or night. And there's not a lot you can do about it except to learn to accept and enjoy the cacophony.

Personal space or lack thereof: Another issue we see new expats struggle with is the concept of personal space. We're more comfortable standing at arm's length to converse, for example, but in many places of the world, standing so far away would make you seem rude and standoffish. And heaven forbid you should try to leave a bit of comfortable space in front of you in a queue. Do that, and someone will invariably squeeze into it.

And you know, of course, that the United States and Canada are undoubtedly the most convenient places in the world in which to live. With a simple phone call or e-mail, or by walking into a store or office and quickly stating your business, you'll get answers and solve problems. Not so elsewhere in the world. In fact, your matter-of-fact, brusque, time-saving approach may be considered offensive.

Polite society: Instead of being the hard-charger, it's best to spend the first few minutes of any meeting making polite conversation about each other's health and well-being. In the developing world especially, personal relationships matter more than money or time . . . something we North Americans may have trouble getting used to. By the way, unless you are in the most laid-back little beach town, and you see the locals dressing casually, it's not the best idea to wear shorts and a tank top when you visit your banker or attorney. You'll indicate your respect (and earn some in return) if you dress in a more formal manner.

Road rules: North Americans are also so used to pedestrians having the right of way that they will sometimes walk out into the street without even thinking. But don't try this elsewhere in the world, where streets are for vehicles and anyone trying to cross them on foot does so at their own risk. General protocol is that the biggest vehicle has the right of way (which can also make for some interesting driving), and since pedestrians have no vehicle at all, you can understand how much right of way they're given. And by the way, traffic signals are more of a suggestion than a mandate. And that laid-back, *mañana* approach to life we mentioned earlier? It goes right out the window when someone gets behind the wheel in Latin America or Asia, where speed becomes the name of the game.

Bodily functions: Offended by seeing people urinate in public? In more than a few foreign locales, it is customary (for men) to go whenever and wherever the need arises. Not in the middle of busy sidewalks, of course, but in an alley or against a wall or in a vacant lot or in front of your car . . . no problem. Same for women and breastfeeding. In most of the world, breastfeeding is not only essential economically but so natural that you'll see women breastfeeding their babies anywhere any time . . . on a bus, in line to pay the electric bill, or while they're doing business with you.

A Hug Here, a Smooch There

One of the things we love about living in Latin America is that people are demonstrative in their affection for one another. Learn to address everyone you pass on the street with a friendly hello. And when you meet someone you know, greet them with a hug and/or cheek kiss.

CAN YOU LEARN TO SPEAK A NEW LANGUAGE?

Unless you move to a country such as Belize or Malaysia where English is the official language, your overseas experience won't be as rich as it could be unless you already speak or can learn to speak the local language. You won't be able to have a meaningful conversation with your neighbors. They will be going about their daily business, the news will be broadcast, your contracts and agreements will be written, and doctors and telephone repairmen and bus drivers will ask you questions in a language you don't necessarily understand . . . unless you make an effort to learn to speak at least a bit of it.

It's true that English is a common second language in many countries, and it's possible to get along without learning the local language. You will often find someone somewhere who speaks enough English to help you. But if you are unable or unwilling to learn the native language of the country you move to, your daily life will be more difficult and your social interactions will be restricted to other English-speaking expats and a few bilingual locals. There are so many fun and interesting ways to learn a new language that there is really no excuse for not at least trying.

———

IS YOUR "SIGNIFICANT OTHER" ONBOARD?

We were lucky in the fact that we were both 100 percent in agreement with the idea of moving to a foreign country. Over the years, we've been able to help each other through some of the challenges that each of us independently might not have handled so well. If you have a partner like this, you're ahead of the game. If you try to make the move with someone who is reluctant, it's almost guaranteed that things won't go well.

What can you do if you want to make the move, but your significant other doesn't?

- *Involve them in the planning.* This is a big decision and deserves careful thought and planning by all involved. Talk, talk, and talk some more about it. Make sure you're *both* as informed as possible and involved in the decisions about where to move, how to live, and so on. Spend time together and separately perusing online forums and other resources. If your motivation is economic, make sure you both understand what's going on with your financial situation.

- *Compromise with a "no strings attached" test drive.* Nothing is scarier than cutting the ties completely. If your partner is reluctant to do that, consider giving the new life a test drive. Before you sell your house or buy that one-way ticket, rent an apartment in the new locale for three months or more.

- *Don't sugarcoat the challenges.* Discuss the difficulties you'll face along the way, and work together on solutions. For instance, you may want to take some foreign language classes before your move. Try out voice and video over Internet protocol (VOIP) technologies like Skype so you can easily stay in touch with family and friends. If you're retiring, do some budget planning. There will still be unexpected challenges, but by working together, problem solving can be part of the fun.

- *Help ease the transition.* Once you've moved, take an active approach to learning as much about your new community as you can. Be sure your partner has an opportunity to meet other expats and locals with similar interests. These days, you can do this in advance of your move through online blogs, forums, and websites. And keep busy—this is the perfect opportunity for you both to try something new. Fortunately, in most expat communities, you'll find your new social life is more active—and more enjoyable—than ever.

- *Remember that attitude is everything.* When challenges do arise, maintain your sense of humor and look on the bright side; this experience will likely strengthen your relationship. (And it will give you great stories to tell later.) So support each other and make a point to have as much fun as possible on this adventure.

ARE YOU OKAY WITH NOT LIVING CLOSE TO FAMILY?

It's a common joke among expats: "The bad news about moving abroad is that you see less of your family. The good news about moving abroad is . . . that you see less of your family."

Keep in mind that some of the best foreign retirement destinations are just a short flight from where you may live now. The flight times to Mexico, the Caribbean, and Central America, for example, are shorter than a cross-country flight from New York to Los Angeles. If your family is already spread out across the United States or Canada, then it may not matter so much where you live . . . you may see them just as often.

If, however, you now live amid friends and family from whom you can't bear to part, you have some serious decision making to do. Kids and grandkids, especially, can be difficult to leave behind. Although the Internet now makes it possible to communicate instantly with anyone anywhere—and even with live video—it may not be enough for you. Only you can make the decision about your ability to cope with separation from your loved ones.

The good news is that the new friends you meet will become like family to you. In our experience, locals love to "adopt" us foreigners. And the bond you'll establish with your fellow expats will be strong. You're all in the same boat, after all, and will come to care for and rely upon one another as family.

By the Way, an Expat Is Not an Ex-Patriot

"I don't like being called an ex-patriot," a neighbor commented one day. About as red, white, and blue as they come, he and his wife love to travel. They moved overseas for the adventure of it all (of course).

But, as he told us in no uncertain terms, he was still a patriot and would love the U.S.A. no matter where he lived. We explained that he didn't have to worry, that he was definitely not an ex-patriot and never would be.

Like *knight* and *night*, or *whole* and *hole*, the words *expatriate* and *ex-patriot* are homophones—spelled differently but pronounced roughly the same. And in fact, the word *ex-patriot* isn't even in the dictionary.

Expatriate, however, is in the dictionary. It refers to those who move from their home country. If you're from the United States or Canada but you live in France, for example, you are an expatriate, and the reason for the move doesn't matter.

But make no mistake . . . being an expatriate does not make you an ex-patriot.

So what is an ex-patriot? The dictionary refers to a patriot as "a person who loves his country, zealously supporting and defending it." So it stands to reason that an ex-patriot is someone who no longer supports or defends his or her country.

We have yet to meet an expatriate from the United States or Canada who fits that definition. Sure, we all may complain about what's going on back home. In fact, many of us did that while we were still there, and moving abroad doesn't change that. We can disagree with something happening back home and even move to get away from it without giving up our rights and responsibilities or loving our country any less.

4

The Most Common (and Avoidable) Mistakes Expats Make

———

IF THERE IS ONE THING *and only one thing* you take away from this book, it's that your primary, overriding motivation for retiring overseas has to be a pure and unadulterated love of adventure and discovery. It just won't work any other way.

Don't get us wrong: It's okay to simply want to live in a place with better weather. It's common sense to figure out how to lower your cost of living in retirement. It's admirable to want to learn a new language or dig deep into a foreign culture. And certainly, some people have difficult personal situations we can't even begin to imagine or understand. But plain and simple, it just doesn't work to try and sweep your problems under the carpet by moving overseas.

As we like to say . . .

―――

TAKE YOUR LUGGAGE, BUT LEAVE YOUR BAGGAGE BEHIND

Several years ago, we met a man who had moved to Ecuador to escape what he perceived as the "burden" of child support payments. He lived there quite happily (if not guiltily) for several years.

About two years into his stay in Ecuador he lost his passport. Now what? He couldn't move forward with his bid to become an Ecuadorian citizen, and he couldn't go to the U.S. embassy to apply for a new passport without the risk of being slapped with legal action. He had become a man with few, and mostly unfavorable, options.

While it's doubtful you're in the same boat, the point is, don't leave home for the wrong reasons. Running from legal obligations is not a good reason to move halfway across the world. It's likely that such a decision will come back to haunt you in the future.

Today, in fact, you cannot get a U.S. passport if you owe $2,500 or more in child support. Laws are a bit murkier when it comes to delinquent taxes you may owe the government or other legally sanctioned debts, such as alimony. If you have any questions about your obligations and rights, consult an attorney *before* you move overseas.

―――

LEAVE HOME AT HOME

Beyond legal and financial issues, what is the most common mistake expats make? We alluded to it earlier. It's something we refer to as "trying to take home with you." In a few words: Don't do it. And this applies no matter if you're from the United States, Canada, or any other country. If you want your overseas retirement to be successful, you have to leave "home" as you know it behind and focus on redefining just what that word means.

Having said that, you'll have days when you long for the positive aspects of your former life. You'll wish you had that favorite brand of beer or cold cream . . . or that high-tech coffee maker you left behind. You'll long for the convenience of accomplishing something with a single telephone call . . . or being able to speak English to anyone and everyone you meet. You'll be frustrated and sometimes fed up. That's just human nature.

Instead, think about why you wanted to move overseas in the first place. Never forget that it's about adventure and new beginnings.

The Most Common Misconception and the Single Most Overlooked Detail

The most common misconception among would-be expats is that they'll have to give up their citizenship when they move overseas. Not so. Instead, you'll get a resident visa in the new country. Eventually you may want to seek citizenship in the new country, and in that case you would have "dual citizenship" of both countries.

Of course, you can officially renounce your home citizenship, but that's a legal process that most expats don't pursue.

The single most overlooked detail is something we mentioned in Chapter 2: budgeting for the up-front costs for your move overseas. You'll have one-time moving expenses, legal fees for residence visas, and so on, and you'll probably need to purchase some items (large or small) for your new home. Don't forget to budget for these items.

THE ONE PERSONALITY TRAIT THAT SUCCESSFUL EXPATS SHARE

Most of us think we'd like a little adventure in our lives . . . to see new places, meet new people, and experience new cultures.

But what if *every day of your life* was an adventure? Seeing new places and meeting new people is one thing, but living in a new culture means that just about everything you're likely to do on a daily basis will be done differently than you're doing it now, from banking and paying the bills to ordering pizza or getting your hair done.

Being an expat requires a true appetite for new and novel situations—or at least a hefty tolerance for them—because it's unlikely you'll ever clear up a confusing or unfamiliar situation by saying, "This isn't the way we do it back home."

Successful expats thrive on novelty and unfamiliar situations. They relish the challenge of figuring out how to get things done, often in new—and possibly better—ways. They say this "keeps them young." We've certainly found this to be true ourselves . . . figuring out how things are done in a new place keeps us on our toes and engaged with just about everything that's going on around us—and that's almost a definition of "young."

YOU MAY BE MORE ADVENTUROUS THAN YOU THINK YOU ARE

You will never *really* know if you are cut out to be an expat until you try it. And "trying it" doesn't mean you need to make a major, all-or-nothing commitment. It's okay to test the waters a little bit at a time. Once you're actually on the ground in a likely spot, you may surprise yourself with how adventurous, flexible, and ready for a new life you really are!

We often joke that if you wear a watch—and actually use it to keep appointments—you may not be cut out for life in a foreign country, where hardly anything ever happens on time. (Kind of like a doctor's appointment in the United States or Canada.)

Show up on time for a concert, a soccer game, or an appointment with your attorney and you'll certainly end up waiting . . . and waiting . . . We've arrived promptly at the posted hour to watch a parade or festival inauguration only to have it start two hours (or more) later!

If you show up at someone's home at the appointed time for a party, you may be embarrassed to find the host in the shower or, even worse, not even home yet. You have to learn to shrug it all off—and over time you will. You'll learn that doing most things at a specific time really doesn't matter that much. More importantly, it's the quality of time spent. And remember, it's all about the adventure. And sometimes adventures can be challenging.

ATTITUDE IS EVERYTHING

Mostly, what it boils down to is attitude. If you're the kind of person who typically sees the glass as half full rather than half empty . . . if you embrace that childlike sense of wonderment at new sights and experiences . . . and if you enjoy meeting new people and not knowing exactly what might await you around the next corner, then you're cut from the right cloth to be a successful expat.

And if you're not quite sure you've got what it takes? That's okay, too. Some of us just need to ease our way in. You have to take baby steps before you learn to run.

Most of all, remember that this needn't be a one-way trip. We've known a few people who've moved overseas only to find it wasn't what they expected or that they weren't quite suited for the place they chose. (It's happened to us, in fact.) You can always move on and try on another country for size. And should you decide to go back home, that's fine, too. You should at least have wonderful memories and great stories to tell.

5

Health Care
Myth versus Reality

"EARLY TO BED AND EARLY TO RISE," the saying goes, "makes a man healthy, wealthy, and wise." But we'd add that moving overseas might do exactly the same thing.

Not only will the lower cost of living in many foreign countries save you money overall, but you'll find vast savings on health care costs. Does that mean you have to compromise on quality? Absolutely not.

In many countries you'll find excellent health care, with doctors and other practitioners who have studied at the world's best medical schools and hospitals. Our own physician in Ecuador, for instance, received his PhD from the University of London, and did postgraduate work at the University of Miami School of Medicine, the Royal College of Physicians of London, the London School of Hygiene and Tropical Medicine, St. Jude's Children's Research Hospital, and Harvard Medical School, among others.

Many of the doctors we've visited since we've been living overseas have similarly impressive resumes. As you'd expect, they speak excellent English and have no problem communicating. Certainly, there are physicians in foreign countries who haven't studied internationally and don't speak English. But in the major hospitals—especially those accredited by The Joint Commission International (JCI)—you will find multilingual health care professionals.

How Will the Affordable Care Act Affect Expats?

As this book goes to print, the IRS indicates that, in general, U.S. citizens living outside of the United States for at least 330 days in a given year and those who meet the IRS requirements to be a bona fide resident of another country are exempt from the health-insurance mandate that comes with the Affordable Care Act. (You'll find the full list of requirements for bona fide residence in Form 2555 on the IRS website.) And we'll post updates on this subject at www.internationalliving.com.

We can personally vouch for the quality health care we've received, as well as for its affordability. Dan had a torn rotator cuff in his shoulder repaired in Quito in 2002. Total bill, including an overnight hospital stay, anesthesiologist, and surgeon fees, came to $2,300. Dan's mother had the same surgery done in Omaha a few months later, but her bill was almost $14,000.

More recently, Dan had cataract surgery in Panama and a retinal vitrectomy in Quito. In 2013, we both had an executive health checkup that was so thorough it included an overnight hospital stay—a literal stem-to-stern look into the darkest recesses of our bodies. We'll leave that to your imagination except to say in addition to all the blood and other fluid tests, it included an EKG and stress test, sonogram, ultrasound, endoscopy, colonoscopy, and on and on . . .

The total bill for both of us was $3,951.39. We've compared this to prices for similar executive health assessments in the United States, and determined we paid about half the going U.S. rate—and far less if you factor in the overnight stay in a private double room.

Looking for Top-Quality Health Care
Providers Overseas? Start Here.

Created in 1994, JCI has a presence today in more than 90 countries. It works with health care organizations, governments, and international advocates to promote rigorous standards of care and provide solutions for achieving peak performance through accreditation, education, and advisory services. The World Health Organization (WHO) has partnered with JCI to establish international patient safety solutions. You can find a list of globally accredited organizations at www.jointcommissioninternational.org.

But it's not just affordability that impresses us and other expats who are devoted consumers of health care overseas. We also appreciate the ability to get an appointment quickly and the personal, caring attention we receive from doctors.

Make no mistake: Excellent health care is available in the United States. But a visit to a specialist there that can cost $200 or $300 out of pocket costs just $25 to $45 in Latin America, and around $16 in Asia. In the States you may have to call multiple doctors' offices just to book a visit. You may wait months for an appointment, and once you get to the doctor's office, you'll likely spend longer in the waiting room than in the examination room.

Our doctors in Latin America, however, typically see us right away. Our doctor in Mexico even made same-day house calls, at a charge of just 500 pesos—about $40. And we've never been rushed through an appointment. Often the doctor himself will take your vitals—height/weight, temperature, blood pressure, and so on—and he'll spend as much time chatting about your health issues as you like. No fuss, no rush.

And by the way, it's fairly common practice for doctors to give you their personal cell phone numbers so you can contact them after hours or with follow-up questions.

―――――

THE U.S. AND CANADIAN HEALTH CARE SYSTEMS
ARE NOT HEALTHY AT ALL

The U.S. Is Overspending and Underperforming

According to the Commonwealth Fund, which has conducted a performance survey of international health care systems every two years since 2004, "the United States underperforms on the major dimensions of health care performance—quality, access, efficiency, equity, and healthy lives, despite spending twice what other countries spend per capita on health care."

It's no secret that the U.S. health care system is not healthy at all. Neither is Canada's, where you're lucky to even get an appointment to see a doctor before it's too late . . .

It is also not a secret that you can find just as high-quality—or at times even superior—health care in other parts of the world.

And sure, comparing and contrasting health care systems around the world is a gargantuan (and relatively thankless) task. But if any organization should have the resources to do this, it's the World Health Organization (WHO).

In 2000—the last time they compiled their rankings of the world's health systems—the United States came in at number 37. The results were so controversial that ever since, the WHO has declined to rank countries in their World Health Report.

But the point is, WHO data indicated that *there are 36 countries in the world with a better health care system than the United States.* For reference, Canada ranks at number 30—better than the United States, but not by much.

France and Italy earned the top two spots. Spain is number seven. Even tiny countries like Malta, Greece, and Morocco are rated as having better health care systems than the United States and Canada!

And this lackluster performance comes despite the fact that the United States spends more on health care—and charges its consumers more—than any other country in the world.

Take a look, for example, at the costs of some common procedures. And just for the sake of comparison, let's compare the average prices in the United States with the average prices in France and Spain, the countries ranked by the WHO at numbers 1 and 7, respectively, in its best-quality global health care index:

- One *single day in a hospital* in the United States costs, on average, $1,514 (to as much as $12,537), while in France it costs $853 and in Spain it costs $476.

- An *appendectomy* in the United States—including physician and hospital bills—costs $8,156 on average (to as much as $29,426). The same procedure in France costs $4,463 . . . and in Spain $2,245.

- *Hip replacement surgery* costs an average of $25,061 (to as much as $87,987) in the United States, but just $10,927 in France and just $7,731 in Spain.

- Costs for an *angioplasty* in the United States average $16,533 (to as much as $61,649). In France: $7,564. In Spain: $9,446.

- Median price for *bypass surgery* in the United States is $46,547 (to as much as $61,649). In France the average cost is $22,844, and in Spain, $17,437.

By the way, a *routine doctor's visit* in the United States? The average cost is $95 (to as much as $176). In France, though, you'll pay $30. And in Spain? Just $11!

And these aren't just arbitrary numbers. They're from data compiled by the International Federation of Health Plans, the leading global network in the industry, with more than 100 member companies from 25 countries. Prices for Spain are from the private sector. For France, prices reflect a blend of private and public sectors. Prices in neither country vary much above the average price.

The prices we've listed from the United States, however, are given as a range and reflect over a million paid insurance claims . . . and as you can see, prices vary widely.

In fact, in many places of the world, you can get excellent quality medical care and buy your prescriptions for even less:

- Private hospital-room charges in *Malaysia*, for instance, start at $28, but for $90 a day you can have an ensuite room with cable TV on a flat-screen TV. Zocor, the high-cholesterol medication, will cost you less than $22 a month, while the generic, simvastatin, costs less than $5.50 a month.

- A full dental cleaning in *Ecuador* costs just $30 to $45. Partial plates run about $325, and a complete set of dentures costs about $900, including office visits, fittings, lab work, and impressions. Teeth bleaching costs $25. A porcelain crown is just $250.

- In *Nicaragua*, you can have lab work done for as little as $8. An overnight stay in an internationally accredited hospital cost about $100. An electrocardiogram is only $25. And a doctor's visit routinely costs as little as $10.

What About the Costs for Typical Medications You Might Take?

Many medications are available over the counter in other countries, without need of a prescription. Comparing the same dosage and quantities:

- Cymbalta, taken for depression, anxiety, and fibromyalgia, costs an average of $149 in the United States (to as much as $317). In Spain it costs $70 and in France it costs $47.

- Lipitor, taken for high cholesterol, costs an average of $100 in the United States (to as much as $145). In France it will cost you $48 and in Spain just $13.

- Nexium, taken for acid reflux, costs $187 on average in the United States (to as much as $373). In France it costs $30 and in Spain it's $18.

HIGH QUALITY AND LOW COSTS: WHY FOREIGN HEALTH SYSTEMS WORK

Why are health care costs so much lower outside the United States and Canada? Primarily because the laws and court systems of most other countries don't allow for frivolous lawsuits. Suing someone can take years, and judges have no incentive to dole out multimillion-dollar awards. Thus, malpractice insurance is very low, as are doctors' and health workers' fees and hospital and clinic charges.

And in other countries, the government sets prices centrally. Most everyone, no matter where they live or their insurance arrangement, pays the same amount. But in the United States, each insurer negotiates its own prices—and consumers unfairly end up paying wildly different amounts.

There are other reasons, too, that you'll find lower health care costs in other countries. In most of the rest of the world, for example, health care expenses are relative to the local cost of living. *It just costs less to live in Asia, Latin America, or certain parts of Europe than it does to live in the United States.* Housing and construction costs are lower. Taxes are lower. Food costs less. And salaries are lower. Foreign doctors often make a sixth of the salary of their U.S. counterparts. For all these reasons and more, you'll save on overseas health care costs as well as on general costs of living.

Questions to Ask about Health Care in Any Location You May Be Considering

When you're doing your research on moving overseas, there are two basic questions you should ask about health care:

First, what's available? For instance, are the hospitals modern and well equipped? Do they have affiliations with well-respected international hospitals? Is there a good network of clinics? Can you find the drugs you need?

Second, just how good is the care? Is the staff well trained? Do the doctors stay on top of the latest treatments? Will you find the right specialists? How long will you have to wait for appointments? Does the country have national standards for accepted practice?

―――――

PUBLIC VERSUS PRIVATE HEALTH CARE SYSTEMS

The countries around the world that expats favor offer affordable, good—and in many cases outstanding—health care. As we've said, doctors in these locales are well trained. And you'll find hospitals with modern equipment and with standards similar to what you'd find at home.

The Money You Save on Health Insurance Alone Can Fund Your New Life Overseas

When friends of ours were considering their retirement options, they were facing health insurance premiums in the United States of at least $1,800 a month for the two of them—with a high deductible. ("And we're healthy people," they said.)

But in Costa Rica, where they now live, they pay just $100 a month ($50 each) for a full-coverage health insurance plan through the public health care system, *La Caja Costarricense de Seguro Social*, or *Caja*. And there is no deductible at all.

That's $20,400 per year they're saving in health insurance costs alone—an amount that goes a long way toward their total cost of living in Costa Rica.

What may not be the same as at home, though, is how some health care systems are organized, and how you pay for treatment. One major difference—particularly as compared to the United States—is that you may have access to a *public health care system* as well as to *private health care*.

Many expat-friendly countries, especially in Europe and Latin America, have a public health care system that is funded by the government. Health care is free (or very low cost) to the country's citizens and to most, if not all, foreigners who are legal residents there. And frankly, having access to this low-cost, public health care system is a big reason *why* these countries are expat favorites.

(You'll find more information about health care options in specific countries later in this book.)

But all of these countries also have private health care, just as the United States does. That is, there are doctors in private practice, and private hospitals and clinics, where you can receive medical care. You then pay in cash or through an insurance policy for your treatment.

In a few countries, private hospitals or hospital chains offer insurance plans strictly for their hospitals. These are generally among the best hospitals in that country . . . hospitals that you'd probably choose anyway.

You're not limited to a single choice, of course. Many expats mix and match these health care options to get the biggest bang for their health care buck.

IS A PUBLIC HEALTH CARE SYSTEM RIGHT FOR YOU?

Nationalized public health care systems provide a useful, low-cost health safety net, and for some expats, it's their primary source of health care in their new country. Others use the public system together with other forms of health care, such as their U.S. Medicare, their Canadian health coverage, or private health insurance that is valid in the country they're living in.

(Note: With small exceptions, Medicare can only be used in the United States. See "Medicare: You Can't Take It With You" sidebar later in this chapter.)

There are pros and cons to any health care system. Is public health care right for you? Here are some points to keep in mind:

Can I Get an Appointment Quickly?

Public systems provide health care for an entire country's population. For poorer people, it is the only form of health care they have. As a result, clinics are usually busy. You may have to wait several weeks to get an appointment, or even longer to schedule a nonessential surgery.

If you want ready access to doctors, without long wait times, you may want to go to a private doctor.

If you have a medical condition that requires frequent checkups, you may also prefer a private doctor—and shorter wait times. On the other hand, frequent checkups may be *exactly* why you'd want to consider the public system . . . since the checkups would be free. It's up to you.

(And note that some doctors in the public system do also have private practices. They may work at a public clinic in the morning and take private patients in the afternoon.)

Do the Doctors and Staff Speak English?

As we've explained, many doctors in the countries you may be considering understand some written English. That's because so many important medical journals are written in English. A doctor therefore will probably know the medical terms for his specialty in English.

However, some who work in the public health sector don't need fluent English to serve their local patients. As a result, you're less likely to find fluent, English-speaking doctors in the public health system than you will in private practice.

It's also likely that public system support staff—nurses, lab technicians, orderlies, and the like—will not speak English. In fact, many support staff in the *private* health care sector don't speak English, either. So if this is important to you, ask.

One tip: Doctors, dentists, and hospitals that deal with many foreigners and/or rely on medical tourism as a large part of their practice are more likely to have English-speaking support staff.

Am I Covered outside the Base Country?

Public health care systems generally won't cover you for medical treatment outside that country.

But as an expat, you can expect to be going back to your home country now and again. You may also want to explore other countries, too—it's one of the pleasures of being an expat.

For trips to other countries—including back to your home country—expect to pay cash for health care, or have separate insurance to cover it.

What Does It Cost?

One of the big pluses of public health care systems is their low costs. In Central and South America, for instance, fees for belonging to the public health care system average from about $25 to $50 per month per person. In some countries you pay the fee month by month. In others you must pay an entire year's premium up front.

Either way, it's a very affordable fee for a health care safety net.

YOUR BEST PRIVATE HEALTH INSURANCE OPTIONS OVERSEAS

If you plan to use private health care overseas instead of a public system, it's always a good idea to have health insurance. Even when health care costs are low, as they are in the most popular foreign retirement destinations, a major illness or surgery can quickly run to thousands of dollars.

Medicare: You Can't Take It With You

Some U.S. expats in countries with low-cost health care rely on Medicare for major procedures, flying back to the States for treatment. Keep in mind that, if you are relying on Medicare for your major medical, it's a good idea to have Medicare Part B (medical insurance) and Medicare Part D (prescription drug plan), as well as Medicare Part A (hospital insurance).

If you don't plan to get Social Security as soon as you turn 65, be sure to sign up for Medicare three months before your sixty-fifth birthday. You can do this online at www.socialsecurity.gov/medicareonly.

You can incur long-term penalties if you sign up for Medicare Part B after your initial sign-up period has ended. Likewise, remember that you'll have monthly premiums for Medicare Parts B and D; make sure you arrange for automatic payments while you're abroad.

Health insurance companies everywhere have a few things in common: They tend to exclude pre-existing conditions, and they tend to have an age limit (usually 65) for issuing new policies. A few companies issue new policies up to age 75. And any company that accepts pre-existing conditions builds that risk into the premium you pay.

For these reasons, always first check whether your existing insurance plan, if you have one, covers treatment abroad. If it does, consider maintaining it. If you are coming from the United States or Canada, you most likely can't use your current health care plan when you move abroad. Canada's nationalized health care system generally doesn't cover treatment abroad. And most U.S. health insurance companies don't cover medical care outside the country.

As a result, you'll most likely need to look at other health insurance options when you move abroad, especially if you plan to live there full-time. Here are some to consider:

International health insurance: These plans are truly global, covering you anyplace in the world. Some companies also offer a semi-global option, excluding certain high-priced countries in exchange for a lower premium. When this option is offered, the United States and Canada are always on the excluded list. You may want an international plan if you travel for long periods to several different countries, or if you live in a small country with limited health care options and will need to go elsewhere for care. Premiums vary, but for a healthy, 60-ish individual, expect to pay roughly $3,000 to $5,000 a year.

National, in-country health insurance: These plans, offered by national or regional insurance companies, provide in-depth coverage in a given country. If you plan to spend most of your time abroad in a single country, a national plan can be a good option. Ask whether the plan includes a travel-insurance component to cover health emergencies when visiting other countries—such as vacations back in the United States or Canada. Premiums in Latin America generally run 10 to 35 percent less than international plans, while in Asia they can cost $1,000 a year or less.

Hospital membership plans: Top hospitals in some countries— notably Costa Rica, Nicaragua, Panama, and Uruguay—offer membership plans that provide steep discounts on services at their facilities, including hospital stays, doctors' visits, and prescriptions. While not strictly insurance, these plans serve many of the same purposes. Monthly fees generally run $25 to $75 per month per person.

Whatever health insurance option you choose, be sure to ask these questions:

- When does coverage start? And is there a delay for coverage of some things? (Wellness visits or maternity care, for instance, may only be available starting in year two of a policy.)
- Is the policy renewable? Some policies are renewable automatically, while others are renewable only at the company's discretion. And is coverage cut off after a certain age?
- Does the company "pre-authorize" payment? Pre-authorization means that claims are sanctioned before you have treatment.
- Will the plan pay up front for medical care or must you submit claims after the fact? (This can be a big issue if you have an accident or a surgery that runs up large bills. As mentioned earlier, hospitals generally want payment in full before you're released from the hospital.)
- Are pre-existing conditions covered?
- Is there an age limit for signing up? (Many companies only issue *new* health insurance policies to those aged 64 and younger.)
- Does the plan include doctor's visits and other wellness care, or does it strictly cover major medical?
- How do you submit claims, and how are reimbursements handled?

___

THE GOOD NEWS: MOVING OFF THE COMFORT
COUCH CAN IMPROVE YOUR HEALTH

All this talk about moving off your comfort couch to a new life overseas may sound stressful. But once you get beyond the move itself, you'll find that one of the most overlooked benefits is the healthier lifestyle you'll find. It's often the first thing expats notice about their new life . . . shedding extra pounds, breathing easier, and generally feeling better. And if you live in a place where the climate is warm and pleasant year round, the food is fresh and locally sourced, and you're less stressed, then it's hardly a surprise that your general health improves.

As a Canadian friend now living in Panama told us, "Winter in Toronto was becoming a real physical burden. Having to shovel out the driveway after every snowfall or being trapped in the house because of miserable weather was no fun. In Panama, we can be . . . and are . . . active every day. Carrying an umbrella during rainy season is nothing compared to the northern alternative."

We all know how sunlight can brighten our moods, of course, but you'd be surprised how much warmer weather affects your well-being. Instead of shoveling snow and running the risk of slipping on the ice or overexerting yourself, you can spend more pleasurable time outdoors being active.

Another acquaintance who traded the stress of corporate life in the States for beach living in Costa Rica says he and his wife are far healthier now. "We've adjusted well to the slower pace of life. Living near the ocean, there isn't a day we don't go to the beach or take a 10-minute bike ride to the grocery store for necessities. Another benefit of living in a tropical climate is the diet. The fresh produce and bountiful seafood has improved our health. We're still working a bit via the Internet, but now, our blood pressures are lower and our tans are better."

Like this couple, most expats we know no longer own a car since public transportation is safe, reliable, and affordable. After all, who needs a car to explore the cobbled streets of a colonial town or make the most of miles of white-sand beaches? If you retire to a place where you can fill your time with fun activities like snorkeling, fishing, golfing, hiking forest trails, or taking a routine dip in the ocean every morning, you'll be healthier for it.

6

The Challenges of Language and Culture

Είναι όλα τα ελληνικά μου. It's all Greek to me.

You've found your perfect overseas destination. It's beautiful, affordable, and safe.

But they speak a different language than you do. How big of a stumbling block is this? Not as big as you might think . . .

Just about anywhere in the world you might go these days, you'll almost certainly find someone who speaks English. Outside English-speaking nations, many people study the language in school as part of their regular curriculum, and many professionals have made a point of learning English to deal with growing numbers of English-speaking international clients.

American movies, television, and music are so widespread that even people who have never officially studied English often have surprisingly good conversational skills. So in a pinch, and unless you're very far off the beaten path, you can usually find at least basic translation help.

But you really should make a valiant try at learning the local language. Not only will it enrich your experiences living, traveling, and interacting with people in your new home country, but it also will certainly save you money and could even save your life.

One option, of course, is to retire to an English-speaking country like Belize, Malaysia, or New Zealand. You'll find pockets of Mexico like the Lake Chapala area or San Miguel de Allende, and in the Canal Zone of Panama City, where locals, thanks to their long-standing interaction with the many English-speaking residents, commonly speak English.

You'll also find English spoken on most Caribbean islands, including the Bay Islands of Honduras and the Corn Islands of Nicaragua. Along with Filipino, English is the official language of the Philippines. Various other countries in the Asia/Pacific region and Africa also list English as their official language.

But if you're planning a move anywhere else in the world—including Latin America—then you'd be well advised to learn at least some basics of the local language. Sure, as we've said, you'll encounter plenty of helpful people who speak English and will kindly come to your rescue in every situation . . . from asking directions to making an inquiry at the bank or a doctor's office to requesting a toilet plunger at the hardware store, or—heaven forbid—something of an even more personal nature.

(Pantomime works, yes—but only so far—and, in some cases, at what damage to your self-respect?)

WHY SHOULD YOU LEARN THE LANGUAGE?
FOR FUN . . . AND BASIC SURVIVAL

Just knowing your numbers is a good start. As beginning Spanish speakers, we admit we had difficulties with *dos* (2) and *doce* (12). Pronounced *DOHSS* and *DOHSS-ay*, they sounded similar enough to our untrained ear that when we were quoted a price, we had to stop and think—was it $2 or $12? No doubt we may have erred once or twice and spent more than we should have.

And once, on a small island off the coast of Venezuela, we waited in the hot sun for the ferry to take us back to our hotel on another island. It leaves at "*dos*," they told us. At least that's what we thought they'd said. So off we went to grab a bite of lunch and when we returned at 2 PM, we learned the ferry had come and gone, at . . . you guessed it . . . twelve noon.

These are minor inconveniences, of course. But if there hadn't been a later ferry, we'd have been stuck.

And what if you're awakened in the middle of the night by the smell of smoke . . . and you see that the vacant lot across the street is on fire? Will you be able to summon the *bomberos* (in Spanish) or the *pompiers* (in French)?

At the very least, you must learn your numbers so you can recite your telephone number and address. It's not at all hard to do. In fact, that's the reason we were taught to count as children. Numbers are about the easiest thing to learn.

So right along with all the other things you do to prepare for your move overseas, we heartily recommend getting a head start on your basic language skills. Certainly, we know of many people living in other countries who think it is too difficult to learn a new language. Some have never even tried.

They're living quite happily in their new home country without any real local language skills . . . but think how much better their experience might be if they would just try. And the truth is that they probably know more than they think they do. But half the battle is getting out there and, yes, making a fool of yourself. And as we all know, that's not difficult at all.

START WITH BABY STEPS . . . AND BABY TALK

There's a movie called *The Mexican*, in which actor Brad Pitt plays a character named Jerry who has a series of misadventures in Mexico. At one point, in a sticky situation, Jerry—who can't speak Spanish—runs up to a Mexican driver and says, "I need to take a ride-o in your el-truck-o to the next town-o."

Nice try, Jerry, but no *cigarro*.

While there are many words that are basically the same and can be translated from English to Spanish simply by adding an *o* or an *a*, like *carro* (car), *problema* (problem), and *programa* (program), there are others for which that just doesn't work.

Go into a store and ask for *sopa* or *pulpo* in your orange juice, and you won't get soap or pulp. Instead, you'll get soup . . . and octopus. Eeyew.

Should you make these mistakes, no need to be embarrassed. But if you ever are, don't say you are *embarazado*. Because that doesn't mean you are embarrassed, but that you are pregnant. And that *could* be embarrassing.

Truth is, it's easy enough to learn basic Spanish or French or even something as exotic as Chinese or Thai, if you have the right teacher or guide. And if you think you're too old to learn another language—or that children are the only ones capable of acquiring language skills—think again.

Take a Lesson from the Kids

You have a lot of lifelong learning experiences on your side, but when it comes to learning a new language, one advantage children have is a complete lack of expectations about how long it should take or how easy or hard it should be. They have no concepts of deadlines or performance measures or success or failure or embarrassment. They just do it. And so should you.

Remember, you needn't be perfect and mistakes are unavoidable. So get out there and start swinging. If you're like most expats, you'll quickly acquire what we call "taxi and restaurant" language skills. You'll be able to go where you need to go and order what you want to eat with minimal effort.

Children do acquire language skills quickly, but they have an advantage: They don't have that far to go. Many adult expats in Latin America, for example, speak what we call "baby Spanish," using the simple phrases a child would use to accomplish basic tasks and fulfill their basic needs. It doesn't take a child long to reach this skill level . . . but it usually takes an adult even less time. They can reach a childlike skill level in months instead of the years that it takes a child to reach the same level.

And there is a good reason for that: You're already a linguistic expert in your own language. You have an adult-size vocabulary at the tip of your tongue that—especially when it comes to Romance languages like Spanish, Italian, French, and Portuguese—can help you decode thousands of words that share roots with English.

You also have incredible reading and writing skills compared to a child, and you can use these to understand things about your adopted language that no child could even express. Plus, you already know how to study. You've done it all your life, with dozens of other subjects and topics.

Our Story: Before we left Omaha we took a six-week conversational Spanish course from our local community college, which happened to be taught by a man from Panama, one of the countries we were considering moving to.

Still, when we actually moved out of the United States, we felt as though we'd been thrown into the deep end of the swimming pool. We met only a handful of expats living in Ecuador the first year we were there, and it really was sink or swim. From that very first night, when we asked a bartender for "*dos besos*" (two kisses) instead of "*dos vasos*" (two glasses), we were in survival mode. We had to learn, or else.

It wasn't until a couple of years later, when we took a series of courses at the Warren Hardy School in San Miguel de Allende, Mexico, that everything started to click for us.

Warren understands that our adult minds work differently than the high school or college-age kids most Spanish learning programs are aimed at. He's developed an entire program that offers shortcuts—some tips and tricks, some cues and clues—that really helped us get to the next step with our Spanish. Maybe he can help you, too. You can take classes in person at his school in San Miguel (highly recommended) or, if you don't have time for that, he's created—in partnership with *International Living*—an online Webtutor course. Details can be found at https://www.ilbookstore.com/Warren-Hardy-Spanish-the-Ultimate-Experience.html.

YOUR BEST LANGUAGE-LEARNING RESOURCES

The best way to learn a new language will depend on several things, including where you happen to be and how *you* learn best. But in general . . .

Before You Go . . .

Take advantage of language courses taught in your home area. Many community colleges offer conversational classes, often taught by native speakers. This is a great way to get a taste of what's to come.

Try a boxed language course from one of the industry giants such as Rosetta Stone, Pimsleur, Berlitz, or another that features audio CDs or multimedia material you can interact with on your computer.

Download some helpful apps and start an online language course. More and more languages are being taught via the Internet, even live via a program like Skype video. You can listen to downloads at your leisure, while doing your chores or out and about on your daily commute.

Just do a quick Internet search and you'll find lots of options. One resource we've found is a website where language programs developed by the Foreign Service Institute for the U.S. government are now available in the public domain. In other words, free of charge.

The materials are a bit outdated (but how much does a language change?) and it's not exactly user friendly, but it's free just the same. You linguists will be in hog heaven. There are 43 languages there for you to learn. You can find all the details at http://fsi-language-courses.org.

Another free language-learning website is Duolingo.com. And should you need to do a quick translation, we've found Google Translate easy to use: http://translate.google.com.

Once You Arrive . . .

There is no substitute for learning a language from a native speaker on his or her home turf, and you'll find local language instructors in nearly every destination that's popular with foreign retirees these days. You'll discover many of those teachers on local bulletin boards, on local Facebook pages, and by talking with other expats.

Here are just a few of our favorite language schools in some popular expat destinations:

Spanish

Costa Rica (Heredia): Centro Panamericano de Idiomas (CPI), www.cpi-edu.com

Ecuador (various locations): Simon Bolivar School, www.simon-bolivar.com

Mexico (San Miguel de Allende): Warren Hardy Spanish, http://warrenhardy.com

Nicaragua (Granada): Casa Xalteva, www.casaxalteva.org

Panama (Pedasí): Buena Vida Language School, www.pedasispanishschool.com

Uruguay (Montevideo): Centro de Capacitación; e-mail marco.moscardi@inc.com.uy

French

France (Paris): Lutece Langue: www.lutece-langue.com

Most Important, Don't Give Up

There is a big difference between being functional or conversant in a language and being fluent. Being able to ask a stock boy where the cream cheese is in the supermarket is not the same as discussing with your neighbor the differences between the fiscal policies of presidential candidates in an upcoming election.

When you become functional—and you will do that quickly, just as a result of living somewhere long enough—don't get stuck there. Take the next step. Converse, talk, and broaden your vocabulary and grammar. It will open up cultural and societal doors you never even knew existed.

PART TWO

Making the Move

It's a Big World . . . Where Should YOU Go?

YOU'RE ALREADY THINKING OUTSIDE THE BOX . . . or you wouldn't be reading this book. In the following chapters we'll introduce you to the corners of the world that make the most sense if you're considering retiring overseas.

We've selected them because they deliver the most "bang for your buck" and offer the attributes most retirees want: a mild climate, modern infrastructure including top-quality health care, and a reasonable cost of living. You'll find the countries we profile to be politically stable and welcoming to foreign retirees. But only you can decide if a place "speaks" to you.

There are organized expat communities in most of these places, and that's usually a welcome advantage. The hard work has been done and you'll have a built-in support network the minute you arrive.

You can, of course, take the "road less traveled." Beyond those we've profiled here, there are many places in the world that deserve your consideration. For instance, you may be drawn to Ireland and Greece . . . and based on recent global economic events, you may certainly find housing bargains there. In South America, the economic powerhouses of Brazil, Chile, and Colombia are all worthy of your attention, as are some Caribbean island locales, particularly the gorgeous Dominican Republic and the Bay Islands of Honduras. In Southeast Asia, the Philippines are an increasingly popular retirement destination. New Zealand also offers some appeal.

The point is, it's a big world and the perfect spot is somewhere out there for you. As for the countries we don't profile in depth on the following pages, you'll find more information on the *International Living* website at www.InternationalLiving.com.

7

Belize

No Shirt, No Shoes, No Problem (and It's All in English!)

———

WHEN WE DAYDREAM ABOUT THE MOST BEAUTIFUL SPOTS we've explored, we find that we're often daydreaming about Belize.

Belize is the place that made the phrase "No shirt, no shoes, no problem" famous, and as many of our fellow expats who've made this tiny country home can testify, that's truly a way of life in Belize. We can't think of a more proudly laid-back and unhurried place to simply enjoy life.

When we reminisce about a walk on the beach, as often as not we'll recall strolling north of the "split" on Ambergris Caye, watching the waves break out on the reef. When we remember great boat rides, we'll often relive blasting full throttle across the wide, placid bay in front of Corozal town. If we're harking back to ancient ruins and cultures, we'll likely think about San Ignacio town and the Maya who still paddle the rivers and farm the fertile hills in this region among the ancient, half-buried cities of their ancestors. And when we're fantasizing about owning a little beach bar and watching the rest of the world go by, we're usually pushing ice-cold Belikin beer to customers across a rough plank bar in Placencia.

Belize Fast Facts

Population: 334,297

Capital City: Belmopan

Climate: Tropical; very hot and humid; rainy season May to November, dry season February to May

Time Zone: GMT-6

Language: English, Spanish, Creole, Mayan dialects

Currency: Belize dollar, pegged 2:1 to USD

We try to visit Belize as often as possible. There are happy memories for us in virtually every corner of the country, and every time we go, we make more. Can you ever really have too many fresh fish dinners, rum punches, amazing reef dives, and concerts at pier bars over the clear Caribbean water, or breezy afternoons swinging in a hammock under a palm tree?

So much variety for such a little country. And to cap it all off, English is the national language . . . although even the way Belizeans speak English is exotic, leaving no doubt that you're in a Caribbean paradise, albeit one firmly attached to the mainland of Central America.

Has Belize changed over the past 25 years that we've been going there? Certainly. San Pedro town on tourist-popular Ambergris Caye is growing rapidly, and is now much more developed than ever. (There are now ATMs and reliable Internet, as well as coffee shops and wine boutiques!) Placencia, too, has evolved. You'll find new residential communities and all the requisite services. Even the mountains and rivers of the Cayo district are being settled, although if you long for wide-open spaces and farming, you'll still find plenty of opportunity.

Thankfully, one thing that never changes in Belize is the feeling of total relaxation that washes over you when you're there. There are just too many little fish shacks and beach bars and jungle lodges to find and enjoy. If you want to build a stockpile of great memories, one visit to Belize is all you need.

And just imagine living there . . .

WHY DO SO MANY EXPATS RETIRE TO BELIZE?

Belize has been popular with sporting types for years, and for many good reasons. The diving, snorkeling, and fishing are spectacular. The world's second-longest barrier reef runs straight down the country's coast, often only a few hundred yards offshore. Many tourists who came for the water sports decided to simply stay. And over the years, other expats have followed.

But, of course, there's more to it than that:

- *English is the official language*—Belize was a former British colony; in fact, it gained full independence just 32 years ago. English is still the official language, although Spanish and the local brand of creole are also widely spoken.

- *No currency conversion headaches*—The Belize dollar is pegged to the U.S. dollar at 2:1, and U.S. dollars are widely accepted.

- *Low, low local taxes*—Belize charges no income tax on foreign-derived income, no capital gains tax, and no inheritance tax.

- *The reef*—Belize's entire 190 miles of coastline is marked by the Mesoamerican Reef System, one of the largest in the world, making Belize a fantasy world of picturesque islands and cayes and spectacular sea life. The reef is the country's number 1 tourist draw.

- *Varied geography and history*—Belize isn't all coast. You'll find fertile plains, stunning river valleys, dense jungle, *cenotes* (limestone sinkholes), caves, caverns, and some of the most impressive Mayan ruins in existence. Belize was part of the central homeland of the Maya culture, and more magnificent ruins are being discovered every year.

THE TOP EXPAT DESTINATIONS IN BELIZE

Ambergris Caye—*La Isla Bonita*

Ambergris Caye (pronounced "AMber-griss key") and small neighboring Caye Caulker (also popular with expats) are among the most beautiful islands in this part of the world. Imagine soft, silky white sand, gently swaying palm trees, and impossibly brilliant turquoise waters, accompanied by a lilting reggae beat . . . and they're home to some of the friendliest, happiest people you'll ever meet.

As word spread about how easy these islands are to reach from the United States and Canada, Ambergris in particular has become Belize's center for ocean sports during the day and for partying at night.

San Pedro town, the major population center on Ambergris Caye, has about 4,000 part- and full-time residents. Golf carts and bicycles are a favorite means of transportation along the sandy streets from home to the beach or to dozens of restaurants, nightclubs, Internet cafés, and friendly mom-and-pop shops. At about 25 miles in length, Ambergris is the largest of some 200 Belizean islands, and to reach its shores, you'll take a ferry or a quick 15-minute flight from the mainland via one of Belize's two domestic airlines.

Despite being a popular tourist destination, you can still find real estate bargains on Ambergris Caye. Prices start at about $150,000 for a one-bedroom beachfront condo and range upward from there. For a long-term rental, you'll spend anywhere from $450 a month for a furnished apartment with no water view to $800 and up for a water-view apartment. You'll find prices about the same on the smaller (and even more relaxed) Caye Caulker, just 12 miles to the south.

Corozal—Laid-Back Bayside Living

At least several hundred expats live full time today in Corozal District, the northernmost district in Belize, with their numbers swelling during the winter snowbird season. Most are retirees. In fact, Corozal may be the most popular destination in Belize for expats who retire on a budget.

Another advantage Corozal has it that is receives less rain than most areas of Belize to its south.

Corozal town (the capital of the district) is a quiet village with a population of about 12,000. The majority are Mexican, Maya, Mestizo, Creole, and Garifuna, with an increasing number of expats from the United States, Canada, Asia, and Europe. Since it's only about 10 miles from the Mexican border city of Chetumal — with warehouse stores like Sam's Club and Wal-Mart, a mall with department stores, movie theaters with films in English, and excellent medical care — you'll find a large percentage of Spanish-speaking residents.

If you want to experience the town's diverse background, go to the open-air market. It's a place where residents often mingle, at least when they're not sailing, fishing, or swimming in the Bay of Corozal.

You'll find the water of the bay to be more opaque green rather than Caribbean turquoise, and Corozal is not nearly the tourist destination that Ambergris Caye, Placencia, and other of Belize's Caribbean frontage destinations arc. Many are put off by its mostly rocky beaches.

With fewer tourists visiting this part of Belize, you won't find many upscale hotels and restaurants. What you will find, though, are more affordable real estate prices, especially on waterfront lots. For example, a nearly 2.4-acre waterfront lot in the Four Mile Lagoon area of Corozal town is currently selling for $160,000. Small long-term furnished rentals start at about $500 a month.

Cayo—The Great Outdoors

The heart of the Cayo District is less than a 2-hour drive west from the coast, but Cayo couldn't be more different from coastal Belize. Instead of beaches, Cayo offers mountains, rivers, waterfalls, and caves. Locals and tourists alike enjoy hiking, canoeing, and exploring. Days can be spent riding horses, biking, visiting ancient Mayan sites, and cave tubing. Farming and timber are the big industries in this area, which produces some of the world's finest hardwoods as well as citrus fruit and vegetables.

Cayo also has a more diverse foreign population—North American, Guatemalan, French, Dutch, German, Asian, and many others. It is, in fact, the fastest-growing district in Belize, but since it also comprises the largest geographic area—2,061 square miles—the population density is still low. National parks and nature preserves also make up a large part of the district.

Most of the growth is taking place around the major towns, including San Ignacio, the capital of the district, and the neighboring village of Santa Elena. Spanish Lookout, where there's a large Mennonite-run hardware store, supermarket, and dairy, is just 12 miles away.

For many residents, a big advantage of this area is the climate. Temperatures during the day are similar to those along the coast, but breezes from the hills make nights a bit cooler and less humid. It's cooler yet to the south of San Ignacio where the elevation rises.

You can rent a basically furnished two-bedroom home in San Ignacio for, on average, $500 or $600 a month, or buy one in town starting at about $75,000. Homes on large properties are reasonably priced, too. A two-bedroom home on 20 acres, and just two miles from downtown San Ignacio, is currently listed for $199,000.

Placencia—Rum, Reggae, and Relaxation

For many years, Placencia has ranked with Ambergris Caye as one of the coastal areas that attracts the most expats. Driving down the Placencia Peninsula, a 19-mile spit of land that parallels the mainland, it's easy to see its appeal. The water here is vivid blue, the beaches white sand. Palms sway in the breeze. And with the vast open sea to one side and tranquil lagoon to the other, the peninsula offers nearly unlimited waterfront vistas.

Despite the many new resorts, condo developments, and sophisticated restaurants, Placencia hasn't lost its rustic charm. And the sea is ideal for fishing, diving, snorkeling, boating, or just enjoying the sunshine.

In fact, Belize's central and south coast retains more of its Caribbean atmosphere than you'll likely find on Ambergris Caye.

Food, entertainment, and the area's general appearance all have Caribbean flavor. Beaches are wider and whiter and, in many places, almost empty except for the occasional egret or ibis. And while you'll sporadically hear creole or Garifuna accents on the streets of San Pedro, they're consistently heard all along this stretch of coast.

At the south end of the peninsula is Placencia village (population about 1,000), with its brightly painted wooden buildings that house typical Belizean restaurants, bars, bakeries, and ice cream shops. You'll also find new low-rise resorts, more sophisticated restaurants, and a growing number of expats.

If you buy a Belizean-style wooden home on stilts, you can do very well, price-wise. A four-bedroom, two-bath home just 400 feet from the sea is currently on offer for $160,000. Or you can rent it, with basic furnishings, for $500 a month. And, of course, you can spend as much as you want; brand new beachfront villas with all the bells and whistles sell in the $1 million range.

Hopkins and Dangriga

North of Placencia—and closer to Belize City—are the seacoast towns of Hopkins and Dangriga, strongholds of Garifuna culture. Their music, language, and customs give the Stann Creek district coast a unique atmosphere.

There's not a lot to Hopkins. There are about 1,000 residents, along with a supermarket, a police station, and numerous restaurants. The road into town is badly rutted, and buses here are infrequent. But the locals, always smiling, are considered among the friendliest in Belize. The pace is slow, the beach is at hand, and the Maya Mountains are just a short drive away. Most notably, the way of life is special: Hopkins is considered the cultural heart of Belize's Garifuna culture.

Hopkins is a popular tourist spot. Hostels and B&Bs—some of them expat-run—handle the tourist trade. There are also at least two large resorts—Hamanasi and Jaguar Reef—that keep Hopkins on the map (though they close during low season).

For those who prefer town living, Dangriga is the biggest town around. Like Hopkins, Dangriga is right on the coast. You won't find white-sand beaches here — the sand is gold-brown and coarser. And the water often is murky near shore, especially during rainy season, due to the rivers that flow into the sea. But the sun is warm and the sea view expansive. With an airport, a small hospital, banks, and supermarkets, Dangriga is the big city in the area.

In addition to the airport, which connects it to Belize City, Dangriga is just off the Hummingbird Highway, the east-west road through the interior that connects Dangriga with the capital, Belmopan.

What about Belize City and the Capital, Belmopan?

In our opinions, neither Belize City nor Belmopan is worthy of attention as a place to put down roots. If you move to or retire in Belize, you will spend time in both places getting visa paperwork and other official government business done. But for most expats, the appeal of these towns ends there. The crime rate in Belize City in particular is high, and the city has been ravaged several times by hurricanes. In 1961, Hurricane Hattie caused such destruction that Belmopan was built as the new capital, farther inland, to escape the storms. Neither city is especially picturesque.

BELIZE'S MUCH-TOUTED QUALIFIED RETIRED PERSONS PROGRAM

You may have heard of Belize's Qualified Retired Persons (QRP) Program. Administered by the Belize Tourism Board, it offers some advantages to those looking to establish residence in Belize, including the ability to bring your personal goods into the country duty-free and to pay no Belizean taxes on any foreign-earned income.

To take advantage of the QRP Program, you have to be at least 45 years old and have a minimum monthly income of $2,000 from a pension or annuity (including Social Security) generated outside of Belize. Despite the name, you don't necessarily have to be retired. You can learn more about this program and its incentives at belizeretirement.org.

There's another option for residence in Belize, and that's the permanent residence visa, administered by the Department of Immigration and Nationality Services. There are several benefits to this program, too, including the ability to work and earn income in Belize.

If you're interested in obtaining residence in Belize, we'd recommend that you don't rush into either program. Instead, carefully calculate the advantages of each one, keeping in mind your income, lifestyle, desire to work in Belize, and the anticipated frequency of trips outside the country. Also keep up to date with changes—or even the prospect of changes—in both programs.

HOW MUCH DOES IT COST TO LIVE IN BELIZE?

Cost of living can vary widely in Belize, and that has a lot to do with location. If you're on the islands, you'll have the higher costs associated with having to import almost everything. (Belize has very little local manufacturing. Aside from beer, concrete, and citrus fruit, just about every consumer product you can name is imported.) However, you get all the savings that come with living in a tropical country next to one of the most fertile fishing grounds in the hemisphere.

Although we know some expats in Belize who live on a small amount, they're living more rustically than most of us would like to do. As a couple, we'd budget a little more than $3,000 a month to live in Cayo and $4,000 a month to live along the coast or on Ambergris Caye, including rent. You'll do better in Corozal, where you can certainly live comfortably from about $2,500 a month, including rent.

You'd do well to budget $500 to $1,000 for a typical two-bedroom furnished rental in Cayo or Corozal, and $1,000 to $1,500 a month for a furnished rental on Ambergris Caye or Placencia.

━━━━━━━

HEALTH CARE IN BELIZE

Medical care in Belize generally gets a poor grade. The good news is that this shortcoming is usually easy to deal with.

Minor ailments and many emergencies can be treated by physicians, public clinics, and/or Red Cross (*Cruz Roja*) emergency stations—all of which are found throughout the country. The cost of medical treatment in Belize is almost always low. Nearly all doctor's office visits will cost less than $50, and most private hospital rooms are $250 a day or less. Prices are also low at pharmacies, and in the larger towns they're generally well stocked except for specialized medications. To be on the safe side, it pays to bring your prescription medications to Belize, just as you would when traveling to most other countries.

Several years ago the government of Belize launched a program to improve the country's health care system, and U.S.-based Project C.U.R.E., a nonprofit organization, has delivered some $5 million in supplies and equipment to medical facilities throughout the country. Still, most residents say the health care system needs much more improvement. For anything serious, Belizeans and expats alike travel to Guatemala or Mexico for medical treatment.

Learn more about Belize at http://internationalliving.com/countries /belize.

8

Costa Rica
Your Easiest *Choice*

COSTA RICA HAS A VERY SPECIAL PLACE in our hearts. In 1997, having never been there before, we flew off on somewhat of a whim to be married at the Don Carlos Hotel in San José. It's nothing fancy, and the "ceremony" itself was laid back and casual, just like Costa Rica itself.

From San José, with a map but no itinerary, we headed north in a rented Suzuki Samurai on our two-week honeymoon. At the time we didn't know that "one of us" wasn't completely comfortable traveling without at least an idea of where he would lay his head or take his meal that night. If we don't have a plan, how will we know where we are going? What if there are no hotels with vacancies? What if we get lost?

Needless to say, we learned a lot about each other on that trip. And we did get lost . . . more than once. We also had the time of our lives.

We spent the night in a little hotel on the south side of the Arenal Volcano where we awoke in the night to see the majestic volcano spouting great red spurts of lava. We drove the "Monkey

Road" between Playas del Coco and Playa Flamingo where we did, indeed, find monkeys at play. We visited the beach towns of Samará, Jacó, Quepos, Dominical, and the gorgeous Manuel Antonio National Park.

Costa Rica Fast Facts

Location: Central America between Nicaragua and Panama

Population: 4,695,942

Capital City: San José

Climate: Tropical and subtropical; dry season December to April, rainy season May to November; cooler in highlands

Time Zone: GMT-6

Language: Spanish (official), English

Currency: The *colón*, trading at about 500:1 USD at date of this publishing. See XE.com for current exchange rate.

From the balcony of our cozy cabana at El Toucanet Lodge, somewhere in the mountains past Santa Maria de Dota, we watched a glittering spectacle of thousands of fireflies twinkling in the night—a perfectly magical ending to our wonderful Costa Rican adventure.

Fortunately for us, we're able to return to Costa Rica often, as it's one of the favored destinations for *International Living* readers, and we often host conferences there to help others learn about the ins and outs of retiring in the country.

We tell you all this for a reason, of course. When you visit, we expect that you will fall in love with Costa Rica, as we did. Possibly you already have, and you know that much has changed since we were married in San José in the spring of 1997.

Many of those sleepy little beach towns we visited slumber no longer. (Jacó in particular is literally bustling with tourists and nightlife.) The roads throughout the country are now (mostly) in better shape—including a new highway from San José to Jacó and another from Manuel Antonio south to Dominical and beyond. This new Southern Highway is opening Costa Rica's lush southern coast in a big way to retirees, vacation-home buyers, and investors.

But Isn't Costa Rica Real Estate Expensive?

Despite what you may think, real estate prices in Costa Rica are affordable—comparable to Mexico and other popular Central American countries like Belize and Panama.

As anywhere in the world, prices are higher in high-traffic tourist and resort destinations. That's the rule of supply and demand, after all.

But if you relocate to Costa Rica, it's doubtful you'll settle in a tourist destination. Most expats settle in the Central Valley, and there, you'll find prices extremely affordable.

Rents are reasonable, too. Paul and Gloria Yeatman spend just $500 a month to rent their furnished three-bedroom mountain-view home in San Ramón. Another couple we know pays $1,400 a month to rent a furnished 3,000-square-foot home near Playa El Coco in Guanacaste with a 50-foot lap pool and a "killer" view of the ocean.

Costa Rica now has two international airports, in San José and Liberia, and another on the drawing board—with environmental and feasibility studies in process—in the southern Osa province near the town of Palmar Sur.

On one of our most recent visits, we especially loved our time in the Lake Arenal area, where we met many outgoing expats and locals alike, and enjoyed many extraordinary meals at the Gingerbread Hotel and Restaurant and an unforgettable overnight stay at the Rancho Margot eco-lodge.

If you're serious about finding a new life and new opportunities overseas, Costa Rica is definitely one of the easiest and most enchanting places to make it happen.

COSTA RICA TICKS ALL THE BOXES ON YOUR RETIREMENT CHECKLIST

Long stretches of deserted and undeveloped beaches on the Caribbean and Pacific Coasts . . . dense jungles teeming with exotic wildlife . . . towering volcanoes, lush green valleys, and hundreds of crystal-clear lakes, rivers, streams, and waterfalls . . . mesmerizing sunrises, sunsets, and star-filled evening skies . . . All these things, and much more, have been drawing retirees to Costa Rica for generations.

Back in the1980s and 1990s, Costa Rica was one of the first countries to create a program that targeted foreign retirees. Its *pensionado* program brought tens of thousands of foreign retirees, mostly Americans, to the country. While the *pensionado* visa is still available in Costa Rica, many of the special perks it once offered have been discontinued.

Still, Costa Rica ticks almost all the boxes on any retirement checklist:

- *Conveniently close to home*—With many direct flights to its two international airports (and a third in the works), it's close to the United States and Canada, at less than three hours from Miami.

- *Excellent weather*—From the temperate Central Valley to the beautiful tropical beaches, there's a climate for everyone. Sunny and tropical or temperate and lush. Temperatures average 70 to 90 degrees F.

- *The most stable democracy in Latin America*—No other country has the peaceful history and democratic stability of Costa Rica—and no army since 1949!

- *All the comforts of home*—modern shopping malls and world-class hospitals. Reliable high-speed Internet is available just about everywhere, as is 3G and even 4G cell service—so bring your smartphone.

- *Low, low taxes*—You'll pay zero income taxes on foreign-earned income. If you buy a home in Costa Rica, your annual property taxes will be no more than $100 to $200 in most cases. *And there's no capital gains tax.*

- *Affordability*—With one of the world's lowest poverty indexes and a high standard of living, Costa Rica offers a surprisingly low cost of living.

Sure, some of these attributes are also true of many Latin American countries, which are all more affordable than the United States. Some are even closer geographically than Costa Rica to the States (but not by much). And while many have democratically elected governments, few have as long-standing a history as Costa Rica or offer the top-notch medical care you'll find there.

COSTA RICA OFFERS MANY ADVANTAGES YOU MAY NOT BE AWARE OF

- *A built-in community of English-speaking locals and expats.* According to official government figures, as many as 16,000 legal residents from the United States live in Costa Rica. When you count part-timers and those who live on tourists visas, that number may come closer to 40,000.
- *It's healthy.* Outside the capital of San José, you'll find little pollution and lots of clean water and fresh air. Costa Rica is one of the only countries *in the world* to reverse deforestation, and 99 percent of its energy comes from renewable sources. The government's goal is to be completely carbon neutral by 2021.
- *Adult literacy is practically 100 percent.* Thanks to the well-educated, well-informed workforce, many international companies have offices, factories, and call centers here—contributing to the strong and stable economy.
- *The happiest people in the world live here.* Sociologists from the Happy Planet Index say Costa Ricans "report the highest life satisfaction and have the second-highest average life expectancy of the Americas (second only to Canada)."

- *Respect for seniors and the disabled.* Older residents and those with disabilities are given head-of-line privileges at banks and government offices by law and in grocery stores, on buses, and the like.

COSTA RICA'S TOP EXPAT DESTINATIONS

Costa Rica has so much to offer that it can be tough to choose the single perfect place to live. You may very well want to try more than one, and many expats we know have done just that. They've tried out different areas of the country . . . moving from city to beach or vice versa to determine which appeals most. In fact, you'll find expats just about everywhere in Costa Rica, making integrating into your new life there that much easier.

These are six of the country's most popular and comfortable expat destinations:

The Central Valley—Ideal Climate and Convenience

Costa Rica's Central Valley is actually a high-altitude plateau—with an elevation of more than 3,000 feet—surrounded by tall mountains. In the middle is the country's capital city of San José.

Beyond San José, though, several Central Valley towns have become expat centers over the years. San Ramón, Grecia, Alajuela, and Atenas, to the west of the metro area, are well established. There's Heredia to the north; Moravia to the east; and Escazú, Santa Ana, and the up-and-coming hot spots of Puriscal and Ciudad Colón to the southwest.

What makes this region so attractive? For one, thanks to the elevation, it offers an ideal climate. Despite being firmly in the tropics, the year-round average temperature is the mid-70s F, with some areas at higher elevations even cooler. Another reason is that, because foreigners have been coming here to live for so long, there's a built-in expat "infrastructure," including social clubs, theater groups, poker and bridge nights . . . plenty to keep you busy.

The big city and all its conveniences are also close by. You can be in San José and its suburbs within an hour to 90 minutes at most from just about anywhere in the Central Valley. There, you'll find the best shopping in the country, including North American–style malls and warehouse shopping clubs (like Sam's Club). It's quite common for expats living in the Central Valley to pop in to San José for shopping, dinner, and a movie (new releases in English). If you want to hit the beach, it's an hour or so to the Pacific coast and not too much farther to the Caribbean coast.

The Central Valley is also the country's cultural center. Opera, classical music, jazz clubs, big-name concerts (Elton John and Bob Dylan were there in 2012, Justin Bieber took a turn in 2013), art festivals and museums, and other high-profile events . . . there's something to do every weekend.

About three-quarters of the native Costa Rican population live in the Central Valley. The *Gran Area Metropolitana*, as San José and its suburbs are called, can be crowded and noisy. But get out of the city and you'll find charming villages, bustling market towns, and plenty of quiet rural areas throughout the region. Rolling hills covered with sugar cane fields, cow pastures, and hillside coffee plantations are interspersed with lush river valleys and forests.

Despite the access to all the comforts of modern life, you'll find real estate reasonably priced in the Central Valley. A furnished, 2,000-square-foot, two-bedroom home with a mountain view outside Atenas, for example, is selling for $220,000, while a small, furnished, two-bedroom cabin with views of Grecia and the Poás Volcano can be had for $90,000.

The Gold Coast—Sunshine, Surf, and Beautiful Sunsets

Costa Rica's northern Pacific coast, near the border with Nicaragua, is popular for those seeking a beach lifestyle and warm climate. Known as the Gold Coast, this region receives the least rainfall and has more sunny days than anywhere else in the country.

It takes about five hours to drive to the Gold Coast from San José. But no worries; you'll find plenty of amenities and modern conveniences. And if you're looking for a mix of *Tico* culture and strong, well-established expat communities, this is your place.

Years ago, this coast was dotted with small fishing villages, and vestiges of this remain. Freshly caught seafood is abundant and cheap—sushi-grade tuna for $7 a pound, for example. But you have easy access to plenty of home comforts, too, such as imported foods, sports bars, and specialty restaurants.

You'll also find boutique clothing stores, golf courses, and tennis clubs, thanks to large resorts and residential developments like Hacienda Pinilla, the Four Seasons, and JW Marriott.

The beach town of Tamarindo, first discovered by surfers in the 1970s, retains a funky, laid-back charm despite its growth over the years. Going out to dinner in your swimsuit is perfectly acceptable, and buying groceries barefoot doesn't warrant a second glance. Playa Langosta to the south is higher-end, with plenty of million-dollar mansions fronting the beach.

About a half-hour north of Tamarindo is Playa Flamingo and the adjoining town of Potrero. Flamingo fronts a beautiful beach, with many of the homes and condos here clinging to a small, rocky peninsula jutting into the Pacific. It's more residential community than full-fledged town. At Potrero, about 20 minutes north, you'll find residential communities next to a working-class *Tico* village.

Further up the coast, Playas del Coco is a sport-fishing and scuba-diving center with a thriving expat community. It also tends to be quieter than Tamarindo, which has a reputation for a bustling nightlife scene.

The growing international airport in Liberia, the capital of the Guanacaste province, makes getting there easy, with several flights to and from the United States and Canada every day. Ticket prices can be a bit higher than the main airport in San José. But factor in a five-hour drive before your flight, and you may join the many who choose to fly in and out of Liberia.

By the way, this area was on the forefront of the housing boom in the early and mid-2000s. As in the States and elsewhere in the world, real estate got a bit out of control. But now things have leveled off. In the center of Tamarindo, for instance, a walk-to-the-beach, two-bedroom condo can be purchased for $77,000. If you want beachfront, there's a three-bedroom, 2,475-square-foot home in Potrero for $210,000.

Arenal—Peace, Quiet, and Rural Living

Thousands of tourists visit Arenal every year. For them, it's all about the volcano, which gives its name to the region. The town of La Fortuna de San Carlos sits at the volcano's base on the eastern side. Admittedly, the volcano is a spectacular sight, a cone rising 5,479 feet out of forest and farmland. But most visitors miss the best part of the area: the 33-square-mile lake, also called Arenal.

Lakeside is where the majority of expats live in this region. The shoreline is unspoiled, and the green field and forest on the hills that drop to the lake are dotted with homes. Along the lake road you'll find eco-lodges, B&Bs, and boutique hotels, but only a few villages, settlements, and small residential developments. Lake-view homes are surprisingly inexpensive. A recent listing featured a two-bedroom Costa Rican–style home for $59,000—and it has a lake view. A North American–style home set on the mountains above the lake in Aguacate is selling for $179,000.

The lack of development in the area gives it a rural feel and quietness. In North America, a lake this beautiful would be over-run with jet skis and powerboats, the shore lined with homes and docks jutting out into the water. Not here. Boat traffic consists of ferries taking tourists from one end to the other, some sail-boats, kayakers, and a few fishermen and pleasure cruisers. Every time we've driven the lakeshore road or been on the lake our-selves, we've rarely seen but a couple of boats on the water.

Nuevo Arenal, on the north shore of the lake, is a tidy village with a gas station, bank, pharmacy, grocery stores . . . most every-thing you need for daily living. (Check out Iguanas Tropical Bar and Grill at happy hour to meet locals and expats alike. And don't miss dining at the Gingerbread Hotel.)

The majority of expats in Arenal are clustered in small, gated communities and individual homes on either side of Nuevo Arenal. On the opposite shore, Tronadora and San Luis are small villages with simple but very affordable homes. Church, soccer field, and tidy, spotless houses—not much else. Tilarán is about 20 minutes inland from Tronadora. It's bigger, with larger stores and more medical care.

The Southern Zone—Classic Costa Rica

The southern Pacific coast, known as the Southern Zone, is what most people picture when they think of Costa Rica—steamy rain forest and jungle-clad mountains that drop dramatically to deserted beaches.

There are no large resorts. No high-rises blocking the ocean view. You get the feeling that if humans left the area, the jungle would soon grow over everything they left behind.

And it's the most biodiverse region in an incredibly wildlife-filled country. On our most recent visit we experienced this first-hand as toucans flew past while we drank our morning coffee on the terrace.

More toucans perched on tree branches outside the restaurant where we ate that night. We saw howler monkeys sleeping in branches above the beach and sloths moving slowly in trees next to the road. It's like stepping into a nature documentary—and that's without even visiting a national park.

The nice part about the Southern Zone is that it probably won't change much any time soon. The paving of the two-lane coastal road from Quepos to Dominical in 2010 made access easier—a three-hour journey now, versus the five it used to take. Still, this area gets far fewer visitors than other regions and planned development is low impact. Hit the beach and you'll see the result: You often have it to yourself.

Dominical, a lazy beach town and surfer's paradise at the far north end of this coastal zone, has grown up a bit since our first visit in 1997. But its personality hasn't really changed much. A few restaurants and bars line the beach road. We like nothing more than to relax with a *michelada* (beer and lime juice on ice, with salt on the rim of the glass) and a bowl of ceviche, watching the surfers—a simple pleasure for $5.

Uvita, about 30 minutes south, is the area's commercial hub, where residents do their shopping and other errands. Ojochal, another 15 minutes down the road, is not a town per se. Rather, it's a few buildings scattered in the jungle, crisscrossed with dirt roads—an unlikely place to find a collection of top-notch gourmet restaurants, featuring everything from French to Italian to Indonesian and Mediterranean cuisine. Yet it's happened, thanks to an international cast of expats who love to cook and a community that embraces the benefits.

Most homes in the Southern Zone are perched high on the mountains to catch the cool sea breezes. You can buy a lot with lush mountain views for as little as $50,000 or a turnkey patio home for $150,000. Or build your dream house. Custom construction is currently running about $100 a square foot.

Most homes in this area are built within the jungle or on former cattle pasture that is being reclaimed by trees, without clearcutting for gated communities. The terrain pretty much rules out developments laid out on a ruler-straight grid.

Central Pacific—A Comfortable Beach Lifestyle

Depending on who you ask, you'll hear mixed opinions about the Central Pacific coast. Jacó, arguably the best-known town in the region, can be a bit frenetic. Too much concrete. Too many souvenir shops. A loud and lively nightlife. Of course, plenty of people love that bustling resort-town atmosphere.

Playa Herradura, just to the north, is much quieter, in a sheltered bay with cozy seafood restaurants. And south of Jacó are several very low-key communities like Esterillos, Bejuco, and Hermosa, where surfers mix with retirees enjoying sunset cocktails on the beach.

Manuel Antonio, the town just outside the national park of the same name, offers no shortage of hotels, restaurants, and T-shirt shops. The park is, after all, the most-visited spot in Costa Rica. And the beach here, especially in the national park itself, is unbeatable—the most beautiful in the country, in our opinion. Protected coves, bordered by hills covered in lush green vegetation, aqua-blue water, and white sand—it doesn't get better than that. Despite all this, housing costs are low. A three-bedroom condo with a view of the ocean can be had for as little as $150,000.

It's not hard to understand the appeal of the Central Pacific coast. You can live on the beach and enjoy a "toes-in-the-sand" lifestyle. Plenty of expats do. And San José, with all the medical care and great shopping, the airport, and cultural activities, is just a little over an hour away.

COSTA RICA'S CARIBBEAN COAST—WILD AND RUGGED

Stretching for some 125 miles between Panama and Nicaragua, Costa Rica's Caribbean Coast is an exotic area. It's sparsely populated with splendid beaches, excellent fishing, great water sports, and plenty of opportunities to get close to nature. The Caribbean Coast is also called the Atlantic Coast, and newcomers often wonder which term is correct. Well, they're both accurate, because the Caribbean Sea is part of the greater Atlantic Ocean.

The entire coast is in the province of Limón, a wild and rugged region where the culture is also different from the rest of Costa Rica's. Limón Province was one of the last strongholds of the native population. Then after the installation of a railroad made banana farming feasible in the nineteenth century, plantation owners brought in workers from Jamaica and other parts of the Caribbean. Today the native Indian heritage is still apparent, and Caribbean culture is even more dominant—in music, food, language, and even politics.

The climate is also different on the Caribbean Coast, where it's hot and rainy for much of the year. While real estate prices are generally low in Limón, most expats who live in the area opt to settle high in the hills in one of several residential communities with a view of the coastline. You can buy a large lot starting at just $50,000 and have a top-quality, 2,500-square-foot home built for less than $190,000.

HOW MUCH DOES IT COST TO LIVE IN COSTA RICA?

The short answer to the question of how much it costs to live in Costa Rica is: whatever you want . . . within reason, of course.

Some expats in Costa Rica live on as little as $1,500 per month. To do this, you may have to forego things like expensive restaurants and frequent shopping sprees—but that's not what most people move to Costa Rica for.

As our friend, Jason Holland, who lives in the San José suburb of Escazú, says if you focus on what's important you can live very well in Costa Rica for very little money. He also says that you don't have to "keep up with the Joneses" here.

"Your 'needs' will become simpler here," says Jason. "You can live comfortably with a lot less stuff." Choose to live in the Central Valley where you won't need heat or air conditioning and your monthly expenses will be very low, indeed.

For sure you can live like a rock star in Costa Rica on $4,000 a month. Most expats, though, report they live happily and without sacrifices on a monthly budget of $2,000 to $3,000, including rent.

BEST OF ALL, COSTA RICA OFFERS WORLD-CLASS, *AFFORDABLE* HEALTH CARE

The World Health Organization praises Costa Rica for its public and private health care systems, and has ranked it better than the United States, despite spending 87 percent *less* on healthcare per capita.

Hands down, its universal health care system is one of the best in Latin America and, indeed, among the best in the world. Once you obtain legal residency in Costa Rica, foreigners are eligible (required, in fact) to participate in the public health care system, *La Caja Costarricense de Seguro Social*, or *Caja*, as it's commonly called. It's affiliated with 10 major public hospitals in the country and many small clinics in almost every community.

The cost of *Caja* is low. It's determined by your income but typically runs $50 to $90 per person per month. (Current rates are 13 percent of the monthly income amount you indicate during your visa acquisition process.) And that monthly fee covers everything, from prescriptions to doctor visits to testing to surgeries. Keep in mind that although the public health system has a large network of clinics and hospitals throughout the country, wait times for some routine procedures can be up to several months. Emergencies are, of course, treated right away.

As a result, many expats use a combination of the public and private health care systems. In the private system, wait times are practically nonexistent and doctors are very accessible.

You can also buy private insurance through the government-affiliated *Instituto Nacional de Seguros* (INS). Like most private insurers, INS excludes pre-existing conditions and does not take new policyholders aged 75 and older. Most plans cover dental work, optometry, and cosmetic surgery in the case of an accident. Prescription drugs, certain medical exams, sick visits, and hospitalization are covered at 70 percent cost, and surgeon and anesthesiologist costs are covered at full cost.

Annual premiums for INS are in the low $2,000s for those aged 55 to 65, and up to the $5,000 range for those aged 76 to 80. Many U.S. and European insurance plans are also accepted in Costa Rica, which has three JCI-accredited hospitals, all in San José. Most of the specialist doctors and services are concentrated here.

CIMA Hospital is affiliated with Baylor University Medical Center in Dallas, Texas, and *Clínica Bíblica* is affiliated with Jackson Memorial Hospital in Miami and EvergreenHealth in Washington State. And don't worry about language issues—many doctors speak English and have received training in Europe, Canada, or the United States.

Costa Rica's Quality Health Care Can Be an Affordable Lifesaver

One couple we know was paying $1,200 a month for health insurance in California before moving to Costa Rica. Now, living in the Central Valley town of Atenas, they pay just $88 a month (and that's for both of them) to be in the *Caja*. The husband has multiple sclerosis, but the *Caja* covers all his treatments and medications. With the money they don't spend on insurance, they can afford to have a private, full-time nurse, which would cost $9,000 or more per month in the States.

Learn more about Costa Rica at http://internationalliving.com/countries/costa-rica.

9

Ecuador

Something for Everyone

IN 2001, OUR HOME-BASED MARKETING BUSINESS in Omaha was doing great. But us . . . not so much. We were burned out. And each autumn, with the looming promise of another gray, bone-chilling Nebraska winter ahead, we dreamed about living in a place where we'd never again have to shovel snow or listen to the furnace burn money 24 hours a day to keep us from freezing to death.

Ecuador, however, wasn't part of those dreams. It was not on our list of possible places to retire.

Sure, we'd been reading about Ecuador in the *International Living* magazine we'd subscribed to, but we'd not considered living there. We were leaning toward Mexico or Belize, or maybe elsewhere in the Caribbean, and we had pestered the publisher of *International Living* to hire us to provide editorial coverage from one of these places.

Ecuador Fast Facts

Population: 15,439,429

Capital City: Quito

Climate: Tropical along coast, becoming cooler inland at higher elevations; tropical in Amazonian jungle lowlands

Time Zone: GMT-5

Language: Spanish (official) and Amerindian languages (especially Quechua)

Currency: U.S. dollar

Still, when we got a call asking if we wanted to change our lives completely, close up our current business, leave the States and all our family and friends, and move to Quito, Ecuador, to work for *International Living*, we said "yes." And then we attempted to learn all we could—as quickly as we could—about this fascinating and diverse little South American country.

Our first year in Ecuador was spent living in Quito and exploring the country from north to south, from east to west. We quickly discovered it was one of the best value-for-dollar locations in the Americas . . . especially since it had adopted the U.S. dollar as its official currency in 2000. The rampant inflation that had previously plagued the economy was quickly stabilized, and Ecuador embarked on an economic upturn that continues to this day, although prices for just about everything, from food to fuel to real estate, have remained remarkably low.

The word has quickly spread about Ecuador's incredible combination of value, weather, scenery, culture, and variety. The result: Ecuador now tops the list as one of the world's best retirement destinations for North Americans as indicated by *International Living's* annual Global Retirement Index.

AN EXCELLENT RETIREMENT VALUE PROPOSITION

What makes Ecuador such a great place for North Americans and others to retire? In our opinion, it's the country's incredible overall value proposition. There are few other countries where you can get so much for so little and enjoy it all in your climate of preference. We personally feel that there is no place on earth with better weather than the mountains of Ecuador. It makes for healthy living, and there's nothing more important than that.

More benefits of Ecuador:

- *Easy to get to*—Ecuador looks far away from North America on a map, but it's surprisingly quick and easy to get there, with two international airports, one in Guayaquil near the southern coast and the other near Quito, the capital city high in the Andes Mountains.

- *Stable government*—For years, Ecuador couldn't seem to keep a president in office. Some couldn't complete a first term before being chased out by disgruntled yet remarkably nonviolent demonstrators. Rafael Correa, a democratic socialist, changed all that by winning not one . . . not two . . . but *three* consecutive presidential elections. Democracy in Ecuador has become increasingly transparent during his terms in office, and Ecuadorians now have a true taste for political stability and the economic stability that comes with it.

- *All the comforts of home*—Ecuador's major cities offer all the shopping and entertainment opportunities anyone could want, along with theaters, symphonies, operas, pop concerts, art galleries and museums, and more. High-speed Internet is, for the most part, available and reliable countrywide. Roads are constantly being improved and upgraded, and the new Mariscal Sucre International Airport near Quito is modern and efficient.

- *Low property taxes*—We pay less than $53 a year in property taxes for our 1,100-square-foot condo. Need we say more?

- *Affordability*—In Chapter 2, we shared our monthly budget with you. From our own personal experience, a couple can live comfortably on $1,500 to $2,000 a month in Ecuador. We know some who live happily on even less . . .

- *A large community of like-minded expats*—There are communities of foreign retirees throughout Ecuador—most from the United States, but also from Canada, Europe, and as far as South Africa and Australia—so you won't want for English-speaking companionship or support.

- *It's a healthy place to live*—This bears repeating. Because of Ecuador's excellent weather, we find we spend more time outside, taking long hikes and short walks to the market where we stock up on fresh fruits and veggies. (Every town has at least one *mercado* where you can get farm-fresh produce, eggs, poultry, and meats.) With less fast-food temptations and more exercise, most expats find they lose weight and experience an overall improvement in their health.

Ecuador even offers some nice retiree benefits: While not the caliber of Panama's top-notch *pensionado* program, Ecuador does offer significant benefits to people over 65, including foreign residents. Discounts are offered, for example, on domestic flights and international fares for flights that originate in and return to Ecuador.

Other 65-and-older savings include:

- 50 percent reduction on public transportation, such as buses
- 50 percent reductions on admission to certain sporting and cultural events
- 50 percent reduction on utility bills

With some extra paperwork, those over 65 can also qualify for a refund of the sales tax (up to a certain amount) that they spend on purchases each month.

One of the best parts of being 65 or older is that you never have to stand in line. If you're a senior citizen, when you make a bank deposit or pay your utility bill, it's the law that you go directly to the front of the line.

The World's Best Climate

Okay, okay, "best weather" is totally subjective. But we unequivocally give this award to Ecuador, which lies right on the equator, and therefore enjoys 12 hours of direct equatorial daylight 365 days a year. (And yes, there is a rainy season, typically December through May, although it rarely rains all day.)

The climate you will experience, of course, depends largely on where you are in Ecuador, since on the mainland (not including the famous Galápagos Islands) there are three distinct geographical areas to choose from—the Sierra (mountains), the Oriente (eastern rainforests), and La Costa (Pacific coastal plains).

The capital of Quito, for instance, is less than 20 miles south of the equator, but at an elevation of 9,250 feet (2,900 meters). The climate is therefore spring-like year round: 50 degrees F (10 degrees C) at night and 69 degrees F (21 degrees C) during the day. Other Sierra locales, such as Cuenca and Cotacachi, enjoy similarly nice weather conditions. (While it suits us perfectly, some find Ecuador's mountain climate too cold. Vilcabamba, at a lower elevation, is warmer.)

The beaches and rainforests, on the other hand, enjoy the tropical temperatures that one would expect from equatorial lowlands, with highs ranging between 80 degrees F and 90 degrees F (26–32 degrees C). It can be hot and humid at the coast from November through April.

ECUADOR'S TOP EXPAT DESTINATIONS

Ecuador's most popular destination for foreign retirees, hands down, is the southern Andean city of Cuenca. You'll also find expats in Quito (which is where we lived in 2001 and 2002). Both cities offer an abundance of cultural activities, shopping, excellent medical facilities, and the perfect climate in which to enjoy it all. For those looking for country living, smaller communities like Vilcabamba and Cotacachi are top choices.

Ecuador has more than 1,400 miles of shoreline, and several beach communities are also drawing newcomers. Three of the most popular are Salinas, Manta, and Bahía de Caráquez.

Cuenca—The Colonial Heart of the Southern Andes

The blue-tiled domes at the back of Cuenca's New Cathedral are the city's most-photographed landmark. But there are many worthy others—a good deal of the city's colonial architecture remains intact, which is why Cuenca, founded in 1557, was declared a UNESCO World Heritage Site in 1999. It's chock-full of stunning colonial architecture, narrow cobblestone streets, shops, restaurants, and museums.

"We No Longer Have to Worry about Having Enough Money to Do the Things We Want to Do"

In 2010, Edd and Cynthia Staton moved to Cuenca, Ecuador, where, says Edd, "We can live a very comfortable retirement on our savings and small income here. And the truth is that even if we win the lottery, we can't imagine living anywhere else. Life here is that good."

The way Edd looks at it, "These are the best years we have left, and we're acutely aware that if we fritter that time away, shame on us. In Ecuador, we have the time and money to do the things we want to do. We live *very well* on $1,800 a month (including rent), and that's with extras we once considered luxuries."

The tempting aroma of little bakeries entices you. Just-cut flowers from nearby greenhouses overflow at the market behind the new cathedral. People relax on benches in Parque Calderón, Cuenca's lovely central square. Nighttime, when things quiet down, is great for a leisurely after-dinner stroll. Beautifully lit churches and prominent old buildings along the way are truly enchanting.

This historic area, known as El Centro, is also where you'll find some of the city's best restaurants and bars. Calle Larga, next to the Tomebamba River (the quintessential babbling brook), is party central until the wee hours of Thursday and Friday nights.

Understandably, most foreigners who relocate to Cuenca (and there are said to be several thousand now) want to be within walking distance of El Centro. But make no mistake; Cuenca's beauty is not just skin deep. It has long been known for its rich intellectual, artistic, and philosophical traditions—as famous for its many colorful festivals as for its breathtaking scenery.

As Ecuador's third-largest city and the economic center of the southern Sierra, Cuenca has leaped into the international spotlight in recent years. *International Living* named it the world's top retirement destination for five consecutive years beginning in the fall of 2009, adding to its other recent distinctions. In 2007, an international association of urban planners designated it as one of the two "most livable" cities in Latin America, citing its culture, low crime rate, and "middle class" feel.

To many Ecuadorians and expats alike, Cuenca represents the best city life in Ecuador. It's smaller than Quito, with fewer of the typical big-city problems, but with a total metropolitan population of more than 500,000, it's still large enough to offer urban cultural activities and infrastructure conveniences.

The growing expat community appreciates Cuenca's modern amenities, too. Along with its many open-air *mercados*, there are plenty of modern supermarkets and malls, great restaurants, excellent medical clinics and hospitals, handsome new condominium projects, and comfortable suburbs. Rental prices range from about $300 to $800 (unfurnished) for a two- or three-bedroom apartment close to El Centro. You can often find furnished rentals in this price range, too.

Quito—South America's Most Beautiful City

If your only experience of Quito is spending time stalled in traffic on your way in or out of this city of 2.2 million people, your opinion may not be high. But spend a few days or more getting to know Quito and we think you'll agree that it's a very special place.

Do Not Miss . . . Old Town Quito

If you have but a limited time to explore Ecuador's capital city of Quito, take our word for it—don't miss its amazing Old Town.

Along with Kraków, Poland, in 1978 Old Town Quito was the first-ever locale to be designated a UNESCO World Heritage site. Extending over nearly 800 acres, it's the largest historic center in the Americas and you can spend days exploring this colonial masterpiece. We highly recommend an organized tour with a knowledgeable guide from a company such as NuevoMundoExpeditions.com.

Two of the highlights of Old Town are the amazing La Compañia de Jesús Church with its gilt interior, and the neo-Gothic Basilica del Voto Nacional.

Often called the "most beautiful big city in South America" for its location in the palm of a valley cupped between towering Andean peaks, Quito has so many parks and plazas it's hard to pick a favorite. But ours would have to be the 14,000-acre Parque Metropolitano, bordering the city's Bellavista neighborhood. It's the largest urban park in South America. (For comparison, New York's Central Park is just 834 acres.) Hiking here, in the maze of forested paths, is a nature lover's delight. The air smells of eucalyptus and pine and, from atop the eastern ridge, the views of Quito to the west, and of the valley and volcanoes beyond to the east, are an experience you'll not soon forget.

On a clear day in Quito, in fact, you'll see the snow-topped Antisana, Cotopaxi, and Cayambe volcanoes looming over the city. (That's the way it appears, but they're actually some distance away.)

Quito, too, is one of the world's most affordable cities. We've rarely ever spent more than $5 for a taxi, and for an evening meal at a truly gourmet upscale restaurant, you probably won't spend more than $50 per person, and that's including wine or cocktails. *Almuerzo*—a fixed-menu lunch, typically soup, salad, meat/rice/vegetables, dessert, and beverage—can be found in many small neighborhood restaurants for $2 to $4.

First-rate health care is inexpensive, too. Even at one of the best medical clinics in the city, you'll never spend much more than $40 or $50 for an office visit — and that's with a top-notch English-speaking specialist.

And for a blossoming world-class city like Quito, property prices are also a real bargain. As a rule of thumb, you can expect to pay, on average, $75 to $100 per square foot for an older Quito apartment. Brand new apartments will fetch more. As for rentals, depending on the neighborhood, size and amenities of the property, and whether it's furnished or not, expect to pay $300 to $1,000 a month long-term for a desirable location.

Some of our favorite Quito neighborhoods include La Floresta, González Suárez, La Carolina, Bellavista, Quito Tenis, and El Batán. Near the city, but at a bit lower elevation, the valleys of Tumbaco, Cumbayá, and Los Chillos are popular with many upper- and middle-class Ecuadorians and expats alike.

Throw in the year-round perfect weather, and plenty of parks and outdoor venues in which to enjoy it, and if you're a true urbanite, you'll not find a nicer place to live.

Cotacachi—The Quintessential Mountain Village

Cotacachi has a special place in our hearts. It's the town where we've lived for the past several years; our little hideaway and respite from the rest of the world and whatever craziness is going on in it.

Cotacachi is a small town with a real sense of community. It's the sort of town many of us remember from our childhoods. There are a couple of barbers, a small health clinic, and a couple of small plazas. At night, the artisans' shops close up and only a few restaurants and small mom-and-pop shops stay open, although we now have more restaurants, and even a bar or two. . .

Still, you'll need to provide your own entertainment in Cotacachi. Except during fiestas (of which there are many), it's an early-to-rise, early-to bed kind of town. After a day of work in the 8,000-foot-elevation mountain climate, nighttime is for sleeping.

Near the popular market town of Otavalo (Ecuador's second most popular tourist destination, after the Galápagos Islands), and just two hours by car north of Quito, Cotacachi is a leather-artisan center, and its main street is lined with shops selling coats, handbags, boots, and more—if something can be made with leather, you'll find it here.

Few Expats in Ecuador Own a Car

Public transportation costs in Ecuador are low, so few expats go to the expense and hassle of owning and maintaining a car. From our home in Cotacachi we can take a bus to Otavalo, about 25 minutes away, for just 25 cents. From Otavalo to Quito, bus fare for the two-hour drive is just $2. Taxis are inexpensive, too. Even in Quito, taxi fares are low. (Taxi fare from the new airport into the city, a 45-minute drive depending on traffic, is usually just $25 to $30, depending on your destination.)

And by the way, if you do own a car in oil-rich Ecuador you'll currently pay less than $1.50 for a gallon of gas. This could change, as President Correa has proposed eliminating the subsidies that keep gas prices low.

In recent years, Cotacachi has also become one of Ecuador's most active expat communities. Certainly, that's caused some growing pains in our little community. Estimates are that about 400 foreigners live here full-time and many more are coming to check it out or spend part of the year here. That's not many foreign residents in a community of about 9,000 people, but the result is that petty-crime rates have risen proportionately.

The expats who live in Cotacachi generally tend to be outgoing and relaxed, since there's not much to worry about. Very little traffic, few wild temperature swings, almost no pesky insects, and low prices for just about everything. On average, rentals cost anywhere from $350 to $700 for a modern, two- or three-bedroom furnished home or apartment.

Vilcabamba—Fabled Valley of Longevity

Tucked away deep in southern Ecuador is Vilcabamba, in the country's southernmost province of Loja. The Incas referred to this area as the Sacred Valley, but today it's better known as the Valley of Longevity, because the locals commonly live into their nineties and hundreds.

Surely, they live longer, healthier lives because of the perfectly temperate day-in, day-out climate, the fresh air, clean water, and heart-stimulating benefits of walking up and down these mountain trails. At a perfect elevation of about 5,000 feet, Vilcabamba enjoys glorious weather all year with daytime temperatures typically in the 80s and with moderate rainfall.

The cornucopia of taste-bud-pleasing fruits and vegetables that grow here—and the many medicinal plants—also contributes to a healthy lifestyle. Cultivated for centuries without chemical additives, you'll find everything from sugarcane and corn to every fruit imaginable, including bananas, papayas, chirimoya, blackberries, oranges, limes . . . and even that elixir of the gods, coffee.

Over the years, Vilcabamba has attracted almost 250 North Americans and Europeans, who've purchased riverside or valley-view homes—most with enough land to grow a good amount of fresh produce or maintain a menagerie of animals. The mellow lifestyle, small-village atmosphere, and wide-open spaces were exactly what they were looking for.

While property prices have risen considerably in recent years, an affordable lifestyle can still be had. Our friends, John and Sue Curran, live in Vilcabamba, and while they own their home (and therefore don't pay rent or a mortgage), they say they live comfortably on a budget of less than $1,000 a month.

"With more gringos moving in, prices have gone up for restaurants, construction, stores, services, etc.," John says. "Fortunately, heating gas and gasoline are government subsidized, so those prices don't change."

John pays less than just $1.25 a month for gas for cooking and hot water. His monthly water bill is just $1.70 and electricity adds another $30 to the monthly utility bill. Thanks to the temperate climate, there's no need for heat or air conditioning. As we've mentioned, gasoline in Ecuador costs less than $1.50 a gallon.

John and Sue are careful with their spending. They don't go out often, and they do as much of their own vehicle maintenance and home repairs as possible.

"We don't have household help," says John (although the going rate for a common laborer is $10 a day). "Sue cuts my hair and I cut hers. It's not that we have 'extra' money because of the low cost of living, it's that we are able to retire here at an early age because our costs are low."

The Pacific Coast—Blazing New Trails

Coastal Ecuador continues to offer some of best investment opportunities in the country. While prices of coastal property in much of the rest of the world soared out of the reach of many buyers during the property boom of the early 2000s, they barely stirred in Ecuador, although experts say they've increased an average 10 percent per year in the last several years.

Ecuador's tourism and government officials are now making a concentrated effort to promote the country's coastal area. They're going all out to attract tourists, and behind that effort are highway improvements and new infrastructure projects. For instance, construction of the new bridge over the Río Chone has made one stretch of Manabí Province's beautiful coastline more accessible than ever before.

What does this northern Manabí coastline look like? Imagine stretches of the coasts of Mexico and Costa Rica . . . those areas where the mountains come right down to the sea, with rocky cliffs and wide, deserted beaches . . . and you'll have some sense of the beauty of Ecuador's northern coast. Along the flatter southern coast, beaches are wide and pretty, and in some areas seem to stretch forever.

And when we say "deserted" beaches, that's exactly what we mean. Much of Ecuador's coast is undeveloped, which is great if you own a horse, or want to speed from town to town along the beach on your bike or in your Jeep at low tide. If you're looking for a highly developed ocean-view resort area, however, your options are limited.

What about Weather along the Coast?

You'd think that anyplace at sea level on the equator would be unbearably hot, but that's really not the case in Ecuador. For much of the year, the Humboldt Current coming up from the Antarctic keeps the temperatures in the 70s and 80s. (Unfortunately, it also brings lots of clouds, and Ecuador's coast is often overcast.) We've been at the beach in August, in fact, when the temperatures bordered on chilly and jeans and a sweater were welcome attire. But most of the time, you'll find temperatures hovering right around 85 to 90 degrees F, with higher temperatures and some bouts of high humidity from November through February.

Ecuador just doesn't have the massive, multimillion-dollar coastal developments that you'll find in Mexico, Panama, or Costa Rica. Those of us who live here hope it never does. On the other hand, a number of nice small- and medium-sized developments under construction or on the drawing board will have an appeal for adventurous investors and potential expats.

Expats have settled all along the coast, from Tonsupa in the north to Machala, close to the border with Peru. You'll find them in small, laid-back, hippie- and surfer-flavored towns like Mompiche, Canoa, and Montañita, and in fishing villages like Crucita, Puerto López, Olón, and Ayampe.

The most popular coastal destinations for expats include Bahía de Caráquez, Manta, and the Salinas area.

Bahía de Caráquez: This attractive small city sits at the tip of a sandy peninsula with the Pacific Ocean on one side and the bay on the other at the mouth of the Río Chone. The bay is a safe harbor for boats and boatmen from around the world who take refuge in the Río Chone inlet and use time on shore in Bahía for R&R and to restock supplies. Bahía has also become increasingly popular with expat retirees who find its low cost of living suits them perfectly.

The cost to rent a furnished two-bedroom ocean-view apartment in Bahía averages $500 to $900 a month. If you'd prefer to buy, you may still be able to find a two-bedroom/two-bath high-rise condo with balcony and views of the Río Chone for less than $125,000—but they're getting harder to come by.

As a city of about 30,000 people, Bahía is a place where you can really live full-time. You'll find pretty beaches and nice waterfront restaurants. The possibility of a new shopping center and supermarket is helping to increase interest in this city.

Manta—Ecuador's third-largest city has it all: Manta is Ecuador's largest coastal city (260,000 inhabitants) and fastest-growing city—with a skyline dotted by high-rise condos and office buildings—and you'll find all the services and facilities you'd expect. As the busiest and largest commercial fishing port in the world, some of the world's largest fish-processing plants are here, along with several shopping malls, movie theaters showing the latest releases, modern hospitals, and fresh (and very low-cost) seafood restaurants.

You'll find a small and well-organized expat community in Manta, and if you're looking for a rental, you can find a comfortable two-bedroom apartment a few blocks from the beach for about $600 a month. A new oil refinery, however, is now being built near Manta, and local real estate rental and sales prices are increasing quickly as management and construction teams move into the city.

As for Manta's overall cost of living, that's reasonable, too. You'll have to budget a bit more for electricity as you'll probably need and want air conditioning, but you can live comfortably in Manta for about the same budget as you'd need elsewhere in the country.

If you're interested in living close to a city but not in it—and admittedly Manta has the feel of a port or industrial city—consider the nearby beach communities of Crucita to the north and Santa Marianita and Puerto Cayo to the south.

Salinas—Ecuador's beach resort playground: Salinas is Ecuador's largest coastal resort. It offers some great real estate values, and (for Ecuador) a more upscale beach lifestyle. As you'd expect, most of the activities here center around water sports:

game fishing, whale watching, wakeboarding, water skiing, yachting, skydiving, parasailing, and surfing.

Located at Ecuador's westernmost point, Salinas is less than a two-hour drive from the international airport at Guayaquil, and features an impressive row of mid- and high-rise condominiums that line the beach and curve around the *malecón* (seaside road) and crescent bay.

Although Salinas itself has a permanent population of less than 40,000, the number swells to more than 100,000 on holidays such as *Semana Santa* (the week before Easter), Christmas, and New Year's, when condos, rentals, and hotel rooms are filled to capacity. (Salinas is at the tip of a peninsula shared with cities such as Santa Elena and La Libertad. Combined, the population of the peninsula approaches 250,000.)

During holidays and high season (December to March), beaches are so jam-packed with people that virtually every inch of sand is covered by a towel, umbrella, or oil-slicked body. Streets are clogged by cruising cars bringing even more sand fans, and the *malecón* is wall-to-wall with vendors hawking everything from ice cream to sunglasses and shark-tooth earrings to shrimp on a stick, hot off the grill.

If you're the least bit agoraphobic, then, the low season, from mid-May to December, is the time to go to Salinas. During this time, Salinas feels like a small town. There is a good-sized expat community living in the area, although instead of in Salinas itself, most expats tend to live in the nearby communities of Santa Elena, La Libertad, Ballenita, and Punta Carnero, where you're more apt to find comfortable waterfront homes and low-profile condo buildings.

ALL THIS, AND *AFFORDABLE* HEALTH CARE, TOO

One of the great perks for foreign residents living in Ecuador is low-cost health care. An Internet comparison of health care costs from around the world found that Ecuador's costs are lower than those in China, Malaysia, India, Mexico, and Panama. In general, you can except to pay 10 to 25 percent of what you would in the United States.

Although Ecuador is technically a developing country, you'll find excellent health care in the major cities of Guayaquil, Quito, and Cuenca. Many services may not be available in rural areas. In addition, the quality of health care may not be as good in rural areas as in larger towns or cities. Keep this in mind if you are considering a move to Ecuador and have a condition that may require specialized services.

It's common, in fact, for doctors in smaller cities and towns of Ecuador to refer seriously ill patients to hospitals in one of the larger cities. For example, patients in Esmeraldas, Cotacachi, and Ibarra would go to Quito, those in the Salinas area would go to Guayaquil, and in Loja and Vilcabamba they would be sent to Cuenca. Health care experts also report that Cuenca picks up extra patients from all parts of the country—including Quito and Guayaquil—because of lower costs. A hospital administrator in Quito estimates that costs for care in Cuenca are typically 10 to 20 percent less than in Quito and Guayaquil.

You can rest assured that you'll find excellent care from doctors at Ecuador's best metropolitan hospitals. They've often been educated in the United States, Europe, Argentina, Chile, and Cuba, and continue to train around the world.

Ecuadorian doctors commonly work in both private practice and the country's public health system, and they don't expect to become instant millionaires. According to a Quito medical association, the average income for doctors is about $65,000 a year. In many respects, the medical system is reminiscent of that in the United States in the 1950s or 1960s. House calls are not uncommon, and office visits take as long as the doctor *and* patient feel is necessary.

Health insurance is a bargain in Ecuador, too. A review of comparable insurance policies for a 60-year-old man in the United States and in Ecuador tells the story. In the States, the man would pay a monthly premium of $1,200; in Ecuador he pays $70. A woman aged 50 to 60 would pay $72 for the same policy in Ecuador.

Learn more about retiring to Ecuador at InternationalLiving.com/countries/ecuador.

10

Mexico

The Top Foreign Destination for U.S. and Canadian Retirees

IN 2000, MARVIN GOLDEN CONVINCED HIS WIFE, Barbara Mercik, to take a work sabbatical. Just for a year, he told her. His plan was to travel from their home in Toronto through the United States and to Mexico.

Mexico Fast Facts

Population: 116,220,947

Capital City: Mexico City

Climate: Varies from arid to tropical

Time Zone: GMT-8 to -6

Language: Spanish

Currency: The *peso*, trading at about 13:1 USD at date of this publishing. See XE.com for current exchange rate.

Down the length of the Baja Peninsula, they went, towing their 31-foot travel trailer. They headed south along the Mexican mainland and the Sea of Cortez through Guaymas, Bahía Kino, and Mazatlán. On the Pacific coast, they spent time in San Blas and Sayulita before heading east into the mountains. When they arrived at Lake Chapala, the deal was sealed. They were staying in Mexico.

"We're no different than other baby boomers," Marvin says. "Mexico has all the amenities that we're accustomed to, like high-speed Internet access, satellite TV, newly released movies."

Plus, Barbara adds, "there's an emphasis on friends and giving back to the community—and a richness in learning about a new culture and language. And, of course, there's the fabulous food and a much lower cost of living."

Today, Marvin and Barbara live in a large mountainside home with panoramic lake views, a garden, and a casita.

"We have a life we could never afford in Toronto," Barbara says. "For a low cost we have a housecleaner and a gardener to help with our chores. Living outside in fresh air is a lot healthier than living in dry heated air in the winter and recycled air condition-ing in the summer. Not only that, but it usually takes us less than 10 minutes to visit our friends, and less than five minutes to go to work, and in sunshine and surrounded by brilliant color. We're here to stay."

Marvin and Barbara are just two of as many as 1 million U.S. and Canadian citizens who already call Mexico home or own vacation properties there, with more joining them all the time. In terms of numbers, Mexico is the most popular expat destination for North Americans *in the world*. (And yes, we know . . . Mexico is actually part of North America and not Central America as many people assume.)

For a place that gets such bad press in the United States, this may seem surprising . . . unless you've lived in any of the delightful—and safe—locations popular with expats throughout Mexico. We've lived in three such places: San Miguel de Allende and Ajijic—both in the central highlands—and Mérida, in the Yucatán peninsula. We've felt as safe in each of these charming places as we've felt anywhere in the States and we'd happily return to any one of them.

Is Mexico experiencing a terrible drug war? Of course—it's adjacent to the largest market for illegal drugs on the planet, and the profit margins for supplying that market are just too high to expect anything else. But Mexico is a huge country. There are small pockets of trouble zones, certainly, but unless you live in or near one of these, Mexico is a safe and lovely place to live, as hundreds of thousands of U.S. and Canadian expats already know.

And there are all those enticing differences that make Mexico so special: the vibrant local culture and rich history; the friendly people and their relaxed lifestyle; the sunny climate; the delicious food and drink; the miles of coastline (nearly 6,000), much of it warm, sandy beach. Mexico's Pacific coast looks much the same as California's, full of dramatic headlands and isolated coves. On the Caribbean coast you'll find some of the finest tropical beaches in the world . . . the beaches of Tulúm are consistently rated among the top five on the planet. Add in miles of Gulf Coast beaches, and you're in beach lover's paradise.

But don't ignore inland Mexico. The colonial highlands in the central part of the country are home to some of the most historic towns in the Americas, and with near-perfect weather year round.

MEXICO'S RETIREMENT ADVANTAGES

In Mexico, you'll find dozens of intriguing retirement destinations, each with its own character and appeal. With all that Mexico has to offer, it's not hard to understand why it ranks so high with so many U.S. and Canadian retirees:

- *It's right next door*—There are direct flights to the United States and Canada from many of Mexico's major airports, and most of them take less than two hours. It's easy to drive across the border. In fact, the border crossing between San Diego and Tijuana is one of the busiest in the world; some people actually commute back and forth to work. If you live in the Lake Chapala area or in San Miguel de Allende, the drive from the Texas border at Laredo takes just 8 to 10 hours.

- *Excellent weather*—The Tropic of Cancer splits the country in two, and northern areas experience cooler temperatures during the winter months while temperatures in the more southern region remain fairly constant all year. The variations that do exist are almost exclusively related to elevation. Because of the country's topography, Mexico has one of the world's most diverse climate systems. Forget about snowfall, but from temperate year-round to warm and sultry . . . you'll find it in Mexico.

- *Top-quality health care*—The quality health care you can expect to find in Mexico's major metropolitan areas equals what you are used to in the States, but it is significantly less expensive. And thanks to its proximity to the States, Mexico is emerging not only as a medical tourism destination, but also as a long-term and elder-care destination as well.

- *A great economy*—Mexico has one of the strongest economies in the Western Hemisphere, and it's surprisingly diversified as well. Oil, manufacturing, tourism, agriculture, and more all contribute to Mexico's economic strength, which translates into many First-World amenities lacking in some other smaller, less prosperous destinations.

- *All the comforts of home*—Speaking of those First-World amenities . . . you'll find supermarkets (with all your familiar brands from home), shopping centers, theaters, museums, great cell phone coverage, and high-speed Internet almost everywhere.

- *Low*, low *taxes*—If you own real estate in Mexico, you'll find property taxes are a fraction of those paid in the United States and Canada.

- *Affordability*—Even with all the modern amenities of a global economic powerhouse, it's still possible to live well in many destinations in Mexico on much less than comparable locales in the States thanks to significant savings on health care, taxes, and utilities, especially in the temperate highlands.

Add to that some advantages unique to Mexico:

- *Lots of English-speaking company*—With major U.S. and Canadian expat communities throughout Mexico, you're never far away from English conversation and like-minded people. Thanks to Mexico's huge foreign tourism industry and global trading capacity, you'll find that many Mexicans speak English as their second language.

- *Familiarity*—Even if you've never been to Mexico, you're probably familiar with Mexico's colorful culture, especially its food, music, and arts and crafts. Visiting or residing in any of Mexico's most popular destinations will not result in major culture shock. And that makes Mexico a relatively easy place to settle.

MEXICO'S TOP EXPAT DESTINATIONS

As we've said, Mexico is a large and varied country, and there are literally hundreds of wonderful cities and towns where foreign retirees have settled. Here are some of the most popular options.

Lake Chapala: Mexico's Most Established Expat Community

For generations now, U.S. and Canadian retirees have been attracted to the small lakeside communities that line the northern banks of Lake Chapala, Mexico's largest lake, cradled in a mountain valley in the state of Jalisco, just 50 minutes south of Guadalajara and 25 minutes from the international airport.

It's estimated that 30,000 or more U.S. citizens, and nearly that many Canadians and Europeans, live in villages like Ajijic (pronounced ah-hee-HEEK), Chapala, Jocotepec (pronounced ho-CO-teh-peck), San Antonio, and San Juan Cosalá.

These retirees are drawn by the temperate climate and the breathtaking scenery, especially from atop the Sierra Madre Mountains looking downward to the lake. With shady cobblestone streets, colonial architecture, and comfortable, Mexican-style homes with gentle arches and hand-painted tiles, the villages burst with flowers of every hue in gardens that bloom year round.

And there's the lake itself—about 50 miles long from east to west but not much more than 12 miles wide at its broadest point. The water is relatively shallow, only about 10 to 13 feet deep. And yes, the condition of the lake is always of concern to people who live here. At one point several years ago, decades of industrial pollution and mismanagement of resources along its main feeder river had helped drive the lake almost to the edge of extinction. Today, though, significant attention is being paid to the lake's health and the water level is back up.

Chapala is blessed by its elevation—roughly the same as Denver at about 5,000 feet (1,524 meters)—and its latitude is about the same as Hawaii. Local legend is that *National Geographic* magazine once referred to this area as having the best weather in the world. Whether or not that's true, there is no denying that the climate really is delightful. January is the coolest month, with temperatures averaging about 71 degrees F in the daytime and about 52 degrees F at night. May is the warmest month, with highs of 84 degrees F and lows of 62 degrees F. It doesn't get much better . . .

San Miguel de Allende—World Heritage History and Highland Charm

San Miguel de Allende—about a four-hour drive east of Guadalajara in the state of Guanajuato and a part of Mexico known as El Bajío—enjoys the same temperate climate you'll find at Lake Chapala. At a slightly higher elevation of 6,200 feet (1,900 meters), however, nights in San Miguel can be chilly enough from November through March that you'll be thankful that most homes have fireplaces.

Straight from a film set, San Miguel still carries the graceful notes of colonial times. Back in the 1500s, it was an important stopover along the silver route between Zacatecas and Guanajuato and on to Mexico City—a safe place for miners to stop and buy supplies. As silver flowed, San Miguel became a flourishing local market center. Whatever you needed or wanted could be found here. Meanwhile, the Spanish built elegant churches, magnificent mansions, and luxurious *haciendas*.

San Miguel soon became a center of revolutionary thinkers, and it was from the nearby village of Dolores that the national uprising began that eventually led to Mexico's independence.

Certainly, San Miguel is now firmly in step with modern times and bustles with artistic and historic energy, thanks in part to its popularity as a tourism destination for Mexicans themselves, especially weekenders from Mexico City, three hours to the southeast. But everywhere, its colonial beauty beckons, from the elegant *haciendas*, with blossomy courtyards and pattering fountains that now house hotels, restaurants, galleries, and boutiques, to its shady plazas with terraced cafés and its soaring, iconic cathedral.

In 1926 the Mexican government made San Miguel and its surrounding communities a Mexican National Monument, and in 2008 it became a UNESCO-designated World Heritage Site. You won't find modern architectural monstrosities here. At the same time, a mixture of foreign and indigenous cultures has created a cultural blend and a remarkable ambience that is rare anywhere in the world.

In the 1930s foreign artists from around the world discovered the wonderful laid-back lifestyle of San Miguel. After World War II came an influx of U.S. GIs who discovered that their education grants stretched further in Mexico at the U.S.-accredited art school, the Instituto Allende, founded in 1950. Many never left. Some renovated colonial buildings into beautiful, comfortable homes, while others built houses in the countryside, making San Miguel famous as a gathering place for artists, writers and other creative types who enjoy the city's many art galleries, excellent musical events, gourmet restaurants, and great bars.

With so much well-deserved enthusiasm, it's not surprising that the population has grown to about 140,000. An estimated 10,000 of those residents are expats. Just a 10-hour drive from the U.S. border, the two nearest international airports to San Miguel are in León and Querétaro, about 90 and 75 minutes away, respectively.

Puerto Vallarta—Star Power Creates a Pacific Paradise

If you're looking for a romantic destination, Puerto Vallarta fits the bill. Elizabeth Taylor and Richard Burton memorably put it on the map in 1963 when they came with hordes of paparazzi in tow. It wasn't much more than a sleepy fishing village then— a place where misty tropical mountains wrapped around the crescent-moon-shaped Banderas Bay and its gorgeous beaches.

Still famous for that gorgeous setting, Puerto Vallarta is now one of the world's top tourist destinations, with an international airport, professional tournament golf courses, designer shops, world-class restaurants, and beautiful people from around the world playing in the blue Pacific waters and strolling its famous *malecón*.

The last 30 years, especially, have brought many foreign residents to Puerto Vallarta. It's estimated that as many as 20,000 expats live there, which makes this the second-largest concentration of expatriates in Mexico, just behind the Lake Chapala area. That means you'll find a host of English-speaking professionals who cater to these foreign residents, and a vast variety of activities to participate in—from cultural offerings like lectures, art walks, and English-language theater to charitable events and volunteer opportunities.

The city lies in the center of Mexico's largest bay, Bahía de Banderas (the Bay of Flags), which is the seventh-largest bay in the world. The entire area—from Yelapa in southern Jalisco up to the bay's northern point at Punta de Mita, in the state of Nayarit—is referred to as Costa Vallarta. And it offers a seemingly endless number of activities, thanks to the natural attractions and the tourist infrastructure that has built up over time.

You can saunter down the *malecón* that stretches along the downtown area and look inside the boutiques, cafés, and restaurants. Or you can spend the day on any of the more than half-dozen nearby golf courses. If you want to escape the heat, the nearby Sierra Madre Mountains offer exhilarating activities such as hiking, biking, and canopy tours that take you swinging from branch to branch. And if you love water sports, options include whale watching, boat tours, fishing, sailing, dolphin excursions, kite-surfing, windsurfing, and parasailing.

The climate in Puerto Vallarta is definitely tropical, but ocean breezes and the nearby mountains create beautiful weather patterns. Sure, it's hot and humid in the summer (May to September) when there can be heavy rains and temperatures hover near 90 degrees F. During the winter (November to April), though, temperatures are delightful, ranging from 80 to 85 degrees F, and there is little chance of rain.

By the way, you'll find an active real estate market here — bursting with condos and apartments in almost every price range, making it easy for expats to find a place to settle in. (A friend of ours recently rented a furnished 1,000-square-foot apartment just a few blocks from the beach in Old Town for $1,050 a month for a six-month high-season term.)

Mérida—Ancient Heritage, Modern Marvels

Not long ago, one of Mexico's best-kept secrets was Mérida, capital of Yucatán State and one of the most charming and livable cities in the country. Today the secret is out.

Just a half-hour from the Gulf Coast beaches, Mérida is a center of commerce but also one of the safest cities in Mexico. Its downside is that it's also hot and humid, with temperatures often in the 90s and above. Heavy rains are common in June, July, and August.

Depending how many suburbs are included, the population of metropolitan Mérida approaches 1 million. But when you walk down the city's tree-lined streets, some paved with hand-laid tiles, you feel as though you are in a city that is much smaller.

Mérida is also an intellectual and cultural center. Home to five universities, several technical schools, and some first-rate hospitals, Mérida's citizens are well educated and relatively affluent. In the city's historical center, you'll find Mexico's second-largest *zócalo* (plaza), second only to the more famous Zócalo in Mexico City. It's surrounded by miles of colonial-style buildings and smaller plazas, all anchored by ancient cathedrals and churches. The Jose Peón Contreras theater, designed by an Italian architect and elaborately adorned, hosts a full season of plays. Art galleries, museums, movie theaters, and free concerts and dances in parks every night of the week offer more opportunities for fun and culture.

Despite the city's growth, infrastructure has kept pace, with new roads and utilities even in the far outskirts of town. The goods and services you'd expect to find in a comparably sized city back home are available here, too. You'll find Office Depot, Home Depot, Sam's Club, Costco, Sears, Burger King, McDonald's, TGI Friday's, Starbucks and high-end shopping malls.

Historic Maya sites like Chichén Itzá and Uxmal are within a couple of hours' drive of Mérida. Few sites offer a better look into the ancient kingdom of the Maya, a people whose influence and culture created much of what Yucatán is today. To the north and west of Mérida are Gulf Coast beaches and authentic fishing towns that haven't yet been overrun by tourists. For this reason, real estate prices are remarkably low—you can find your own piece of white sand for a fraction of what it costs a few hours east near Cancún. (Beachfront lots, depending on size, can typically be purchased for $50,000 to $75,000.)

Direct flights from Miami or Houston to Mérida take only two hours. There are several direct flights a week, and Mérida's modern airport is a pleasure to fly into and out of.

Tulúm and the Riviera Maya—On the Move in the Right Direction

If you're looking for casual beach living in a picture-perfect Caribbean setting, put the little town of Tulúm, about 80 miles south of Cancún, on your radar. The southern limit of Mexico's Riviera Maya and one of its most unspoiled areas, Tulúm is home to some of the most beautiful beaches along this coast. With pure white sand and turquoise waters, these beaches are the stuff of dreams.

For years Tulúm was a mecca for backpackers and others looking for a less-developed, less-expensive alternative to Cancún and Playa del Carmen. Amenities were relatively few. But today, development is coming to Tulúm, and it looks to become the Next Big Thing along this popular coast.

Today a fast highway connects Tulúm with Cancún. A new downtown, called Aldea Zamá, is being built to accommodate new shops, tour buses, and other tourist needs. A new international airport is reportedly in the works. (In the meantime, Cancún's airport—the second busiest in Mexico—is only 90 minutes away.)

Tulúm really does have a lot going for it. In addition to beautiful beaches where you can swim, bodysurf, and parasail, a reef system just offshore provides spectacular diving. For nature lovers, there is the Sian Ka'an Biosphere Reserve: nearly 1.3 million acres of protected jungle, wetlands, mangroves, and plains that's home to hundreds of species of birds and other animals. The reserve is just south of town—literally at Tulúm's back door. There are also plenty of Maya ruins to explore in the area, starting with those much-photographed Tulúm ruins themselves, one of the few Maya cities to have been built on a coast.

Tulúm is developing quite a reputation as an eco-chic destination, and thanks to its location just a few hours by plane from New York or Los Angeles, it's become very popular with fashionistas, film celebrities, and other creative sorts. For dining out, you'll find a number of eclectic restaurants everywhere. You'll also find bohemian-style boutiques and several yoga centers and spas (for those days when you need to relieve the stress of living in paradise).

As trendy as it is, real estate prices here are still affordable, but understandably, they're rising quickly.

___

HOW MUCH DOES IT COST TO LIVE IN MEXICO?

We've said it before, and we'll say it again: You can spend as much or as little as you want to live almost anywhere in the world. That's certainly true of Mexico, which is home to one of the largest cities on the planet as well as some of the tiniest fishing villages. Your costs of living will depend completely on where and how you want to live.

That said, we personally found that our cost of living in Mexico was significantly less than it was in the United States. Most couples will be able to enjoy a comfortable lifestyle on about $2,500 to $3,500 a month, depending where they live. And we know several living on far less. For example, our friend, Gary DeRose (who owns his home outright) and his girlfriend, Kate, live quite comfortably on about $3,000 a month.

It's possible to rent a home or apartment for $400 a month, for example, but we'd rather budget about $800. If you don't need cable TV or Internet, you can save on those expenses. If you live in the highlands you probably won't need heat or air conditioning, a big savings on utility bills. Additionally, you might consider whether or not you'll need a car and what kind of health plan you'll be comfortable with.

And, of course, if you like to eat out frequently, travel, play golf, scuba dive, and the like, you will obviously spend more money. But still, all these costs are much less than you probably would spend for a similar lifestyle in the States. (And with much better weather!)

EXCELLENT—AND AFFORDABLE—HEALTH CARE

In general, health care in Mexico is very good—and in many places it is excellent. Most doctors and dentists in Mexico receive at least part of their training in the United States. (And many U.S. doctors have trained in Mexico, notably in Guadalajara.) Many of them continue to go to the United States or Europe for ongoing training. Every mid-sized to large city in Mexico has at least one first-rate hospital. A big plus is that the cost of health care in Mexico is generally half or less of what you might expect to pay in the United States. The same goes for prescription drugs.

Of course, the costs of medical care will vary by physician, hospital, and the gravity of your condition. In the major cities of Mexico, you can get good-quality medical care for serious medical conditions, including dialysis, major surgery—even live-in 24-hour care—for a fraction of what you might pay in the States.

Another plus is Mexico's national health service, known as the Instituto Mexicano del Seguro Social (IMSS). In some cases expats can qualify for inclusion, and the monthly costs are extremely low. However, the system has all the challenges found with many national health plans . . . long waits, no choice of physician, and some less-than-stellar facilities outside the major cities. But as with national health plans in other countries, many expats find this can be a good safety net.

Because health care costs in Mexico are relatively low, many expats choose to pay out of pocket for many procedures. Many also buy private health insurance. As in other countries, rates for private insurance coverage vary depending on your age, your pre-existing conditions, the deductible you choose, and so on. But to give you a generous guideline, expect to pay between $800 and $3,500 a year for your premium. There are several private insurers in Mexico to choose from. One of the largest is Grupo Nacional Provincial (GNP): www.gnp.com.mx.

And note that you generally cannot apply for a new private health insurance policy once you reach age 65—most health insurance companies don't accept new policyholders after age 64. It would be wise to consult with expats in the area you are considering to get their recommendations.

Learn more about retiring to Mexico at InternationalLiving.com/countries/mexico.

11

Nicaragua
Ready for Prime Time

IT WAS A TIME OF CHANGE IN NICARAGUA. Daniel Ortega, once the leader of the Sandinista rebels and a former president of the country, had won the presidency yet again in a free and fair election in the fall of 2006. The world was holding its breath to see what would happen—especially including more than a few expats in the real estate business in Nicaragua.

Nicaragua Fast Facts

Population: 5,788,531
Capital City: Managua
Climate: Tropical in lowlands, cooler in highlands
Time Zone: GMT-6
Language: Spanish
Currency: The *córdoba*, trading at about 25:1 USD at date of this publishing. See XE.com for current exchange rate.

Having moved into our rented condo in the Pacific coast town of San Juan del Sur on the very day of Ortega's inauguration on January 10, 2007, we were among those who were waiting and watching. It didn't take long to realize that there were no earth-shattering changes in store for Nicaragua . . . life went on under Ortega much as it had under the three presidents who followed him when he left office in 1990.

For us, the six months we spent exploring Nicaragua from our base in San Juan del Sur are implanted in our memories as one of the most relaxed and enjoyable periods of our time living overseas. And that's despite the fact that Nicaragua at that time was still a very poor country with significant infrastructure challenges: terrible roads, frequent power outages, and slow Internet speeds. But regardless of the poverty, potholes, and blackouts, the Nicaraguans themselves were amazingly happy and carefree.

Even then, back in 2007, the country was well on its way to recovering from a brutal civil war that played out in the 1980s and in which the United States figured prominently. You might expect, therefore, that Nicaraguans might hold some resentment toward those of us from the States. And yes, sometimes its zealous president might lead you to believe that. But to the contrary, we have always been warmly welcomed and have always felt completely safe in Nicaragua.

We've returned to Nicaragua often since 2007. Each time, we feel a bit more like Rip Van Winkle . . . like we've gone down for a short nap and awakened years later to find out that everything has changed. Every place we go sparks another "holy cow" moment. For example, many of the major roads that we dreaded driving on in 2007 have now been paved. Power outages are far less frequent, and usually for maintenance. Internet, once spotty and unreliable, is now available practically everywhere and often fast enough for streaming video and more.

Today, the upward momentum and sense of optimism in Nicaragua is practically palpable. It's a nation at peace and one of the safest countries in Central America. Its government is democratically elected, and President Ortega has had the time to demonstrate that he is truly committed to a free-market economy and foreign investment.

"The Only Thing to Fear Is Never Wanting to Leave"

"Isn't there a war going on?" That was the first question Renda Hewitt asked her husband, Ralph, when he suggested a visit to Nicaragua. He assured her that no, there was not. The country's political issues had been solved decades before, in the 1980s.

Indeed, a recent Gallup Poll indicates Nicaragua is the safest country in Central America. The *Economist* Intelligence Unit says Nicaragua is one of the safest countries in *all of Latin America*. After living there for more than a decade now, Renda says, "The only thing to fear is that you'll never want to leave."

We'd concur with that. Nicaraguans know what it's like to go through stressful times, and to live on very little and still be very happy. They're generally proud, kind, and joyful people, and perhaps because of their political history, they're not naturally confrontational or aggressive.

Nicaraguans who left the country during the revolution of the 1980s have now returned—and they've brought First-World business skills and ideas with them. New businesses are popping up all over Nicaragua, adding to the energy and sense of renewal.

Truth is, there's much to admire about Nicaragua. It's one of the most beautiful countries in the Americas, with a dramatic Pacific coastline; long, gentle Caribbean beaches; and volcanoes and freshwater lakes that dot the hilly inland. Colonial cities like Granada and León offer visitors a taste of days gone by. Managua, the capital, is rapidly becoming a modernized city with top-notch theaters, world-class hospitals, and a range of international restaurants.

Complement all this with very attractive real estate values and it adds up to a near-perfect retirement or second-home destination. Whether you want to live quietly near the coast where you can sit back and listen to the waves gently lapping against the sand, or you'd prefer the hustle and bustle of a colonial city with everything you could possibly need (at half the U.S price), you should definitely take a closer look at Nicaragua.

NICARAGUA'S RETIREMENT PLUSES

Hundreds of U.S. and Canadian retirees have made Nicaragua home over the years, as much for the beauty of its beaches and colonial towns as for the low cost of living compared to North America. Here are some other things Nicaragua has going for it:

- *Close to home*—It's in the same time zone (either Mountain or Central Time depending on the season) as the United States. A flight from Miami to Managua takes only two-and-a-half hours and *costs about the same as a U.S. domestic flight*.

- *Convenient*—In its modern supermarkets and shopping malls, you can get all the high-tech products and all the familiar clothing and food brands you're used to finding at home.

- *Safe*—We've said it before, but this bears repeating: A recent Gallup Poll indicated Nicaragua is the safest country in Central America. The *Economist* Intelligence Unit says Nicaragua is one of the safest countries in *all of Latin America*.

- *Excellent health care*—There are good medical facilities throughout the country, including Managua's excellent *Hospital Metropolitano Vivian Pellas* that offers several private health insurance plans for both locals and foreigners, priced from $240 a year if you are 40 or older.

- *Welcoming to foreigners*—Besides a benefit-heavy foreign retiree program, Nicaragua offers many incentives to investors and entrepreneurs.

- *Affordable*—Amazingly, foreign retirees in Nicaragua typically say they can easily and comfortably live on budgets of $1,000 to $2,000 a month.

And the food? Local produce and meat is fresh, plentiful, and extremely affordable. Nicaragua may have almost as many open-air *churrasco* (grilled steak) restaurants as Argentina does. Plus, Nicaragua produces some of the best coffee and chocolate in the world. If you're a rum drinker or a cigar aficionado . . . you'll be in heaven. Flor de Caña consistently ranks as one of the world's best rums. And Nicaraguan cigars rank just as highly as those from Cuba and the Dominican Republic.

By the way, Nicaragua has often been referred to as the "Next Costa Rica." No offense to Costa Rica, says former Nicaragua Tourism Minister Mario Salinas, but "Nicaragua has a culture and diversity of offerings that Costa Rica doesn't have."

The government is doing all it can to position Nicaragua as a unique and intriguing destination all its own, and to "preserve our nature, our culture, our folklore, and our traditions, and to start attracting tourists who stay longer and spend more," says Salinas.

And that includes retirees and vacation-home buyers.

―――

ROLLING OUT THE RED CARPET TO FOREIGN RETIREES . . .

Nicaragua has passed legislation to encourage retirees and pensioners to move to the country. The Law of Resident Pensioners and Retirees (Decree 628) offers you many attractive benefits:

- You may import up to $20,000 worth of household goods for your own home, duty free.

- Any construction materials—up to a value of $50,000—that you import or purchase for the construction of your home are exempt from import or sales tax.

- You may import or purchase in Nicaragua a new car of a value up to $25,000 (and less than seven years old) and be exempt from import or sales tax.

- You can import an additional vehicle every four years under the same tax exemptions.

- Don't want a car? Rentals are inexpensive and as a retiree, you are exempt from paying any sales tax on rental cars.

- And to qualify for a retiree (*pensionado*) visa, you only need to prove a monthly income of $600 or more.

NICARAGUA'S TOP EXPAT DESTINATIONS

Thanks to two long coastlines and its varied interior, there are several great retirement destinations to choose from in Nicaragua. Some of those most popular with expats include the following.

Granada—The Heart of Spanish-Colonial Nicaragua

If it's Spanish-colonial charm you're after, you can't do much better than Granada, one of Nicaragua's most popular destinations. Less than an hour after landing at Nicaragua's international airport in Managua, you can be sitting at an umbrella-shaded table on Granada's popular Calle La Calzada, a cold Toña *cerveza* (just 75 cents) in hand.

There, as the sun casts its good-night light across the façades of centuries-old buildings, you'll be entertained by an endless procession of roving musicians, break-dancers, twirling *gigantonas* (giant folkloric puppets), trinket peddlers, and more.

Horse-drawn carriages still clip-clop atop cobblestone streets past some of the best-preserved colonial architecture in the Americas to the edge of Lake Cocibolca (also known as Lake Nicaragua), the largest freshwater lake in Central America.

Many of the old homes within a few blocks of the plaza have been purchased and rehabbed by both Nicaraguans and expats from all over the world, some of whom have started businesses such as natural food stores, gyms, yoga studios, restaurants, real estate agencies, and art studios.

In fact, ask some of the long-time expats living in Granada and they'll tell you that they "kinda sorta" miss the old days when the café tables didn't spill out into La Calzada and it was necessary to go to Managua for any real shopping or nightlife.

Of course, Granada's local *mercado* offers just as much fresh fruit, vegetables, chicken, beef, and pork as it ever has, and the little local restaurants and shops still feature the same local food and handicrafts they always have . . . and at some pretty remarkably low prices. At one of the best restaurants in town, two of you can enjoy a freshly grilled steak and a salad, a carafe of wine and dessert for less than $40.

León—The Country's Intellectual Capital

With its pretty plazas anchored by Catholic churches and its square blocks rimmed by high-walled buildings and cobblestone streets, León is commonly considered as Nicaragua's "second" colonial city, after Granada. But don't let that fool you into thinking that it's second rate. If anything, León may have at least one historical foot up on Granada.

Two sites here have earned UNESCO World Heritage Cultural designations. One is the impressive Cathedral of León, that anchors the central plaza. The other is the ruins of León Viejo, the original city founded in 1524.

Like Granada, León's historic center is filled with colonial archi-tecture, red-tiled-roof buildings, homes with central courtyards, and churches on every block. In fact, León may be home to more colonial churches and cathedrals per capita than any other place in Nicaragua, although as yet, tourists and expats aren't arriving in any great numbers to check them out.

Home to several of Nicaragua's major universities, León blends youthful energy with deep historical and cultural roots. And in the crypts of the Cathedral of León—built between 1747 and 1814 in a colonial-Baroque style with thick walls that have endured earthquakes, volcanic eruptions, and public uprisings— you'll find the remains of some of Nicaragua's most illustrious public figures. Among these are political heroes, musicians, and poets, including Nicaragua's beloved Rubén Dario, who spent his childhood in this city. (Poetry in all forms is one of Nicaragua's best characteristics.)

Still—despite its treasures and charms, León is not a city where you'll find luxury hotels, ultra-chic restaurants, hoity-toity spas, and boutique shops. It's a real, honest-to-goodness working city, not much dependent on tourist dollars. And since León isn't as much of a tourist destination, you're better able to blend in and experience true Nicaraguan life.

Two other bonuses are the nearby beach towns of Poneloya and Las Peñitas, with long stretches of flat, sandy beaches lined with restaurants and vacation homes. They're just 20 minutes from León and provide a welcome escape from the city heat.

San Juan del Sur and the South Pacific Coast—The Next Big Thing

San Juan del Sur, a once sleepy fishing village just north of the Costa Rican border, is where you'll find the main concentration of expats along Nicaragua's southern Pacific Coast.

It's not hard to understand why. The *malecón* runs the length of the nearly two-mile-long protected bay where the town sits. Seafood restaurants line the beach, offering fish fresh from the boat. Steep hills rise sharply from the shoreline at the north and south ends of town. Local fishing boats share space with pleasure cruisers in the harbor.

The town itself is charmingly shabby, with seaside shacks, faded signs, and worn wooden tin-roofed buildings painted in a rainbow of colors. Wear more than shorts and a T-shirt, and you're overdressed. In the heat of the afternoon, you'll be looking for a hammock in a shady spot.

By early evening the *malecón* fills with strolling Nica families, tourists, and local expats heading to dinner. There is a lively nightlife to be had in San Juan del Sur, and for this reason, many of the town's expats live outside the town center.

But San Juan del Sur is just part of the story along this stretch of coast. The excellent surf has beckoned the younger crowd for years, but only recently has the long, dramatic coastline of Nicaragua's Rivas Province drawn major attention from retirees and vacation home buyers from outside the country.

In particular, a couple of large, mixed-use residential and resort communities are maturing into major draws for retirees and vacationers from around the world.

The granddaddy of these Rivas coast projects is Rancho Santana, and full disclosure: It's owned by *International Living's* parent company, Agora Inc. Even if it weren't, it would still be one of our favorite spots in pretty Nicaragua.

Nearly 50 private homes are spread across 3,000 acres overlooking a series of sandy beaches and hidden half-moon bays. Aside from both its part-time and permanent residents, Rancho Santana is a destination resort in its own right, with a new boutique inn and a section of ocean-view condos with close-up views of one of the country's best surfing beaches. And its La Finca y el Mar Restaurant is one of the best in Nicaragua.

Just south of Rancho Santana, an impressive new project called Guacalito de la Isla is being developed by Don Carlos Pellas, the scion of one of Nicaragua's wealthiest families. The 1,670-acre resort features a hotel, spa, beach club, vacation homes, and a par-72 golf course designed by David McLay Kidd. Don Pellas's plan is to put this section of Nicaragua's Pacific coast firmly on the map while benefiting the local economy and helping preserve the environment by incorporating as many eco-friendly practices as possible.

There are other projects and resorts in the southern Pacific zone, as well, all of which can't help but benefit from all this growing attention. There's even discussion of a new airport and local coastal road in the works.

Nicaragua's Caribbean Coast—Yes, It Has One!

Named for the Dutch pirate Henry Bluefeldt who hid out there in the early 1600s, the town of Bluefields sits at the mouth of Río Escondido where it joins the murky Bluefields Bay on Nicaragua's eastern shore. It's the country's principal Caribbean port and the heart and soul of this primarily English-speaking region. If you like hot reggae dance clubs, bustling markets, and strolling along busy seaport waterfronts, you'll like Bluefields. But for many expats and tourists, Bluefields is simply where the plane lands before taking off again for Nicaragua's Corn Islands.

Just about 40 miles from the mainland, the Corn Islands, or *las Islas del Maíz*, are what the Caribbean was like long ago, before the big resorts moved in. Big Corn Island covers just four square miles and is lush with green, forested hills and mangrove swamps in the interior and miles of beautiful white coral sand beaches on the fringes. Its 8,000 inhabitants—descended from European pirates, British landowners, and African slaves—are friendly and welcoming.

The island's main population center is on the west side in and around the main town of Brig Bay, while the east is sparsely populated, with sections of rocky coast, lagoons, and mangrove swamps. Prevailing easterly winds keep the nights cool and comfortable.

As for the economy, it was based mainly on palm oil production until 1988, when Hurricane Joan's 125-mph winds destroyed most of the island's palm trees. Today, the islanders make their living plying the seas for lobster, and tourism is just starting to take off. And when we say "just starting" we mean it . . . there is but one dive shop on the island even though one of the world's largest underwater reefs is just offshore. There are no coffee shops, no Internet cafés, and no grocery stores with anything but the most basic supplies.

Little Corn Island is smaller than Big Corn, as you might guess from the name, and it is every bit the tiny Caribbean hideaway. Ringed with sparkling white sand beaches and clear blue waters, it's a pristine destination for those who travel well off the beaten track. There's excellent fishing, world-class diving, mouth-watering seafood, and the companionship of a lively but small group of hard-core travelers. Only about 800 acres in size, there are no motor vehicles on Little Corn, and only about 250 visitors can be accommodated at one time.

Development is happening in the area, on both Little and Big Corn and on the coast near Bluefields, but it is happening slowly and not in any large-scale way. We expect the area's unique and off-the-beaten-path character to carry on for some time yet, which is just fine with the few expats who have found their way here.

Managua—Nicaragua's Big City

Managua's recent history has been shaky . . . literally. A fault line runs under the city and there are active volcanoes nearby. A 1972 earthquake leveled much of the city, including its historic old-town area, so Managua lacks much of the Spanish Colonial charm of many other Latin American capitals.

Managua is halfway between León and Granada, two towns that were adversaries for the location of Nicaragua's capital city, and it was originally built in 1852 as a compromise to settle that rivalry and to ensure that the capital is equally distant from just about anywhere in the country.

Today, it's the economic and political hub of Nicaragua, and the location of the Augusto C. Sandino International Airport. You'll find the country's best health care offerings here, too. This makes Managua a natural base for expats who enjoy city living or are involved in businesses such as manufacturing, shipping, or tele-communications. With a population of over 2 million, Managua has a large potential workforce, and the services and offices needed by foreign investors can all be found here.

Of course, major shopping malls and supermarkets can be found here, too. In Managua you'll find many familiar brand-name products and all the services and amenities of a modern-day city.

HOW MUCH DOES IT COST TO LIVE IN NICARAGUA?

Nicaragua, as Ecuador does, offers a tremendous value proposi-tion. We've met people living in Nicaragua quite comfortably on as little as $1,000 a month. Carol Dorsett, who owns a home at Rancho Santana, says she's doing exactly that . . . and that includes her $100 a month homeowners' association dues, her weekly housekeeper fees, and gas for her car.

A couple paying rent, though, should probably budget $2,000 a month. It's hard to think of how you might spend more, unless you have a large home and run your air conditioner full-time and/or you have expensive dining and entertainment tastes.

Why is the cost of living so low in Nicaragua? Things just cost less. Labor costs are low, as are construction costs and just about everything else. Small and very modest furnished rentals start at about $300 a month and range upward. Typically, you might expect to pay $800 to $1,000 for a long-term furnished two- or three-bedroom rental in either Granada or San Juan del Sur.

Health care and health insurance costs are about one-fifth of what you'd pay in the States. Car insurance costs are low, too . . . and it's a small country so you won't spend much on gas to get anywhere you want to go. Many foreign retirees find they don't even need a car.

As for groceries . . . sure, you can buy your favorite imported brands—and pay more. But eat like a local and you'll not only be healthier, but you'll also save money. Anything you could possibly want is produced locally, from exotic fruits and vegetables to free-range cattle and chicken to absolutely fresh, delicious seafood.

WHAT ABOUT HEALTH CARE?

On our most recent visit to Nicaragua, we were impressed with the stories expat retirees shared with us about the quality health care they're receiving in Nicaragua. Surgeries . . . emergencies . . . routine checkups . . . treatments that "on the first try actually cure what ails you," as one expat said, "and doctors who give you their cell phone numbers and say 'Call me anytime' . . . and they actually mean it!"

In towns like Granada and San Juan del Sur, you'll find doctors, dentists, well-stocked pharmacies, and clinics that are adequately equipped to treat everyday illnesses and provide emergency medical services. León, being a city of 175,000 people, takes it up a notch, with excellent hospitals and medical personnel.

If you need high-tech, advanced medical care, it's likely you'll go to Managua—and that's easy to do since Nicaragua is a small country. Granada is less than an hour from Managua. León is just a bit farther. From San Juan del Sur, you're only about two hours from Managua—and that's via good roads all the way. (Quick and efficient helicopter service is available for serious emergencies.)

There are several excellent hospitals in Managua, including the Hospital Bautista, the Military Hospital, and the Hospital Metropolitano Vivian Pellas—one of only six hospitals in all of Central America to earn JCI accreditation.

The Vivian Pellas Hospital, as most people refer to it, is well equipped with all the latest technology and everything you might expect in a truly first-class hospital. Just about every specialty or procedure you might need is offered, and it's staffed by excellent doctors. Most studied or did residencies in the United States, Europe, or elsewhere, and many speak English. Every expat we spoke with who's had occasion to use the hospital raves about the quality of care and the personal level of attention they received.

Best of all, the Vivian Pellas Hospital offers an amazing discount program (what we commonly think of as a hospital-based plan) for a very small monthly fee . . . as low as $20 if you're 40 or older. Depending on your age and health condition, you can buy into this program and receive discounts of up to 80 percent, and that's on everything from doctor's visits to lab work, MRIs, surgeries, and prescriptions. And you needn't to be a resident of Nicaragua to participate.

Learn more about retiring to Nicaragua at InternationalLiving.com/ countries/nicaragua.

12

Panama

The World's Best Retirement Program (and Much More)

COMING INTO THE CITY AT MID-AFTERNOON, the plane flies low across the bright sky over the sparkling Pacific Ocean. Below, the Pearl Islands lie strung across the azure landscape like the jewels they are. Lush with green jungle and surrounded by golden beaches, one has just a rickety wooden boat dock, another is large enough to support a small village, and all 100-plus are stunningly beautiful.

Once on the ground, the shuttle van speeds from the airport toward the gleaming city, and eyes again are drawn to the ocean view whizzing by to the left where daredevil pelicans circle and then, in an instant, fold their wings and plunge like arrows into the surf.

It's always good to be back in Panama, where we lived for most of 2006. The tiny nation on the southern edge of the Northern

---

Panama Fast Facts

Population: 3,559,408

Capital City: Panama City

Climate: Tropical maritime (with temperate regions in Highlands); average temperature 88 degrees F; wet season May through November, dry or summer season December through April.

Time Zone: GMT-5

Language: Spanish (official), English 14 percent (many Panamanians are bilingual)

Currency: U.S. dollar

Hemisphere is one of the only countries to bridge two continents . . . and the *only country in the world* where you can see the sun rise over the Pacific Ocean and set on the Atlantic in the same day.

If you didn't know that, don't worry—there are so many things unique to Panama that it's hard to track them all. For instance . . .

Panama is the *only* country in Central America with no hurricanes. It uses the U.S. dollar as its official currency, though it is locally referred to as the *balboa*. (Panama mints its own coins, which are used alongside U.S. coins.) And it's the *only* country in the world where you'll find a protected, tropical rainforest within city limits.

Panama is also the only country in the world with a $2 billion revenue stream on its doorstep—although "stream" is not the right way to describe the wonder of the world that is the Panama Canal—making Panama the *only* country with a waterway that connects the Atlantic and Pacific Oceans (and a huge reason for this country's economic stability and growing economy).

We could go on and on. Every month, it seems, Panama tops another index, whether for its solid GDP, technology and infrastructure, globalization, tourism. . . So far, it's the only country in Central America to build a light rail commuter system in its modern capital city. You'll also find the first Waldorf-Astoria Hotel in Latin America and Frank Gehry's first Latin American design, the Bridge of Life bio-museum.

As you might imagine in the country that's home to one of the world's most crucial and busiest shipping routes, Panama boasts the most advanced and modern infrastructure in Central America. Tocumen International Airport, home base and hub for Copa Airlines, is a nexus for connections to North, Central, and South America. Major airlines fly in and out of Tocumen, too, including directly to and from the United States, Canada, and Europe.

So it's no wonder that Panama is called the "Hub of the Americas," and this is one quality that expats appreciate most: Panama is quick and easy to travel to and from, and its communications networks are the region's most reliable.

But the attribute that should be of most importance to you is this: Panama offers one of the world's best retirement programs, and foreign retirees with resident visas are welcome to participate. If you're looking for a place where you can live more affordably, but you don't have to give up real First-World amenities, put Panama at the top of your list.

MONEY-SAVING DISCOUNTS AND MORE

Panama's long-standing *pensionado* (retiree) program, widely regarded as the best retirement program in the world, offers significant discounts to retirees. To qualify, you simply need documentation of a guaranteed pension income of $1,000 a month from a government agency (e.g., Social Security, disability, armed forces) or corporation. If you opt to buy a home in Panama valued at $100,000 or more, that amount is reduced to just $750 per month. (Keep in mind that requirements and benefits may be adjusted at any time.)

The details: As a qualified *pensionado* in Panama, you're entitled to the following:

- 50 percent off entertainment—such as movies, theaters, concerts, and sporting events, anywhere in the country
- 50 percent off closing costs for home loans and more
- 50 percent off hotel stays from Monday through Thursday
- 30 percent off hotel stays from Friday through Sunday
- 30 percent off bus, boat, and train fares

- 25 percent off airline tickets
- 25 percent off at restaurants
- 20 percent off medical consultations
- 20 percent off professional and technical services
- 15 percent off hospital bills (if no insurance applies)
- 15 percent off dental and eye exams
- 10 percent off prescription medicines
- And more. . .

You're also entitled to a one-time exemption from duties on the importation of your household goods (up to $10,000).

EVEN MORE REASONS TO APPRECIATE PANAMA . . .

For a number of years now, Panama has been a popular destination for foreign retirees, thanks yet again to the Canal. As you may know, the Canal was under U.S. jurisdiction until as recently as 1979 when it became a joint operation of the United States and Panama. In 1999, Panama gained control of the Canal, thanks to a treaty signed in 1977 by U.S. President Jimmy Carter, who has often vacationed in the country. (We crossed paths with him and his wife, Rosalynn, out for a stroll on Contadora Island during the Christmas holidays of 2006.)

The Canal Zone of Panama City was a separate entity, populated for many years by U.S. military members and their families as well as many others working in connection with the Canal. Many of these "Zonians" and their families chose to stay in Panama after the zone reverted to Panamanian administration. Today, the tie between the United States and Panama remains strong, and the long-standing familiarity with and acceptance of foreign nationals makes Panama a consistent top-ranking destination on *International Living's* annual Global Retirement Index.

Certainly, Panama is a place where cultures converge. Walk the bustling, cosmopolitan streets of Panama City and you'll commonly hear English and other languages spoken. And just about anything you might be looking for in the way of international cuisine can be found in Panama's modern supermarkets and restaurants.

In fact, Panama offers many reasons for your consideration:

- It's close to the United States (just a two-and-a-half-hour flight from Miami)
- It's politically stable and business friendly
- You'll find excellent weather, with a climate for everyone, from tropical beaches to temperate mountains . . . and no hurricanes
- It offers top-quality healthcare—the gleaming new Punta Pacifica Hospital is affiliated with Baltimore's renowned Johns Hopkins Hospital
- You'll pay no income taxes on foreign-earned income
- You can drink the tap water most everywhere
- A wide range of newly constructed residential properties carry a 15-year property tax exemption from date of completion
- It's affordable—you can live comfortably on $2,000 to $3,000 a month

---

Yes, You Can Bring Your Pets to Panama

Satisfy all the typical requirements (immunizations, international health certificates, etc.) and it's easy to bring your dogs and cats to Panama. But be aware that Panama is one of the only countries requiring an "in-house" quarantine for 40 days. Basically, this just means that the pet must be under your care at your place of residence for the first 40 days you are in the country. During that time you may receive a phone call from officials to check on the health of your pet, but we've never heard of an in-person visit being made.

ALL THIS, AND AN AFFORDABLE COST OF LIVING

You may be shocked when you first arrive and see the clusters of skyscrapers that define the Panama City skyline. But even though every modern convenience is available, you can still take a taxi across town, get your hair cut, or see a first-run English-language movie for just a few dollars. Dinner for two with a bottle of wine can be had at one of the city's most enjoyable restaurants for little more than $40.

As we've said before, we'll say again: You can spend as much or as little as you like anywhere in the world, depending on your personal lifestyle. But most expats in Panama report that they live comfortably on $2,000 to $3,000 a month, and some on even less. Ellen Cook and her husband, John July, who own their own home in the Pacific Coast beach community of Coronado (and therefore don't pay rent), say they live happily on a monthly budget of no more than $1,500. That includes utilities, insurances, property taxes, Internet, gas for the car, medical bills, and so on.

It even includes food, Ellen says. "We mostly eat at home but we go out to dinner once a week." Evenings out, she says, are spent at a nearby pizza place listening to live music. John is a musician himself and enjoys sitting in on occasion. Their nights out rarely cost more than $20 to $25 total, thanks to their *pensionado* discount. (Remember, retirees in Panama get 25 percent off restaurant meals.)

While you may spend more, depending on your lifestyle or if you choose to live in bustling Panama City, for example, there are also areas of the country where you may spend even less. In little Santa Fe, a rural pueblo in Veraguas Province, for instance, where there are few restaurants or other expensive diversions to spend money on, you will find the cost of living to be extremely affordable.

PANAMA'S TOP RETIREMENT DESTINATIONS

Outside Panama City, you'll find two beautiful coastlines, bordered by the Atlantic Ocean to the north and the Pacific Ocean to the south. But there's more to Panama than a bustling city and gorgeous beaches. There are rolling green tropical mountains, lush rainforests, and fertile countryside that supports just about any type of crop. And there are many small and mid-sized towns where you can find your perfect laid-back retirement lifestyle.

Some of Panama's destinations most popular with foreign retirees include the following:

Panama City—One of Latin America's "Hottest" Cities

If you're looking for inexpensive cosmopolitan living—but with the conveniences you'd expect in a modern city—Panama City fits the bill.

Along with being the heart of the "Hub of the Americas," it's a major international commerce and banking destination, home to some 80 national and international banks. It's also the Latin American base for giant multinational corporations such as Federal Express, 3M, Dell, and the like.

You can dine in five-star restaurants; attend plays, symphonies, or the ballet; and shop at the many malls and unique boutiques. And in Panama City, you can enjoy these First-World luxuries at about half the price you'd pay in any U.S. city.

The city offers a number of distinct neighborhoods where you can find just about any type of housing option, from historic renovations in the colonial Casco Viejo area to ultramodern high-rise living in a planned community like Costa del Este. And, of course, everything in between.

Average rental prices in Panama City's nicer areas tend to be in the $800 to $1,800 range, but a little legwork can yield some bargain results. If you're looking to buy, you should know that Panama City's real estate market is notoriously stable, and has been for many years. As a very generous rule of thumb, and depending on how big a property and which city neighborhood you're considering, you should be able to find a comfortable home or apartment for $100,000 to $300,000.

If there are any drawbacks to Panama City, one is that traffic can be a problem. The city's street system has simply not been able to keep up with the number of cars on the road. But recent bypasses and the new mass transit project should help. For some, the tropical heat and humidity and fast city pace aren't appealing. Others love the sunny, sultry ambience and the excitement of a city coming into its own.

Coronado and the Pacific Coast Beaches—Fun in the Sun

Just over an hour by car along the Pan-American Highway from Panama City, you'll find the country's most popular Pacific Coast beaches. This area is called the *Arco Seco*, or "Dry Arc," because it receives slightly less rain than the rest of the region and you'll enjoy sunny weather most of the year (even during the May-through-November rainy season).

Dotting this section of coast are many small beach towns, such as Gorgona, Farallon, and Santa Clara, but the most popular—and the commercial nucleus of this area—is Coronado. The expat community is large and active, and if you settle there you won't lack for social engagements. There are opportunities for community service and social outings, and activities ranging from tennis to mahjong (a type of tile game) to golf. (The Coronado golf club features a championship course designed by Tom Fazio.) There's even an Olympic-sized pool and an equestrian club.

For a small home outside the gates of Coronado, you'll spend about $150,000. Inside the gates and close to the oceanfront, prices rise dramatically. Still, bargains can be found. For example, a four-bedroom, three-bathroom home of nearly 2,250 square feet on a 9,000-square-foot lot is currently on offer for $225,000.

You definitely won't lack for modern comforts in Coronado, which may be the fastest-growing area outside Panama City, and services have improved drastically in the last decade. You'll find shopping centers with at least two mega-modern supermarkets, clothing stores, and all the services you could want.

Importantly, there's a new clinic equipped to offer a wide range of services including X-rays, CAT scans, ultrasounds, lab tests, and more (all of which used to require a trip to Panama City). A full-time dentist and ophthalmologist also work out of the clinic, which has English-speaking doctors on staff. A visit can cost as little as $15.

El Valle and Sorá—The Garden Spot

El Valle (pronounced el VAH-yay) and Sorá (so-RAH) are lush, green, slightly higher-elevation settings (and therefore always a few degrees cooler) than Panama City.

Sorá, about an hour and 15 minutes west of the city, is a small town with very few commercial outlets. Just a bank, a small grocery store, a hardware store, a community center, a couple of small restaurants, a couple of veterinary clinics, and a small health center that provides basic general care and emergency services. But no worries, it's only a 25-minute drive to all the commercial amenities at Coronado.

There are perhaps 150 expats who live in the Sorá area, most in mountain-view homes tucked here and there in the gated community of Altos del Maria.

On the other hand, El Valle, a bit farther on (about a two-hour drive west from Panama City), is more developed. The town has excellent infrastructure—high-speed Internet and satellite television are nothing new—and offerings include a few small supermarkets (with pharmacies), hardware and construction stores, two gas stations, livestock and pet supply stores, a small 24-hour medical clinic, a dental clinic, a post office, and a library.

Many of Panama's oldest and wealthiest families have weekend homes in lush, green El Valle, which sits in an inactive volcano crater and is home to a famous open-air market, a riot of color bursting with flowers and perfumed by sweet, tropical fruit.

There's also a growing expat community, and in the past few years, El Valle has come into its own, with new small businesses like cafés and delis adding an extra touch to the town offerings. There's not much nightlife, although the expat community is active and hosts lots of fun activities, from festivals and charity work to concerts and gourmet cooking classes. Larger activities are often coordinated with the expat community in Coronado.

You can still find nice homes for sale in El Valle for under $200,000 . . . it just takes a little legwork, as most are advertised via signs or word of mouth, not online. In Altos del Maria, near Sorá, home-and-lot packages start at about $210,000 for a nearly 1,873-square-foot home on a lot of just under a quarter acre.

New Airport to Serve Popular Beach Areas

Panama is growing as a tourism destination, and several hotel resorts can be found along the coast in both the Chame District and the Coclé Province. To meet the future needs of increased tourism—and the growing number of residents along this coast—an airport to serve domestic and international charter flights has been recently opened on a former military base site at Rio Hato, just 25 minutes by car from Coronado.

Boquete and Volcán—Perfect-Climate Mountain Living

In Panama's Chiriquí Province, Boquete (pronounced bo-KET-ay) may be Panama's best-known destination for foreign retirees. That's thanks to its elevation (4,000 feet or 1,200 meters) and temperate year-round climate. Daytime temperatures typically hover in the mild, spring-like range of 70 to 80 degrees F.

Located at the base of Panama's tallest peak, the Barú Volcano, Boquete is set amid lush green hills, flowing rivers, and waterfalls that also help make it one of the most picturesque retirement retreats in the world. The Caldera River rushes through the middle of town and out to the Pacific Ocean, less than 30 miles away. From the upper rim of the valley, you can see the ocean and the border of Costa Rica in the distance, as well as the storybook village below.

If there is any downside to Boquete, it's the frequent misty afternoon rain called *bajareque*. But that keeps everything green and makes it easy to grow just about anything. Locally grown produce is available daily at the farmer's market from the farmer who picked it that morning. You can buy ahi-grade tuna, freshly caught, for $3 a pound (back home you might pay as much as $30), and big shrimp for $6 a pound. If you don't feel like cooking, get a savory, satisfying Panamanian meal of meat, beans, rice, and plantains for about $3. (And if you love coffee, some of the world's best is grown here.)

"If You're Bored in Boquete, It's Your Own Fault"

That's what an expat who lives here says. And it's true. Boquete is an ecotourism destination, with hiking, rafting, bird-watching, and more at your fingertips. There are annual flower and jazz festivals, a new theater and community center with shows in English, and much more.

You'll find numerous shops and restaurants offering a variety of cuisines: Mexican, Peruvian, Chinese, French, Italian, and more. And you'll find a wide range of professionals, from Web designers to dentists to attorneys and more. There are even a couple of golf courses . . .

To get to Boquete, drive a bit less than six hours west of Panama City by car or via a $15 air-conditioned bus. A quicker way is to take a short 55-minute Air Panama flight (see AirPanama.com) from Panama City's domestic Albrook Airport to the modern city of David (dah-VEED), with a population of about 150,000. Round-trip flights cost about $200, and the drive from David to Boquete takes about 35 minutes.

The smaller town of Volcán is a 45-minute drive up Volcán Barú from David. Though Volcán doesn't offer all the amenities you'll find in Boquete, it does offer a similarly mild climate, and real estate prices that are, on average, up to half those of Boquete.

Largely an agricultural town, Volcán has about 10,000 inhabitants, about 250 of whom are expats. You'll find a couple of supermarkets and hardware stores, three banks (two with ATMs), and many small restaurants. There are two full-time doctors, four pharmacies, two dentists, and a new 24-hour emergency clinic.

For medical care, most expats in both Boquete and Volcán opt for a hospital plan from Hospital Chiriquí in David. Depending on your age, you can purchase a membership plan for as little as $70 a month for 100 percent accidental coverage and up to 70 percent coverage for other care. A co-pay for a doctor's consult is $15 and an EKG can be as little as $20.

As for real estate prices, you'll find homes in Boquete in every price range, but they start at about $150,000 for a basic traditional Panamanian country home and go up to about $450,000 for a luxury European-style chalet. As mentioned, you'll find lower prices in Volcán.

And More . . . Pedasí, Santa Fe de Veraguas, Boca Chica, Bocas Del Toro

Because Panama is such a small country, you'll find foreign retirees in just about every corner. Besides the locales we've already mentioned, other popular destinations include the beach towns of Pedasí—a small fishing village on the Azuero Peninsula—about five hours by car west from Panama City, and Boca Chica (a personal favorite) on the coast near David in the province of Chiriquí.

As for Bocas del Toro, if you like the feel and look of the Caribbean, this is your place. White sands, turquoise waters, Rastafarians, and surfers are the name of the game. Bocas town on Isla Colon is a favorite jumping-off point to explore the many islands of this archipelago. But a word to the wise: Property titles here are hard to pin down and much of the land is rights of possession or owned by the government and you cannot readily acquire *titulo de propiedad* (formal titled ownership).

If we were personally looking for a place in Panama to hang our hats, we'd consider the tiny rural town of Santa Fe, just 35 miles north of Panama's fast-growing city of Santiago—and just 155 miles (or a three-and-a-half-hour drive) west from Panama City. At an elevation of about 1,300 feet, you'll find a temperate climate and lush green hillsides crisscrossed by babbling rivers and streams.

YOU'LL FIND EXCELLENT HEALTH CARE OPTIONS IN PANAMA, TOO

Panama offers high-quality medical care and modern hospitals in its major metropolitan areas. The Johns Hopkins–affiliated Punta Pacifica Hospital is the most technologically advanced medical center in Latin America.

In the city of David (near Boquete and Volcán), there are two medical centers with modern facilities. You'll also find good medical centers and clinics in growing cities and towns like Chitré, Santiago, Penonomé, and Coronado. As in much of Latin America, many Panamanian doctors—at least those who work in the major medical centers—have studied in the United States, Canada, or Europe. The standards and quality of care at these top hospitals compare favorably to care you might receive in North America.

Private health insurance is available in Panama and much less expensive than insurance in the United States, primarily because doctor's fees and hospital visits are much cheaper. Prices for prescription drugs are also low because manufacturers price them for the market. (The average salary in Panama is around $500 per month.) You'll find some drugs that require prescriptions elsewhere are available over the counter in Panama.

The good news is that if you are retired from the U.S. military, Tricare is accepted at Hospital Nacional in Panama City.

Learn more about retiring to Panama at InternationalLiving.com/countries/panama.

13

Uruguay
More First World Than the United States?

SIPPING A CAPPUCCINO AT A SMALL TABLE in a shady plaza outside our hotel, we flashed back to days and evenings spent similarly at sidewalk cafés in Europe. Lined by stately nineteenth-century Neoclassical- and Baroque-style buildings with wrought-iron balconies and curtains waving gaily through massive wood-framed windows, this was the perfect perch to contentedly watch the world go by.

On the other side of the famous Avenida 18 de Julio, yet another shady plaza was rimmed with currency exchange outlets, shops selling clothes, housewares, and electronics, and even more sidewalk cafés offering pasta, pizzas, and *chivitos*—something like a Philly cheesesteak, but piled high with ham, bacon, lettuce, tomato, cheese, and a fried egg, slathered with sauce, and all atop a bed of French fries. Take that, dear arteries!

Uruguay Fast Facts

Population: 3,324,460

Capital City: Montevideo

Climate: Four seasons. Can be cool in winter, but freezing temperatures are almost unknown

Time Zone: GMT-3

Language: Spanish

Currency: The *peso*, trading at about 22:1 USD at date of this publishing. See XE.com for current exchange rate.

We ordered more coffee and sat back to savor the moment—no need to rush. As in European cities or neighborhoods of Manhattan or Chicago, whatever is needed or wanted can be had within these 10 square blocks. How absolutely civilized.

We honestly didn't expect to like Uruguay as much as we did. But the drive from the airport into Montevideo immediately set us at ease. Unlike much of Latin America, this is no developing nation.

As we drove along the *rambla* (shoreline road) we passed chalet-style homes with tidy manicured yards, which gave way to stylized high-rise condo buildings as we neared the city. Arriving just before sunrise, joggers and dog walkers were already about their morning rituals, as silver streaks of light crisscrossed their way across the massive body of water next to which Montevideo sits. Is it an ocean? A river? In actuality it's a little of both, although it doesn't look like any river we've ever seen.

While Montevideo's seven-mile coastline is not technically oceanfront, it certainly appears so. Beaches are wide and sandy and there are waves and tides to contend with. At the height of the Southern Hemisphere summer, beaches were beset with sunbathers and water lovers.

As we explored not just Montevideo but Uruguay's entire stretch of coastline and beyond, into the interior, we came to the same conclusion others have . . . that Uruguay does indeed offer the "best quality of life in Latin America."

But Isn't Uruguay Far from Home? Expats Say "No!"

If there's any real drawback to Uruguay, it's that for North Americans, it can feel like it's far from home, at least distance-wise. A nonstop flight from Miami takes nine hours. But as expats who live there explain, this is something you get used to.

Our friend David Hammond reports that "most of the flights between Miami and Uruguay are at night. I get on a plane in Miami, eat dinner, watch a movie, and then get some sleep. They wake me in the morning, I eat breakfast, and the plane lands. Right now, when it is spring/summer in the Northern Hemisphere and fall/winter in the Southern Hemisphere, there is only a one-hour time difference between Miami and Uruguay—so there's really no jet lag."

Uruguay is arguably the most progressive and advanced country in South America, with safe highways and a modern, reliable public transportation system—in fact, all-around terrific infrastructure and technology. And the people are warm and welcoming . . . with far less noticeable poverty than elsewhere in this hemisphere.

Expats who live in Uruguay really love it there (at least those we met). And that's whether they're enjoying the sophisticated amenities of the capital city of Montevideo, living in a historic colonial river town or on a small farm or vineyard, or spending their days beachside along the sunny Costa de Oro or in an Atlantic Ocean beach resort like Piriápolis or the glamorous Punta del Este.

Something you'll notice right away that certainly adds to its appeal is Uruguay's European influence, especially in the charming capital city of Montevideo.

In one of Montevideo's many shady plazas, for instance, you can grab a cappuccino at a small café and happily watch the world go by. The only way you'll know you're not in Europe is when you hear the tango music.

This continental ambience—and a primary reason the Uruguayan government has thrown its arms open wide to foreign retirees and other immigrants—is because practically every Uruguayan can trace their roots to Europe. Most are of Spanish, Italian, or Portuguese heritage, and the European culture is prevalent in sidewalk cafés, classical music, and European cuisine accompanied by great wines.

When dining out, in fact, you'll be spoiled for choice, especially if you're a beefeater. Uruguayans love their *carne*, and you'll find open-air barbecue restaurants, called *parilladas*, on every corner. But thanks to that bountiful ocean offshore, seafood of every delicious variety is plentiful, too, as is handmade pizza, ravioli, gnocchi . . . you name it. (Again, the European influence is strong.) And as for cooking at home, the supermarkets and specialty food stores are well stocked.

If you're a wine lover, you'll have another reason to love Uruguay. Like its neighbors, Argentina and Chile, Uruguay is a superior producer of fine wines. Tannat, the signature wine of Uruguay, is not to be missed. And it's very affordable—you can pick up a bottle of excellent vintage in stores for just $7 or $8 or so. . . even less for a good Cabernet.

But all this talk of food is throwing us off track. Let's tell you more about why Uruguay makes so much sense as a retirement destination.

WHY CONSIDER URUGUAY FOR YOUR RETIREMENT HOME?

If you're looking for a safe and captivating place to spend your retirement years . . . with a temperate climate, excellent health care, and a stable economy . . . move Uruguay to the top of your list. It meets all those criteria and more.

The economy is strong, and tax advantages are many. Plus, it's a physically safe place to live . . . although it must be said that as elsewhere in the world, crime rates have increased in recent years, especially in the capital city of Montevideo.

All in, Uruguay is a First World, progressive country where you'll find mile after mile of modern highways, good food, pure water right from the tap, and reliable electricity, telephone, and Internet service.

So it's no wonder more and more foreigners—including a good number of retirees from the United States and Canada—are deciding to call Uruguay home. Some come for the convenient city living. Others come to settle in the vast stretches of rolling *pampas* (grasslands), or along the beautiful Atlantic Coast beaches.

Plain and simple, more and more people are coming in search of a quality lifestyle—a safe place to live in a country that's conflict-free, with mild weather, sustainable agriculture, and a solid financial system.

And that's the beauty of Uruguay . . . it's *all* here.

So where exactly is Uruguay, you may be wondering? Grab your map of South America—you'll find Uruguay tucked between Argentina and Brazil, near the bottom of the continent. The next landmass to the south is the Falkland Islands, and then across the South Atlantic Ocean, Antarctica.

Its location doesn't mean it's cold in Uruguay. Far from it. At between 30 and 35 degrees in the southern latitudes, you'll find the weather similar to the Carolinas and Georgia in the Northern Hemisphere. You'll enjoy four seasons just as you would in those states—but no major risk of snowstorms or natural disasters.

Is it Utopia? Nah, no place is. But Uruguay has a lot going for it. If you're looking for a retirement destination that's "just about" perfect, put Uruguay on your short list.

URUGUAY'S TOP RETIREMENT DESTINATIONS

Montevideo—Uruguay's European-Flavored Capital City

Montevideo (moan-tay-vee-DAY-oh) has everything you could want in an urban setting. Enjoy the opera, symphony, or ballet at the 150-year-old Solís Theater . . . or watch tango dancers in one of many plazas for free. The city is easy to navigate and public transportation is safe, reliable, and totally modern. On modern buses, you can travel anywhere in the city for little more than $1. (By the way, cross-country buses are equally clean, comfortable, and inexpensive, and have *free* Wi-Fi. Did we mention how civilized Uruguay is?)

You'll find yacht clubs and marinas, golf courses, ultramodern shopping malls, and world-class hospitals with English-speaking doctors who studied in the United States or Europe. Best of all, there are gorgeous parks and stunning beaches where you can happily while away your time without any bother. We never saw a panhandler the entire time we were in Uruguay.

In the city's Ciudad Vieja (Old Town) neighborhood, the architecture is a reminder of the city's colonial past. The Portuguese, Spanish, French, and British all tried to stake a claim here at one time or another. Many of the old buildings, especially along Calle Sarandí, have been renovated in recent years. Antique shops, art galleries, and boutiques occupy ground floors, with upper floors home to stylish, one-of-a kind apartments with shuttered windows and beckoning, sunny balconies.

Despite the aesthetic appeal of Ciudad Vieja, most expat retirees in Montevideo prefer living in the trendy neighborhoods of Pocitos and Punta Carretas. Both border the city's best beaches, and Pocitos especially has an urban neighborhood feel, with little shops and restaurants and its own nightlife.

The Costa de Oro and Piriápolis—Your Value-Priced Option

If you're looking for value-priced beach living, you'll find it along Uruguay's amazing Costa de Oro or "Golden Coast," so named for the golden sand beaches that begin just 22 miles outside Montevideo and extend along the coast for about 30 miles. The small seaside towns here—called *balnearios*—are clean, shady, and quiet, with tall sycamores and pines growing right up to the edges of rolling sand dunes that give way to wide, sandy beaches.

Long a popular vacation-home destination with middle-class Uruguayans, this stretch of coast is also attracting a growing number of foreign retirees for its affordability and proximity to Montevideo.

What to Know about Real Estate along the Coast

The seashore is a popular vacation destination for Montevideo residents, and many of them own homes along the coast that they use only in summertime. In fact, many of the homes are built for summertime living only. Many have fireplaces, but if you plan to live here year-round, you may need to augment walls and add insulation.

If you want to rent before you buy, remember that this is a prime area for summer vacation rentals. Many property owners earn big money to rent their homes during the high season months of January and February. They use the property themselves during December and March.

The rest of the year, you can most likely rent one of these properties very inexpensively. Keep in mind that off-season and long-term rates are almost never given on the Internet; you need to negotiate them in person, case by case . . . and just about any offer will be considered.

Atlántida—named for the mythical continent of Atlantis—is the largest town along the coast, with a permanent population of around 6,000 (and growing) that increases to more than 20,000 during the peak summer vacation season.

There's a good-sized expat community here, and in a stretch of a few blocks near the beach, you'll find hardware shops and pharmacies and, of course, the requisite *parilladas*. Close to the highway are modern supermarkets and medical clinics. La Floresta—also popular with expats—is just six miles farther east.

Continue east to the seaside town of Piriápolis (pee-ree-AH-polis), just 50 miles from downtown Montevideo. This was Uruguay's first seashore resort and its beautiful hillside may remind you of a little European seaside village.

While summertime Piriápolis is lively with vacationers who come to enjoy the waterfront boardwalk, busy seafood restaurants, casinos, and of course the beaches and marinas, wintertime here can be the best of all seasons . . . when you'll have the beach and *rambla* practically to yourself. You'll find a good-sized community of foreign retirees here, as well.

Punta del Este—South America's Hottest Resort Destination

No trip to Uruguay is complete without a stop in hip and happening Punta del Este. If you visit in January, at the height of the summer season, you'll have plenty of company, as vacationers arrive en masse to play and party in the sunshine. This is a grown-up, glitzy, and glamorous resort town—at least in the summertime—with miles of sandy beaches and blue waters, the country's hottest nightclubs, its best casinos and shows, and the highest concentration of fine restaurants.

There is no better place to see and be seen—at least if you're Uruguayan, Argentine, Brazilian, or any level of celebrity—than "Punta." That's because, as one expat explains, "It's clean. It's safe. Although no place on earth is totally crime-free, you can drive an expensive car and have little fear of robbery or anything else."

And while property and rental prices are higher in Punta than anywhere else in Uruguay, as is the cost of living, expats here say they wouldn't live anywhere else. And if you're a real estate investor, you may be interested to learn that in two months alone—during the height of the summer vacation season—properties can rent for up to *five times* what they will at any other time of the year.

Wintertime, though, is when expat retirees living in Punta say they enjoy it most. As one expat told us, "It's so sleepy here in June and July that they turn off the traffic signals . . . there are that few cars on the roads."

Many of the restaurants close down. But the movie theaters, casinos, and those beautiful beaches don't . . . and for several months, you can have them pretty much all to yourself.

Note: A new private university opened in Punta last year, and an Argentine software company is opening new offices there. Quite a few Argentines and Brazilians are relocating full-time to Punta del Este. As a U.S. expat living in Punta explained, "My building has 280 apartments. Last year there were 12 occupied in the winter. This year there are 56 occupied."

Rocha—The Final Frontier

To truly get away from it all—especially during the winter—head farther east along the coast to the department of Rocha.

This is where you'll find Uruguay's last, vast stretches of undeveloped beaches. The ocean is clear and blue, the sand is white, and the beaches are relatively deserted. Rocha feels much more remote than it really is; the highway is not far away, and you're still within three hours of the international airport in Montevideo.

While true beachfront land is rare in Uruguay, and there are just a few places where you can build adjacent to the water, you'll find more opportunities like this in Rocha than anywhere else.

The small beach towns of Rocha you may want to investigate are La Paloma, La Pedrera, Punta del Diablo, Barra de Valizas, and Aguas Dulces. And when we say small, we mean small . . . especially in the winter once the tourists have gone. Only about 70,000 people live full-time in the entire department—and most of these are farmers in the interior and the 26,000 inhabitants of the capital, also called Rocha.

If you were to buy a beach home in Rocha, you might be a bit lonely in the winter, although some say winter here makes for the perfect time to stoke the fireplace and take long walks on a beach you have all to yourself.

"You can pretty much do what you want to do in the winter," says an expat who lives in Punta del Diablo, "because nobody else is really around."

Summertime is where it's at, though. Rocha definitely has a more laid-back, bohemian vibe than Punta del Este. Young people from all over the world throng Rocha's small seaside towns with their small hostels and makeshift cafés. Happy travelers sell jewelry, wind chimes, and smoking paraphernalia. Nightclubs don't even open until 3 AM and partiers straggle home long after the sun comes up.

Rocha is definitely Uruguay's next frontier. It may not be quite ready yet for prime time, but it very well may be a place to invest now for future growth, as it's in the path of progress of development moving west along the coast from Punta del Este.

Colonia del Sacramento—Historical Treasure

Just 28 miles across the river from Buenos Aires, Argentina (a 50-minute ferry ride) and a two-hour drive northwest from

Uruguay's capital city of Montevideo, Colonia del Sacramento—or just "Colonia," as it is commonly called—is right off a picture postcard with its cobblestoned, shady sycamore-lined streets, massive colonial-style buildings, fine shops, galleries, great restaurants, and *parrilladas*.

Unlike any other city or town in Uruguay, Colonia is a faithfully restored city of seventeenth-century Portuguese architecture that's earned its status as a UNESCO World Heritage site. Also unlike coastal Uruguay, Colonia is "open all year." It never closes, even in the winter. There's a high season between December and March, but even in July you can find the nicer hotels booked solid on the weekends, especially with Argentines who find Colonia an easy and safe weekend getaway.

Many Argentines, in fact, have purchased vacation homes in Colonia. More and more English-speaking expats are also finding their way to Colonia. And they're not just visiting; many are settling here. Three neighborhoods of most interest are Barrio Histórico, Centro, and Balnearia.

Barrio Histórico is the original settlement, and if you'd like to buy or restore a historic building, this is the place to do it, although real estate here is much more expensive than in any other sector of the city.

Centro lies just outside of Barrio Histórico, although it's home to its own fair share of historic and antique buildings, and is noted for its quiet, tree-lined streets, restaurants, and parks and its bustling commercial center.

The Balnearia area runs along the *rambla* beside Río de la Plata, which is very wide here and looks very much like the ocean. In this traditionally residential area, you'll find quiet neighborhoods, elegant homes, and stunning water views—especially at sunset. If you're looking for a new single home with a large yard near a nice beach, this area is a good bet.

IN URUGUAY, YOU CAN IMPROVE YOUR QUALITY OF LIFE AND LOWER YOUR COST OF LIVING

While Uruguay isn't the least-expensive retirement destination on our radar, in our opinion it very well may offer the highest quality of living in the Western Hemisphere. That old adage "you get what you pay for" is certainly true here. But in the case of Uruguay, the lifestyle you can afford is top notch.

Almost anywhere in the country, you can rent a nice unfurnished home or apartment from $500 to $1,000 a month. In a desirable Montevideo neighborhood, that $1,000 will get you a small one-bedroom unfurnished apartment. Two-bedroom city apartments rent for $1,500 a month and up, unfurnished. And in summertime Punta del Este, of course, you'll pay dearly for a furnished rental, with prices dropping considerably the rest of the year.

Property prices aren't inexpensive, either . . . but if you have $200,000 to spend, you'll do well along the Costa de Oro and certainly in Rocha. The good thing is that you'll save on big-ticket items such as property taxes and capital gains, which are low in Uruguay.

Since Uruguay's mass transit system is efficient and affordable, many expats choose not to own a car, thus saving on car maintenance and purchase costs, taxes, insurance, and high gas prices. And health care expenses are low while quality is high. (Doctors still make house calls for as little as $12.)

The tale of the tape: If you own your own home or apartment, you can live comfortably in Montevideo on $2,500 month—and for less in other parts of the country. Or live luxuriously if you prefer. One expat couple reports that in the Montevideo penthouse they renovated in the city's upscale Pocitos neighborhood, their monthly expenses average $3,000 to $4,000 a month.

HEALTH CARE IN URUGUAY: THE ICING ON THE CAKE

Expats in Uruguay say one of the best things about living there is the quality and affordability of health coverage.

Uruguay has a public health care system that serves as a social safety net in the cities and assures the availability of medical services in the most rural parts of the country. The most popular health care option for working and retired Uruguayans, as well as expats, is a private hospital plan called a *mutualista*.

A *mutualista* is different from health insurance. There is no middle party between the hospital providing service and the member. There are no big deductibles, no lifetime cap, and no complicated terms to decipher.

Mutualistas mainly serve employed persons and their dependents. In Uruguay, health care is a social security benefit. Like a voucher system, an employed individual can choose a participating private hospital that offers *mutualista* membership. The health care portion of the worker's social security benefit is then paid to the private hospital that, in return, provides the worker with complete care. Individuals who are not employed (including retired expats) can become members of a *mutualista*, and directly pay the hospital the monthly fee—usually about $90.

Another choice in Montevideo is the British Hospital (Hospital Británico), one of the country's best hospitals. The British Hospital is not a true *mutualista*, but has a similar hospital plan called the "Hospital Scheme."

It's important to note that each private hospital in Uruguay sets its own acceptance standards for new members. Some are strict about age restrictions and pre-existing conditions . . . and some are very lenient. While you may not get your first choice of hospital, we have never heard of a persistent expat who didn't find membership in one *mutualista* plan or another. And that's despite pre-existing conditions such as diabetes, heart issues—even cancer.

While the British Hospital is one of the stricter hospitals for accepting new patients, one expat couple reports that despite pre-existing conditions, they pay just $1,700 a year for a policy through the British Hospital that's similar to one that cost $17,000 a year in the United States. Co-pays at the British Hospital are about $7 for a doctor's visit and $15 for an emergency room visit.

And make no mistake: As elsewhere in Latin America, Uruguay's hospitals are top quality and doctors are well trained.

Learn more about retiring to Uruguay at InternationalLiving.com/countries/uruguay.

14

Europe

All the Ingredients for the Good Life

YOU CAN'T DENY THAT EUROPE HAS MUCH TO OFFER . . . great food; graceful, stately cities full of history and culture; stunning country landscapes where life is quiet and relaxed; awe-inspiring mountains for skiing; and soft, sandy beaches for lazing away summer days.

"But isn't Europe expensive?" That's the question we're most asked about Europe and the answer is yes, Europe can be expensive . . . unless you know the right places to look. For instance, it's still possible to buy a house in France for less than $100,000. Obviously that won't be in Paris, but rather in a part of the country that's just as historic, romantic, and beautiful in its own way.

In Italy and Spain, too, you'll find areas of the country where a romantic European lifestyle needn't break the bank. Certainly, Europe has been hard hit by the recent global economic crisis, so if you know where to look you can find some exceptional real estate bargains. (Spain especially comes to mind.)

And once you're on the ground and become part of the community, you'll find ways to reduce your daily living costs. You'll find the best butchers and flower shops, the best places to buy your fresh strawberries and asparagus—and of course, those delicious and affordable Mediterranean wines.

So don't despair. If it's an affordable retirement location you're looking for, or even a part-time vacation home, there are still pockets of Europe where you can find exactly that.

YOUR COST OF LIVING MAY BE LESS THAN YOU THINK

Your cost of living anywhere in Europe, as in the rest of the world, will depend on your own lifestyle and where you plan to take up residence. Opting for the high life in Paris is likely to make larger holes in any budget than living in a quiet corner elsewhere in the country.

Generally Speaking . . .

Housing costs aside, singles can enjoy a comfortable lifestyle in Europe on an annual income of $25,000 to $35,000 a year. Couples may be more comfortable with an annual budget of $35,000 to $50,000.

You'll find lots of statistical surveys that compare living costs in the world's major cities. One website to check out is Numbeo.com.

Although Paris isn't particularly inexpensive, it does compare favorably with London and New York. Likewise, should you choose a small village in Italy or Spain—or just about anywhere in France, for that matter—you can expect your cost of living to be comparable to what you might spend in a similarly sized city in the United States . . . with one exception, and that's health care costs.

Much has been written about the low cost of health care in Europe as compared to the States. Almost every European country offers free public health care to those who pay into national social security programs. And you can buy private insurance for as much as 80 percent less than you may be currently paying in the United States.

Cost of a Doctor's Visit

According to the International Federation of Health Plans (the leading global network in the industry), the average cost for a routine doctor's visit in the United States ranges from $95 to as much as $176. In France, though, you'll pay $30. And in Spain? Just $11.

And in Europe, you needn't worry about the quality of health care you'll receive. The last time the WHO compiled their rankings of the world's health systems, France and Italy earned the top two spots and Spain was number seven. As we explained in Chapter 5, even tiny countries like Malta, Greece, and Morocco are rated as having better health care systems than the United States and Canada, which came in at numbers 37 and 30, respectively.

FRANCE: WHO DOESN'T DREAM OF LIVING *LA VIE FRANÇAISE*?

Imagine relaxing in the garden of your own French home, a pretty stone cottage set among orchards, vineyards, and flowery meadows. Under a shady canopy of trees, your lunch of freshly baked baguettes, ripe Camembert cheese, and a glass of chilled Chablis is spread before you on an old oak table. . . .

Who wouldn't enjoy *la vie française*?

France offers perhaps the best quality of life on the planet: great food and wine, *haute couture*, a welcoming climate, unspoiled countryside, glittering culture, excellent health care, colorful traditions and history, and, as a bonus, the glamour and sophistication of Paris—arguably the world's most bewitching capital.

And the truth of the matter is that France is more affordable than you think, if you know where to look. The trickiest thing is deciding which bit of France holds the most allure for you. It could be the wild, rocky shores of Celtic Brittany, steeped in heritage and tradition . . . or sun-drenched Provence, with its rolling hills and lavender fields, broken by the turquoise waters of the Côte d'Azur . . . or the castles and sleepy villages of medieval holdings in the Dordogne . . .

If good health care, a relaxed lifestyle, and all the modern comforts you enjoy at home are among your top priorities, then France should be on your radar.

France Fast Facts

Population: 65,951,611

Capital City: Paris

Climate: Generally cool winters and mild summers, but mild winters and hot summers along the Mediterranean

Time Zone: GMT+1

Language: French, and near the country's borders, Spanish, Italian, German, and Belgian, are spoken. English is the most common second language, and more English speakers can usually be found in the major cities.

Currency: The *euro*, trading at about .75:1 USD at date of this publishing. See XE.com for current exchange rate.

Yes, France has been hit by the euro-zone crisis, but not as hard as some other countries in the region. With at least 75 million foreign tourists per year, France is the most visited country in the world and maintains the third-largest income in the world from tourism.

Most tourists head directly to Paris, of course. It's one of the world's greatest cities, and if you're a Francophile, there is nowhere better to soak up the flavors and culture of France. So it's no wonder that this is where many expatriates have found a home away from home.

Yes, you'll pay for the glamour and excitement Paris has to offer. But if you have your heart set on this city, there are some neighborhoods that are more affordable than others.

Areas like the tenth arrondissement with its covered Saint-Quentin Market, or the artisan quarter of the twelfth arrondissement, or the eighteenth arrondissement—an area that many see as being the epitome of Paris—all have properties you can buy or rent at very affordable prices. And just because you don't live right in the center of the city doesn't mean that you are missing out. Each arrondissement has its own unique character and, with its good transport system, the rest of Paris is very accessible.

Beyond Paris, though, you'll find other parts of the country that offer sophisticated living at a more affordable price.

The Midi-Pyrénées region

Deep in southwest France, this region of about 2.7 million people is bordered by the Dordogne to the north and the Pyrénées Mountains to the south. Tucked between is a landscape of farmsteads, vineyards, buttercup meadows, and wooded ridges strewn with medieval villages and strongholds. You'll find dramatic river gorges, too, cut by rivers such as the Lot, Tarn, Garonne, and Aveyron, all very popular with canoeists.

This region has felt the fallout of the economic crisis, and if you're looking for a "rescue and restore" property or a picture-perfect gem, their values have plummeted. Now's the time to find a deal. Still, there's no compromise on the good food, wisteria blossoms, or blue skies here. Even in early spring, it's warm enough to enjoy a glass of chilled rosé wine in the garden as the sun goes down.

International Living Europe editor Steenie Harvey tells us that you can snap up a vineyard in this region for just $106,250, "including a tiny cottage that's the price of a vineyard on 1.25 acres in the Gers department of the Midi-Pyrénées region. In 2008, it produced around 4,500 liters of white wine from two grape varieties."

Another example, she says, is in the historic little town of Lauzerte. At the western end of the Tarn-et-Garonne department, it's a traditional stopover on the Santiago de Compostela pilgrim route—and has a number of restored stone-built houses starting at $89,600.

Limousin

Quiet farming villages are scattered throughout Limousin, and the beautiful scenery continues to attract French tourists looking for R&R, especially in the summer season. Winters can be harsh, though, and the more isolated areas can find themselves without electricity for days at a time. But this is part of the charm of the region that has long attracted artists and writers looking for peace and inspiration. This is truly a place where you can get away from it all, and where you may find the country's lowest cost of living.

The Property Purchase Process in France

It's easy and straightforward to purchase property in France, but be sure to hire an attorney to work on your behalf and to complete the title search and all necessary legal documents. Keep in mind that the buyer is typically solely responsible for all legal costs and fees incurred in relation to property transfers.

Health Care in France

The low cost of health insurance and the superb quality of care are why the WHO ranks France number one in their world health report. They say France provides the best overall health care system in the world. And for those who are paying into the French Social Security System, it's a lot cheaper than buying a private health care plan (which North American retirees will have to do). Private medical insurance is mandatory for non-E.U. citizens wishing to take up residence in France.

Once you move to France, you may be able to transfer your private health care plan to a French provider (remember, Medicare is not accepted overseas), or even to one of the many British companies that specialize in providing coverage for individual expatriates. This may prove cheaper. Costs depend on age and medical history, but if you're in good health, monthly premiums for a retiree average $175.

Private medical insurance generally covers hospital treatment, but under some plans you must fund the cost of doctor's visits yourself. Others will reimburse around 75 percent of doctor's fees. As with household insurance, the consular section of the U.S. Embassy (http://france.usembassy.gov/living_in_france.html) can provide you with a list of English-speaking insurance agencies offering health coverage.

Note: If you move to France as an expat retiree, you will be required to show proof of *private* health insurance as a requirement of your residence visa. One way to do this is to join the Association of Americans Resident Overseas (website: www .aaro.org) and buy into their group plan. Once you have a legal residence visa, you can then begin making payments to the *sécurité sociale* to access the public system.

To learn more about retiring to France, see InternationalLiving.com/countries/france.

ITALY: BARGAINS BEYOND THE TOURIST TRAIL

Practically every expat we speak with has dreamt of living in Italy. It's easy to understand why: Italy has warmth, style, and really terrific food. Its excitable people exude a true zest for life. And you can spend years exploring the country's art treasures and the architectural glories of its magnificent past.

Even if you've never been there, Italy is one of those places that tugs at the heartstrings. And once you *have* been there, you're always looking for reasons to go back. It's not hard to imagine spending springtime in Rome or Venice or Florence. But if you're looking to live in Italy, and it's affordable retirement living you're after, you may want to look beyond the major cities.

Italy's countryside landscapes are as gorgeous as they are diverse: historic walled towns, timeless villages set against Cézannesque backdrops, and fields covered with yellow sunflowers.

There are a few drawbacks to Italy, of course. Persistent problems include illegal immigration, organized crime, corruption, high unemployment, sluggish economic growth, and the low incomes and technical standards of southern Italy compared with the prosperous north. But choose the right locale, and you can be very happy, indeed.

Some Locations to Consider

Abruzzo: Fringed by Adriatic beaches, the Abruzzo region, often overlooked by tourists, is a tapestry of mountains, olive groves, vineyards, pine forests, medieval castles and villages, monasteries, and Roman ruins. This really is Italy's premier hunting ground for true property bargains, and you'll find dozens of affordable houses and apartments for sale or rent.

Italy Fast Facts

Population: 61,482,297

Capital City: Rome

Climate: Predominantly Mediterranean; Alpine in far north, hot and dry in south

Time Zone: GMT+1

Language: Italian

Currency: The *euro*, trading at about .75:1 USD at date of this publishing. See XE.com for current exchange rate.

Calabria: The toe of Italy's boot, Calabria has a long coastline along the Tyrrhenian and Ionian seas, with alternating sandy beaches and craggy cliffs. You're never more than 34 miles from the sea here. Property prices are starting to catch up with the rest of coastal Italy, but for now you can still find inexpensive studio apartments within easy reach of a beach.

Le Marche: Hill towns, beaches, mountains, art treasures, a summer opera festival at Macerata, and blessedly few visitors . . . the things that entice many of us to Italy are combined in this east-coast border region between north and south. Few tourists come here, even though medieval cities like Urbino, with the Renaissance magnificence of its Ducal Palace, can easily match famous Tuscan locations like Siena for beauty.

Although Le Marche's villas and farmhouses are much in demand—the countryside is very similar to Tuscany—and have risen to Chianti-region price levels, there are still smaller properties at affordable prices to be had, including country homes to be fixed up.

A Note about the Property Purchase Process in Italy

There are no restrictions on foreigners buying property in Italy, and all residential property is freehold and titles are registered, but it's not the most straightforward country in which to purchase property. The buying procedure is complex and you'll want to have reputable professional help.

Health Care in Italy

As we mentioned, the WHO ranks Italy number 2 in the world, behind France, for quality health services. Italy has both a public health care system and a parallel private system. Although public medical facilities in Italy are adequate for emergencies, many public hospitals are overcrowded and underfunded. In some small towns, particularly in the south, you will only be able to access the public health system.

You are more likely to find private doctors and hospitals in bigger cities, where residents are more likely to have private medical insurance. If having a wide choice of private doctors and private hospital facilities concerns you, then you should seriously consider choosing a home within easy reach of larger cities like Florence, Rome, or Milan.

As in France, citizens of non-E.U. countries (including the United States and Canada) must show proof of health insurance to get a residence permit in Italy. Since you won't be able to join Italy's public health care system as soon as you arrive, this means that you'll need private health insurance. Also note that hospitals do not generally accept credit card payment, though most will agree to bill patients after discharge. There are numerous private clinics offering a wide range of medical services, but charges are generally higher than those applied by public hospitals.

> To learn more about retiring to Italy, see InternationalLiving.com/countries/italy.

SPAIN: ECONOMIC WOES AND EXPAT OPPORTUNITIES

Picture a sun-drenched white house with a shady courtyard, perched on a cliff-top site in Spain. With the deep blue sea beyond, and an olive grove nearby, it's the stuff of which fantasies are made.

Spain Fast Facts

Population: 47,370,542

Capital: Madrid

Climate: Temperate; clear, hot summers in interior, more moderate and cloudy along coast; cloudy, cold winters in interior, partly cloudy and cool along coast.

Time Zone: GMT+1

Language: Castilian Spanish (official) 74 percent, Catalan 17 percent, Galician 7 percent, and Basque 2 percent (official, regionally).

Currency: The euro, trading at about .75:1 USD at date of this publishing. See XE.com for current exchange rate.

Beaches . . . mountains . . . fabulous cities . . . fun festivals . . . and, of course, guaranteed sunshine. It's not surprising that Spain is the most popular country for Europeans seeking a home overseas. Many have bought vacation home properties along the Costa del Sol and other popular seaside destinations. But we'd advise you to look carefully to find the right spot.

There's far more to Spain, in fact, than the Costa del Sol. Venture a few miles into the far-west Andalusian hinterland, along the Costa de la Luz; along the Costa del Azahar in eastern Spain north of Valencia; or along the Bay of Biscay in the far north of the country. The "real Spain" is well worth a look.

Spain was hard hit by the global economic crisis of recent years. Its mixed capitalist economy is the twelfth largest in the world, and its per capita income roughly matches those of Germany and France. But after almost 15 years of above average growth, Spain's economy began to slow in late 2007, and it entered into a recession in the second quarter of 2008. It's been the last major economy to emerge from the global recession.

One of the reasons the recession hit Spain so hard is because of its oversupply of housing. And without consumers to buy properties, many developments, especially in resort destinations, have fallen on hard times. You may find many distress-sale bargains, but be sure to do your due diligence. You don't want to buy in a project that's undercapitalized and with little hope of digging out from under a load of debt. Remember in a distressed sale especially: Don't buy what you are promised; only buy what you can see with your own eyes.

Today's Best Locations in Spain for Retirees

Barcelona: If you love cities, go directly to sun-blessed Barcelona where you'll find an intoxicating medley of old and new. Highlights include Gaudí's eye-popping architecture, the Ramblas street theater, and the atmospheric maze of the medieval Barri Gòtic (Gothic Quarter).

Truly, few other major European cities can deliver on Barcelona's beauty, style, history, beaches, good weather, and arty bohemianism—and also be within a couple hours of ski slopes.

Only a short distance from the French border, Barcelona is Spain's second-largest city, and also the capital of the autonomous region of Catalunya (Catelonia). Home to people of diverse nationalities and backgrounds, it has an entirely different feel than cities such as Madrid and Seville. (And yes, you'll find plenty of English speakers.)

You'll also find cheap eats, fine dining, and—for a city with all Barcelona has to offer—reasonable property and rental prices. Best of all, you don't have to decide between urban buzz or Mediterranean beaches. Barcelona offers both.

Granada: Granada is an even more affordable option than Barcelona. A brand-new two-bedroom apartment in the center of town with a view of the mountains from the terrace sells for less than $200,000.

Warmed beneath Andalusian skies, Granada taps into the emotions as well as the senses. It bridges the worlds of Islam and Christianity, meshing together Jewish and Gypsy traditions along the way. With the Sierra Nevada mountains as a backdrop, it's difficult to envisage a more dramatic setting for a city. Or a sultan's palace . . .

That palace, of course, is the Alhambra, Granada's iconic famous rose-red citadel, built mostly in the thirteenth century. With the Alhambra towering above, the café bars along the riverside Paseo de los Tristes also attract scores of visitors. Look beyond the tourist areas, though, to find the best bang for your buck on everything from rental properties to delicious tapas at a comfy neighborhood sidewalk café.

Bilbao: Nine miles inland on Spain's green north coast, Bilbao is a modern urban miracle. In the last 20 years this industrial port city—the pride of Spain's Basque country—has transformed itself from a gritty metropolis into the poster child for urban renewal . . . and all while preserving its romantic, medieval heart. The transformation has earned it a fistful of awards and an explosion of tourism, and has made it one of the most enviably livable cities you'll see anywhere.

If you like convenient urban living, accessible culture, delectable food, an engaging seaside atmosphere . . . and green, hilly countryside just a short drive away . . . then come to Bilbao.

The building that kick-started this city's renewal is the Bilbao Guggenheim, an offshoot of the New York museum, opened in 1997. A deliriously exuberant hulk of gleaming titanium, it looms over a large park along the estuary that runs through central Bilbao.

Pretty Bilbao has much to offer. You can walk through leafy green space, beside water, from one side to the other of central Bilbao—and many people do. Locals and tourists stroll, bicycle, and skate along this promenade, while children romp in playgrounds. The two sides of the estuary are connected by delicate pedestrian bridges that arc over the water.

In the popular Casco Viejo neighborhood, apartment prices start at about $200,000. But bargain hunters would do well to search for properties across the estuary—just a few steps farther to the Casco's restaurants, shops, and nightlife—where prices are perhaps 30 percent lower.

Málaga: On Spain's southern Mediterranean coast, Málaga is the gateway to the Costa del Sol, long one of Spain's biggest beach-tourism regions. A city of more than a million in the major metropolitan area, Málaga is lovely and lively, with plenty of shops and museums, food to die for, and a rich history. The Phoenicians founded it nearly 3,000 years ago.

But Málaga doesn't use its pedigree as its calling card to fame. It's also a major business and financial center, the fourth-largest in Spain in terms of economic activity. Because it doesn't rely totally on tourism, Málaga manages to remain a "real" Spanish city. Especially outside the center, there is a sense that life goes on as it does anywhere else in Spain (and with non-tourist prices to prove it). And while Spanish is still spoken everywhere, you'll get by in English perfectly well.

For full- or part-time living, Málaga is a great choice if you want big-city life by the sea. As in other Spanish cities, apartments or condos in the city center are small by U.S. standards. Acceptable size for a couple in a two-bedroom apartment is about 90 square meters, or about 969 square feet. (Many Spaniards, in fact, live happily in 600-square-foot apartments.)

Long-term leases in central Málaga start at about $975 a month long-term for an unfurnished two-bedroom apartment.

Short-term furnished vacation leases in the high summer season (July and August) or during year-end holidays will be higher— plan on spending as much as $1,300 a month, or even more.

You'll find lower rents by looking farther from the center and away from the water. You may also choose to look in the sea- side villages along the coast outside Málaga proper. These vil- lages will have their own ambience and real estate market. But bus and suburban train services to Málaga are convenient and frequent.

If you're looking to buy, there's plenty on offer. Prices have dropped and many financially strapped owners must sell. Modern apartments in the 800-square-foot range, right in the historic cen- ter, start in the low- to mid-$100,000s. If you're willing to take on some renovation work, you can find apartments well below $100,000. There are elegant, more expensive properties on offer, as well. In Málaga, there's something for every budget.

Buying Real Estate in Spain

The purchase process in Spain is fairly familiar and straightfor- ward, but do hire an attorney to help you with the title search and other details.

Health Care in Spain

The health care system in Spain is very good. In fact, the World Health Organization ranks Spain seventh in the world for quality of health care. Spanish medical schools are well respected, many Spanish hospitals are modern and well equipped, and Spanish doctors are considered excellent.

Like many other European countries, Spain has a public health care system as well as a private system. Expats from non-E.U. countries like the United States and Canada can access the public health care system if they have a Spanish social security number. (To obtain one, you must hold a residence visa plus have the right to work in Spain, either as the employee of a company in Spain or as a self-employed individual. In both cases you will pay into Spain's social security system.)

However, as almost everywhere else in the European Union, expats from non-E.U. countries are required to show proof of health insurance to get a residence visa. So whether you eventually qualify for *seguridad social* or not, you'll need to consider private health insurance to get your residence visa. There are dozens of insurance companies offering private health insurance for Spain. You can choose national plans that cover only Spain, choose Europe-wide plans, or even opt for full international health coverage. It all depends on your personal needs and situation.

Having a private health care plan will also offer you access to more options for treatment and physicians. And you'll avoid the queues of the public health system, which is excellent but overtaxed.

To learn more about retiring to Spain, see InternationalLiving.com/countries/spain.

WHERE ELSE IN EUROPE MIGHT YOU LOOK?

There's far more to Europe than France, Italy, and Spain, of course. Other destinations that may be of interest to you include Ireland—if you can tolerate long stretches of cold, rainy weather—and sunnier Mediterranean-climate destinations like Croatia, Greece, Malta, and Portugal.

Ireland

Nearly 34.5 million Americans list their heritage as either primarily or partially Irish. That number, incidentally, is seven times larger than the population of Ireland itself (4.68 million). So it's no wonder that so many of us feel such an affinity to Ireland.

Ireland's charm is compelling. Everyone speaks English (even in the few Irish-speaking areas), and the Irish are friendly, hospitable people. The whole nation—but particularly the countryside—takes a small-town approach to life. And right now, thanks to the recession that began in 2008 and hit Ireland particularly hard, the whole country seems to be on sale, and prices are still falling.

If you're looking to pick up an Irish country home, an apartment in Dublin, or a vast acreage with a grand manor, now's the time. Prices are expected to stay low for a number of years to come, as the country has faced large tax increases and sharp spending cuts over the past five years.

Rentals, too, can be had for a reasonable amount. A good Irish website to start your search for a rental is Daft.ie.

And, by the way, if you have at least one parent, grandparent or, perhaps, a great-grandparent who was born in Ireland, you may be eligible to apply for Irish citizenship. This gives you the right to apply for an Irish passport, which grants you membership in the European Union and the right to travel, live or even possibly work in any of its 28 member states.

Croatia

Although many Americans know very little about Croatia, this small maritime country at the heart of Europe offers you the chance to discover the closest thing to the Mediterranean of years gone by.

Unspoiled, relaxed, beautiful, and safe, Croatia is one of Europe's loveliest treasures. Everything you might look for in a retirement destination can be found there: crystal-clear seas, timeless fishing villages, unspoiled beaches, Roman ruins, a pristine lake district, and medieval walled cities.

And if you are under the impression that Croatia is war-torn, communist, backward, poor, or struggling—think again. Such ideas are either completely out of date, or altogether misguided. The war here ended in 1995, and tourists are coming in droves from all over Europe. Croatia and its islands have become one of the hottest new destinations for holidaymakers weary of the crowded resorts and overdeveloped coasts of Italy, France, Spain, and Portugal.

As to where in Croatia you might want to spend time or relocate to, a lot depends on your budget and lifestyle needs. But whatever those reasons, you'll find something here to suit you. Places you might focus on include Dubrovnik and Istria.

Greece

Greece is gorgeous. Of its hundreds of islands and islets, 166 are inhabited—so there is bound to be an island for you. Or consider the Peloponnese mainland—stunningly attractive, but barely known to North Americans.

Greece still holds onto a lot of its customary charm, particularly the islands, with their whitewashed houses on stony hills; black-clad women delivering citrus and vegetables carried by donkeys to local *tavernas*; and leathery old fishermen sitting around in the sun, passing the time of day.

Like Ireland, Greece has been hit hard by the euro-zone economic crisis. Property prices have declined and are likely to continue to fall over the next few years as harsh economic measures affect Greek and foreign buyers alike. But be aware that not many investors have a rosy outlook on Greece. The economic future continues to look bleak, as there is strong public discontent and political instability.

Malta

The Mediterranean Sea, a warm and sunny climate, a peace-ful lifestyle waiting to be lived . . . if you've never been to Malta and maybe have never even heard of it, don't be embarrassed. Anchored almost in the center of the Mediterranean Sea, 50 miles from the Italian island of Sicily, Malta isn't a mainstream destina-tion for North American tourists.

If you have a love of culture, history, and excellent weather, you'll love Malta. Plus, you'll find a tranquil way of life, virtually no crime, and the opportunity to benefit from a considerable reduc-tion in your tax burden. If you meet certain requirements, Malta is a relatively affordable European tax haven to retire to and set up official residence. Plus, it's an English-speaking country.

The Republic of Malta isn't a solitary island, but an archipel-ago of three islands and three islets. The most popular destina-tions include the capital city of Valletta—a World Heritage Site renowned for its excellent architecture, which overlooks the impressive Grand Harbor—and Gozo, a green, rural island of about 31,000 people.

Portugal

Portugal is the size of Vermont with an official population of less than 11 million, making it one of the smallest countries in Europe on both measures.

There are many selling points if you're thinking of living here: the nearly flawless weather; the abundance of golf and water sports (the country's entire west coast looks to the Atlantic); and superb, abundant food, including fresh fish caught daily up and down the 350-mile stretch of coastline.

And probably the biggest factor that keeps many happy here is the relatively low cost of living. The introduction of the euro may have inflated prices, but compared with its other European neighbors like Germany, France, and even Italy, goods and services are still bargains here.

The areas of Portugal most popular with retirees (especially European; fellow North Americans will be few) are the Algarve and Alentejo regions, and the Silver Coast, particularly the attractive seaside towns of Nazaré and São Martinho.

It's perfectly possible for an expat couple to enjoy life in Portugal for around $1,100 a month, not including rent. Rental costs in Lisbon, other major metropolitan areas, and the tourist hotspots of the Algarve are much higher than in rural areas and provincial towns. A one-bedroom rental in central Lisbon, for example, in the Bairro Alto neighborhood averages about $750 a month. In the smaller Alentejo town of Estremoz, two-bedroom properties rent for between $350 and $525 monthly.

If there's a downside to Portugal it's that the official language is Portuguese, a language that most Americans and Canadians don't speak.

You'll find much more information about Europe—cost of living, real estate prices, visa information, and more—at InternationalLiving.com.

15

Southeast Asia

Exotic and Affordable

KNOWN FOR ITS PERFECT BEACHES, low prices, and excellent scuba diving, Southeast Asia usually conjures up images of young, globe-trotting backpackers and sultry nights spent at a beach bar.

But this region is also a vast cultural melting pot with something to appeal to everyone, especially adventurous retirees on a budget. You'll find night markets, floating markets, jade and pearl markets . . . fish markets with things you never imagined existed. You can ride tuk-tuks and cyclo-rickshaws, and take longboat journeys on meandering riverways through the jungle.

At your fingertips, you'll also have sophisticated cities, lush hill towns and rainforests, and some of the best beaches in the world . . . talcum-white sands, swaying coconut palms, and an evening chorus of cicadas. These tropical seascapes far surpass any travel agent's poster.

If you love to explore exotic, offbeat places, play golf or tennis, swim, dive, surf, go fishing or sailing, or dine out frequently—and

---

The Downside . . .

If you crave adventure and the opportunity to see the world from a new perspective, you'll be elated in Southeast Asia. On the other hand, if you're looking for a comfortable and easy alternative to your North American lifestyle, this may not be the place for you. Asian languages are difficult to learn . . . heck, even the alphabets can be a trial.

If a laid-back lifestyle is what you're after, head for the small towns, as Asian cities exude a fully frenetic energy. City traffic, especially, may make you head for the hills.

The biggest challenge may be the distance from back home, although, as one expat says, "Flying across the Pacific is a royal pain, but I can be with my 92-year-old father and my sister in California within 24 hours of leaving my home in Chiang Mai."

And keep in mind: While the airfare may be expensive, your overall cost of living in Southeast Asia will be almost ridiculously affordable.

---

you never want to think twice about being able to afford any of it—Southeast Asia may be the perfect place for you. The good life here, in fact, can be almost unbelievably inexpensive.

We believe three areas of Southeast Asia in particular deserve your attention: Malaysia, Thailand, and the newly emerging expat destination of Cambodia. Whether you're contemplating a long-term overseas retirement or an extended adventure, each offers a cost-of-living jackpot. Pick any one and you'll be living a superior lifestyle—and for much less than you ever did at home.

And of course, there is more to Southeast Asia than just these three locations.

You may find you prefer the clean and ordered island state of Singapore, the longtime expat haven of Bali, or the endless island-hopping opportunities that Indonesia offers (over 18,000 islands to choose from). And, of course, there are the beautiful English-speaking islands of the Philippines. And, of course, there are the beautiful English-speaking islands of the Philippines, the often forgotten and wonderfully laid-back Laos, or beautiful Vietnam.

HOW FAR WILL YOUR RETIREMENT INCOME GO?

International Living correspondent Keith Hockton lives in Malaysia, and he says the low cost of living there is a great benefit. Malaysian prices are fairly representative of all of Southeast Asia, he adds. In fact, prices in modern, upscale Penang, where Keith lives with his wife, Lisa, maybe be even a bit higher than elsewhere in the region.

"Lisa and I rent a stylish three-bedroom, three-bathroom seaview apartment for $950 a month," he says. "It comes with a shared pool and gym. We eat out five nights a week, and our total budget is $1,719 a month. Two people can have a three-course meal here for $10.

"A bagful of fresh fruit costs around $4. We also have a maid that comes once a week for four hours at a cost of $15."

Another expat living in Chiang Mai, Thailand, says, "I live like a king for $2,000 a month." Numbeo, the online database that tracks cost of living in cities around the world, says consumer prices in Chiang Mai are 59 percent lower than in Boston.

MALAYSIA: ENGLISH-SPEAKING, AFFORDABLE, AND TRULY ASIA

Malaysia is definitely something of a surprise package. Summoning all the mysteries of Asia, it's a former British colony that remains as colorful as ever. Beyond the lofty skyscrapers of the capital of Kuala Lumpur, its dramatic canvas is painted with tropical beaches, mountains, dense rain forest, and vividly green tea plantations.

Malaysia Fast Facts

Population: 29,628,392

Capital City: Kuala Lumpur

Climate: Tropical; annual monsoons in the southwest (April to October) and northeast (October to February)

Time Zone: GMT+8

Currency: The *rinngit*, trading at about 3.3:1 USD at date of this publishing. See XE.com for current exchange rate.

While Malaysia is not on many people's radar, it should be. It's an easy place to make friends and integrate, since English is the unofficial first language. It has great infrastructure; foreigners are allowed to own properties freehold; and there is no inheritance tax, property capital gains tax, or tax on income repatriated from overseas.

Obtaining a residence visa is straightforward. The Malaysia My Second Home (MM2H) Program launched by the Malaysian government offers incentives including a renewable, ten-year, multiple entry visa for qualified applicants who wish to live in or spend extended periods in the country. Learn more about the program at mm2h.gov.my.

So it's no surprise that in recent years, Malaysia has steadily moved up *International Living's* Global Retirement Index and now consistently occupies one of the top five spots, thanks in large part to its high score in the "entertainment and amenities" category, its low cost of living, and the ease with which new expats can settle in.

Most of the expats who have moved to Malaysia aren't from the United States or Canada, but instead are from Europe, Australia, and elsewhere in Asia. Along with these foreign expats, the country is home to Malay, Chinese, and Indian Malaysians. And there are still traces of British influence. Throughout the Muslim world, there's probably no more liberal country.

You'll find that the largest communities of expats live in Kuala Lumpur and Penang, and there are numerous organizations that can help you get settled and integrated. For example, members of the International Women's Association (formally The American Woman's Association) of Kuala Lumpur organize activities on a daily, weekly, and monthly basis. On Mondays there are jungle walks, Tuesdays mahjong, Wednesdays sewing. They sponsor trivia night once a week at a local pub and put on a formal ball once a year. For more information, see http://iwakl.org.

Health Care

Penang and Kuala Lumpur are also medical centers of excellence, and every day two planeloads of medical tourists arrive in Malaysia for various treatments. Not only is the health care quality top notch, but it's among the world's least expensive. Prescriptions typically cost one-fifth of what you pay at home.

"The last time I was at the dentist in Penang," Keith Hockton says, "I got a filling and a cleaning, which cost $22.50. In the U.S. this would set me back around $180."

So what are the favored destinations for expat retirees in Malaysia?

Penang

Many expats who work in Malaysia live in Kuala Lumpur, the country's business and financial center. Many foreign retirees, however, are more tempted to live on Penang Island, a 50-minute flight from Kuala Lumpur—although Penang does have its own international airport. It's also accessible from the mainland by two bridges and a 24-hour ferry.

Buying Real Estate in Malaysia

For foreigners to be able to own property freehold, it must be valued at a certain amount, which varies by state. For example, at today's exchange rate, the minimum purchase price in Penang is currently RM1 million ($315,000) for an apartment, and RM2 million ($630,000) for a house. For this reason, many expat retirees prefer to rent. One place to start your search is at iproperty.com.my/rental/.

One of the oldest outposts of the former British Empire, Penang lies anchored on the Spice Route, just off Malaysia's west coast, and delivers 110 square miles of tropical treasures. A lush, mountainous island oozing history and heritage, Victorians christened it "the Pearl of the Orient."

George Town is Penang's main settlement, and it's one of Asia's most likable cities. Blending old and new, its modern high-rises encircle streets packed with mansions, shop-houses, and Chinese clan houses.

Furnished apartments of four bedrooms and three bathrooms in a high-rise building with a swimming pool, gymnasium, and more can be had for as little as $575 a month.

Malacca

Also spelled "Melaka," Malacca is Malaysia's oldest city. Like Penang, it's another historical gem. A two-hour drive south from Kuala Lumpur, this was once Southeast Asia's greatest trading port. The Portuguese, the Dutch, and the British were attracted here to haggle and barter for spices and make their fortunes.

Malacca's status was enhanced by its location, which guards a vital waterway: the Straits of Malacca, where the trade winds meet . . . and where pirates soon followed the European traders. Some found loot, others found gravestones. With its matching red-brick clock tower, Protestant church, Dutch graveyard, and ornamental windmill, Malacca appears more like a corner of Holland than Malaysia.

Compared to Penang, you'll find some real estate prices even lower in much-smaller Malacca. A furnished three-bedroom, two-bathroom apartment, for instance, can be rented for less than $300 a month. A furnished three-bedroom, three-bathroom house near a golf club rents for less than $400 per month.

To learn more about retiring to Malaysia, see InternationalLiving.com/countries/malaysia.

THAILAND: STEP INTO THE WORLD OF EXOTICA

From the golden beaches to the fabulous food and friendly people, it's easy to see why Thailand is known as "the Land of Smiles." There's much to smile about, and living here is a lot easier than you probably think. It's easy to get around, to get what you need, and to find a community—of both expats and locals—that will welcome you.

Plus, Thailand is safe. Women can travel alone without problems, even at night in the big, bustling city of Bangkok. Best of all, the cost of living is low, and getting a retirement visa is simple. But buying property is tricky. Foreigners can only buy condominiums under a strata or freehold title. You'll have to buy land and houses through a Thai corporation.

Thailand Fast Facts

Population: 67,448,120

Capital City: Bangkok

Climate: Tropical; rainy, warm, cloudy southwest monsoon (mid-May to September); dry, cool northeast monsoon (November to mid-March); southern isthmus always hot and humid

Time Zone: GMT+7

Currency: The *baht*, trading at about 32:1 USD at date of this publishing. See XE.com for current exchange rate.

This is a big reason why so many expats in Thailand rent instead of buy. Renting is easy and affordable, and then if you want to move on and try out a new place, you just pack up and hit the road.

Some foreign retirees choose to live in the hubbub atmosphere of Bangkok. Some live in the north of Thailand where life is quiet, peaceful, and very inexpensive. Others choose the south for its beautiful beaches.

Affordable Living

Living in Thailand can be very affordable, especially when it comes to that most basic human need: food. And while food in Thailand is never "basic," it's always a good value. At street food stalls, for instance, a bowl of *khao gaeng*, or rice and curry, costs about a dollar. Wet markets, found in most neighborhoods, offer a range of fresh fruit and vegetables. You can buy a pound of mangoes for a dollar, a half-pound of cucumbers for less than a quarter, and a bright bunch of orchids for a couple of bucks.

While the Western-style supermarkets selling gourmet and imported foods are best reserved for the occasional indulgence, the international big-box "hypermarkets" offer good value for the money.

Motorbikes, a popular mode of transportation, cost about $800 for a new, mid-range model, and gas is just under $5 a gallon. Metered taxis cost about $2 for a three-mile journey, and air-conditioned buses offer good value with fares averaging around 50 cents or less.

You can easily and affordably indulge in regular luxuries like a Thai massage, which costs about $8 for an hour. And maid services, including having someone cook for you, start at about $320 a month for full-time help.

Depending on your location, you could live on $1,200 a month, although some couples in Chiang Mai, for instance, live on much less. But if you wish for real comfort, then $1,500 to $2,000 a month is more realistic.

Health Care

Most expats we've spoken with have been impressed with the quality, standard, and cost of the medical care they've received in Thailand. In Bangkok and Chiang Mai's private hospitals, you can expect a quality equal to standards in the United States. In recent years, in fact, Bangkok has emerged as a medical tourism destination. With scores of medical facilities and no less than 14 hospitals accredited by the JCI, it's one of the top cities in Asia for quality medical care.

Many doctors in Thailand have received training in the United States, Canada, and Europe, and many who are affiliated with private hospitals carry board certification from Western countries. Most doctors and a high percentage of medical staff at these top hospitals speak English fluently. (Note: You won't find many English speakers at the public government hospitals.)

Health care in Bangkok rivals that of most Western countries — and at a far lower cost. A basic office visit starts at $20. For less than $50, you can see a range of specialists. Something like full knee replacement surgery costs $15,000, including doctor and surgical fees, medicine, lab tests, and room fees. In the States the procedure averages about $45,000. A colonoscopy costs less than $1,000 in Bangkok — it's more like $3,000 back home. And in a plush Thai hospital, coronary artery bypass graft surgery costs $25,000 . . . that's a saving of tens of thousands on what you would pay in the States.

There are also some very good private facilities in Hua Hin, Udon Thani, Phuket, Pattaya, and Koh Samui, where most primary and secondary medical care problems can be dealt with. And of course, you'll also find public hospitals in the largest cities. While these are considered to be perfectly adequate in emergencies, and technologically well equipped, they tend to be overcrowded, underfunded, and poorly staffed after hours.

Our Favorite Destinations in Thailand

Bangkok: Thailand's capital, a former Chinese trading port situated along the banks of the Chao Phraya River, has long attracted expats. Earning its place in history as an R&R spot for American troops serving in the Vietnam War, Bangkok has flourished into a modern and surprisingly cosmopolitan city, with gleaming skyscrapers, luxury hotels, and world-class public transit options. Today, expats flock here for the multicultural vibe and high-on-convenience, easy-on-the-wallet living.

Buying Real Estate in Thailand

Foreigners can't own title to land in Thailand. They are, however, permitted to lease land and homes, on a maximum 30-year lease, with an option to renew for another 30 years.

Foreigners are allowed to buy condos so long as fellow foreigners don't own more than 50 percent of the building or development. Companies registered in Thailand with a majority Thai ownership are permitted to buy land, and foreigners can legally hold a minority stake in such companies.

Marry a Thai and you are also permitted to buy land (although it must be titled in the name of the Thai spouse). In case of divorce, it will become their property; in case of death, it will become property of surviving Thai family members.

The city's large concentration of foreigners, or *farang*, means there's no shortage of social clubs and activities for interests as varied as tennis, language study, and theater. As we mentioned, Bangkok is home to many of the country's top doctors and private hospitals, and local expats appreciate the astonishingly affordable costs for top-quality care.

Due to Thai law restricting the purchase of land and homes in the country (see sidebar, "Buying Real Estate in Thailand"), condominiums are a popular choice. For example, a modern, furnished 1,290-square-foot, two-bedroom, two-bathroom condo in Bangkok's Asoke neighborhood, within walking distance to public transport, will cost about $220,000. If you prefer to rent, you'll pay $1,120 a month for a similarly sized unit. In the suburbs, you can rent a furnished three-bedroom, three-bathroom, 2,580-square-foot home near shopping options and an international school for about $1,000 a month.

Chiang Mai: Located near the foothills of northern Thailand, an hour's flight from Bangkok, Thailand's second-largest city of Chiang Mai is dubbed "the Rose of the North," and it's one of the country's most culturally rewarding regions. With golden *wats* (temples), teakwood houses, dragon sculptures, and intriguing alleyways, this is traditional Thailand. It was founded in 1296, but there's also a modern city outside the historic core.

Best known for its mammoth Night Bazaar, the city attracts scores of wholesale buyers—prices are generally cheaper than elsewhere in Thailand. On average, wholesale discounts are 20 to 50 percent lower than retail. But even retail prices are substantially below what similar items cost back home.

Like any modern center, Chiang Mai is not without its challenges. The area's popularity means overcrowding can be an issue, especially in the Old City. And during the hot season, when rice fields are burned for the coming planting season, the area suffers from reduced air quality.

Many expats live near the city center, where you can find a furnished one-bedroom apartment for as little as $250 for a month's lease. A furnished two-bedroom, one-bathroom condo close to the Night Bazaar and with views of the Ping River typically rents for about $500 a month. Move farther out and $500 a month will rent you a furnished two-bedroom home with mountain views.

Phuket: You've probably heard of this tropical island of over 350,000 people just 8 degrees north of the equator. But Phuket isn't just a sophisticated vacation paradise. It's also a favorite with expats—around 8,000 live here permanently. The main island is circled by 32 smaller islands rich in caves, cliffs, lagoons, and seabirds. The seascapes are surreal. Rising from waters that gleam jade, emerald, and deep turquoise are countless limestone pillars and bizarre outcrops smothered in jungle vegetation.

Phuket isn't the cheapest place to live in Thailand, but it is one of the loveliest—beautiful white-sand beaches, crystal seas, laid-back living, excellent health care, an international school, big supermarkets, and just about every kind of restaurant you can imagine.

Today, little trace is left of the impact of the 2004 tsunami, which devastated Phuket and other locations on Thailand's western coast. Resorts are now back to full capacity, many of which took the opportunity to renovate and upgrade their facilities following the destruction. Since the tragedy, a tsunami warning system has been established in the area to increase safety.

Phuket's expats live in a variety of towns and villages. The Patong area does earn its reputation as a seedy locale for tourists and "sex-pats," but that's just one part of the island. In fact, in Phuket you'll find a very nice range of family-friendly locales like Chalong and the Nai Harn/Rawai area.

But whatever your budget, there's something for everyone. A furnished two-bedroom, two-bathroom villa with a pool, for example, just a five-minute walk to Kamala Beach, rents for about $650 a month. Sacrifice beach views and you can rent a furnished three-bedroom, two-bathroom home with 1,500 square feet for less than $500 a month on the island's north end, near Nai Yang Beach.

> To learn more about retiring to Thailand, see InternationalLiving .com/countries/thailand.

AND KEEP AN EYE ON . . . CAMBODIA

Angkor Wat is only one of the reasons to visit Cambodia today. The country has put its troubled past behind it and is fast becoming the hottest destination in Asia for expats looking for low costs, good living, and exotic adventure.

You'll find Angkor Wat in Cambodia's north, near the town of Siem Reap, home to a small and growing expat community. Six hours south, in the rejuvenated capital of Phnom Penh, you can live well on just $700 a month. But it's along Cambodia's little-known coast, with stunning beaches and tropical islands, that you'll find the most popular havens.

Buying Real Estate in Cambodia

As a foreigner you can't own land in Cambodia. You can, however, acquire leasehold rights for up to 99 years with an option to renew. And many expats are happy with that option.

You can purchase a house, land, or property with land by forming a joint-venture company with a Cambodian citizen or with a Cambodian company, which would then allow you 49 percent of the shares.

For the most beautiful deserted beaches in Asia—and the lowest prices—the Cambodian coast is hard to beat. You can rent a furnished 2,000-square-foot house on a quiet part of the beach, on a secure lot, with free high-speed Internet and all utilities included, for just $150 a month. You'll eat a three-course lunch for $5 and spend all day on a tropical beach without seeing a single soul.

Sihanoukville is the largest town along the coast, and its pristine beaches are the best in the country. It's easy to see why this area is so special, yet hard to understand why there is no one around. It's astoundingly beautiful.

There is already an expat community here, too. It's a mix of older Americans who arrived in the 1960s and 1970s for a little R&R and returned to retire here after the civil war, and the forty-something scuba diver generation who came in search of a Shangri-La–like coast. They all found what they were looking for.

Cambodia is a very affordable option. Just to give you an idea of how outrageously affordable it is to live in Cambodia, one expat living in Sihanoukville shared his expenses with us. To rent a furnished two-bedroom house he pays $150 per month. He spends about $50 a month on groceries, and he usually goes out every night. For this, his monthly entertainment bill is $300. Utilities and Internet are included in his rent. He spends $15 a month for his phone and another $10 for gas for his motorbike. His total monthly expenses are *just $525.* Do keep in mind, though, that one thing lacking in Cambodia is quality health care, and most expats travel to Thailand for health care needs.

To learn more about retiring to Cambodia, see InternationalLiving .com/countries/cambodia.

16

Boots on the Ground

Zeroing In on the Community That's Right for You

YOU CAN STUDY ALL THE COLLECTED DATA, analyze real estate statistics, crunch the cost-of-living numbers, study weather patterns and more, but nothing surpasses your gut instinct when it comes to choosing a place to live.

And believe us, your gut can change — especially as you get older. Your needs and interests expand right along with your waistline.

For instance, back in 1997, when we were just married and first started thinking about living overseas, we pored over every *International Living* e-mail and magazine. We compared and contrasted, planned and dreamed . . . Certain we would live in an exotic tropical destination, we wanted it to be relatively close to family and friends back home in the States, who promised to visit often.

Cost of living was important, of course, as it still is. But far more important to us today is convenient access to quality (and yes, affordable) medical care. Over a decade ago — when we were in our mid-forties — we didn't think much about that.

Instead, we were all about sunshine, warm weather, and beach bars where we could while away the hours watching the sun set over the surf, digging our toes in the sand and hoisting a cold one. This is how we spent our vacations, after all.

But as the old adage goes, life is what happens when you're busy making plans. And life isn't a constant vacation. So except for half a year spent high on a hill above San Juan del Sur, Nicaragua, which came with a forever view of the Pacific Ocean, we never have lived at the beach. And we probably never will.

Why? For one thing, while those little beach bars can be perfectly charming for a day to two, they'd never keep us mentally engaged much longer than that. And no matter how tasty those cold ones are, can you imagine how much *more* our waistlines might expand if downing them were our only pastime?

And then there's the sand that gets in every crevice. And mosquitoes. And neither of us can tolerate heat and humidity for long stretches of time. A week of fun in the sun is one thing—and we still love our beach vacations, for sure—but we've grown to love the warm days and cool nights of equatorial mountain climates.

Long-term happiness for us means living in a city or town where there is plenty to keep us busy and where the climate is more suitable to our maturing lifestyle. (It helps our self-esteem, of course, that in the mountains we can eschew skimpy bathing togs for jeans and T-shirts that better hide those ever-growing waistlines.)

In hindsight, too, we've learned that once you get settled in, many of the things that you thought would matter greatly don't matter nearly as much as you thought they would. Sure, it's a great bonus that in Ecuador, where we live, our monthly utility bills—water, gas, and electric—rarely amount to much more than $30 total. And that's spring, summer, fall, or winter. And we love that for little more than $2 each we can take the bus two hours south to Quito or buy a hearty, full meal . . . including beverage.

We've settled in with good medical service providers. We now have doctors, dentists, pharmacists—and one excellent health insurance advisor—who know all about our physical status, issues, and quirks.

And that brings us to the single issue that matters the most when choosing a place to put down roots: community.

Having lived in seven different communities in four foreign countries, we have some expertise in this. More than scenery or weather or cost of living or anything else, the game changer that most affects the success of your move overseas is the friendships you make.

Fortunately, it's easy to make friends when you're an expat. You can't help but stand out, after all. The locals will be curious about you and ask you all sorts of questions. (Show them photos and explain why you're there. A photo of your U.S. home buried under an avalanche of snow is a great icebreaker . . . pun intended.)

And you'll have loads in common with your kindred fellow expats—despite your apparent differences.

Would-be political foes back home become fast friends overseas. Same for those of different age groups or economic statuses. In an expat community, you're all in the same boat. You learn from one another, depend on one another, and more than anything, you tolerate uniqueness and respect one another for the decision you made to try out expat life.

So here's our best advice: Once you've weighed all the factors that are most important to you—beach versus mountains, city versus village, cost of living, health care, and so on—go one step further. Stand in the town plaza and check your gut. If you get a warm little tingle about the people who live there—both local and expat—you've probably found your spot.

WE'LL SAY IT AGAIN: PROFILE YOURSELF RUTHLESSLY

In Chapter 3, we mentioned eight factors to consider as you're searching for your perfect overseas retirement destination: affordability, health care, ease of transition, accessibility, community, housing prospects, climate, and things to do.

Your single most important step, though, is deciding on the community that's right for you. Now's the time to dig in a bit deeper.

Beach versus mountain living: Many people are lured by the sun, sea, and sand. Others prefer mountain vistas and the more temperate climates found at higher elevations. But if you can't handle full-time heat or can't tolerate high altitudes, consider your options and make your decision based on your best interests.

Our Advice: If you want it all and aren't willing to compromise, don't despair. There is such a thing as a temperate-climate beach destination. But you'll need to look beyond the tropics (23 degrees north or south of the equator) to find it. If this is what you're after, we'd suggest you look at Mexico's northern Baja region, the beaches of Europe, and coastal Uruguay.

Small town versus the big city: The benefits of living in either a rural or city environment are pretty obvious, and only you can decide which appeals to you more. Small towns are peaceful, and easy to get around, with little traffic and pollution. And they're typically more affordable than urban environments. But if you're a culture vulture, you won't want to be without big-city amenities such as shopping malls, art galleries, theater, and musical events. And don't forget that your very best health care options will be found in larger cities.

Our advice: If your desire is to live in a city like Paris, and you can afford to do so, then by all means, follow that dream. For more affordable city living, we'd suggest Quito, Ecuador; Panama City, Panama; Mérida or Puerto Vallarta, Mexico; Bilbao, Spain; and in Asia, Bangkok, Thailand and Penang, Malaysia.

Our personal favorite small-town destinations include Cotacachi and Vilcabamba, Ecuador; San Juan del Sur, Nicaragua; Boquete, Panama; Tulúm, Mexico; Placencia, Belize; and in Costa Rica, Arenal, Nosara, Sámara, and Ojochal.

Prefer a mid-sized city where the cost of living is low but with plenty of cultural activities to keep you busy? We'd suggest San Miguel de Allende, Mexico; Granada, Nicaragua; Cuenca, Ecuador; Chang Mai, Thailand; and Malacca, Malaysia.

The small but critically important details: As you're trying to decide where to retire overseas, think about those amenities you simply must have at your fingertips as well as those things you can't live without. For instance, consider your access to quality medical care. If you'll be taking children, you'll want good schools. If you're a golfer or a tennis player, you like to fish, or have other special hobbies you enjoy, make sure you can continue those in your new home. If a religious community is important or you have special dietary needs, or you're concerned about language issues, be sure to do your homework about the destinations you may be considering.

Our advice: The easiest places to retire—in our opinion—are close to home, just a few hours by plane from the United States or Canada (although we can't deny the appeal of Uruguay, despite its long distance from the States). Costa Rica, Mexico, and Panama are well-developed countries where you'll find all the amenities of home, including well-organized expat communities and a good number of local English speakers.

If it's both ease of transition and affordability you're after, we'd suggest you look at Lake Chapala and San Miguel de Allende in Mexico; Costa Rica's Central Valley (specifically the communities of San Ramón, Atenas, Grecia and Escazú); and Panama's Boquete or Coronado.

GETTING THERE—AND ONCE YOU DO, THEN WHAT?

We'll say it again: Before you decide to pick up everything and move somewhere, you have to visit. So here are some travel tips.

Go during the worst season: Whether it's rainy season, windy season, or the hottest season, plan a trip to your proposed destination during the worst time of year weather-wise—normally referred to as "low season." If you like what you find, you can be pretty certain you'll like it even more during its high (or fair-weather) season.

As a general rule of thumb, high season (also often referred to as dry season) in the tropics is roughly November 15 to April 15. Generally during high season you'll pay more for your airfare and accommodation, with spring break, Thanksgiving, Christmas, and New Year's being the most expensive times to travel. (You may have a difficult time finding accommodation at beach resorts in Latin America during *Semana Santa*, the week before Easter, when practically everyone takes a beach holiday.)

While you may encounter wet weather from June to September (low season), it rarely rains all day. The fringe seasons in most destinations (April to June and September to November) can be quite pleasant weather-wise and more affordable, too.

It probably goes without saying, but if you're set on traveling to Europe, high season will be in the summer, same as in the United States and Canada. And if you're traveling to southern South America or New Zealand, high season will be during North America's winter. High season in Uruguay, for example, is during January and February, when everyone goes to the beach and it can be nearly impossible to find last-minute accommodation.

Find the best airfares: As we said, you'll pay more overall to travel to a destination during its high season. You'll also find generally higher airfares and hotel costs from mid-June to mid-August when many people from the United States and Canada take vacations. (This is the most expensive time to travel to Europe.) That's another reason fringe-season travel can be a wise choice.

Traditionally, the earlier you can book your travel, the better chance you'll have of picking up the lowest fares. Keep in mind that airlines change fares constantly, often multiple times a week. So sign up for airfare alerts from your favorite travel websites and start checking fares as soon as you've decided on your travel dates. Then check continuously—at least once a week—to get a sense of pricing. When you find a deal you like, be ready to pull the trigger.

Also understand that, in general, traveling on some days may be cheaper than on others. Tuesdays and Wednesdays are generally the least expensive days for domestic flights and Friday and Sunday are the most expensive. Monday, Thursday and Saturday are in the middle.

And don't forget to check alternate airports. Costa Rica and Ecuador both have two international airports, for instance, and Mexico has many. As an example, if you want to save on travel to Mérida, Mexico, you may find lower fares flying in and out of Cancún. If you're going to Mexico's San Miguel de Allende, you may find discount fares to Mexico City, rather than the closer airports of León or Querétaro. (Buses in Mexico are safe, reliable, comfortable, and very affordable. You'll pay about $25 to reach Mérida from Cancún or San Miguel de Allende from Mexico City.)

Some of our favorite online resources for researching low-cost airfares include Farecompare.com, Kayak.com, and Mobissimo.com. We've also had good luck buying through Expedia.com and Orbitz.com.

Find the best accommodations: You can use the websites we mentioned above to search for accommodations, too. But if you're looking for good recommendations, you might want to check out reviews from travelers who have gone before you. Ask questions on expat forums or check out websites like Tripadvisor.com and Airbnb.com. The latter site is a particularly good one if you're looking to rent a home or apartment and get a true feel for what living in a particular destination may be like.

Other good sites to find vacation property rentals are VRBO.com and HomeAway.com. Keep in mind, though, that these are short-term vacation rentals and will not reflect the prices you'd pay for a long-term stay of six months to a year or more. (Read more about how to find long-term rentals in Chapter 17.)

Our advice: We'd suggest you rent a home or apartment in your intended destination. Not only will you save money by making your own meals, but you can explore local markets and grocery stores and see if local products meet your needs. And budget travelers, don't overlook hostel stays. They're not just for backpackers. Research your options at a site like Hostels.com.

In-country transportation: Unless you are going to be on the road a good distance in a particular destination, you may not need to rent a car. And keep in mind that fees to pick up a car in one city and drop it off in another can be painfully high. You may not want to drive in some countries if you are unfamiliar with the rules of the road or unsure how to get from point A to point B. In some countries like Ecuador, where gasoline averages less than $1.50 a gallon, it may be more cost-effective and far less stressful to hire a private driver or taxi to ferry you about.

Most of the countries we recommend as retirement destinations offer far more advanced public transportation systems than most of us from the States are used to. In our opinion, you'd be well advised to give them a try. Buses in Latin America and Asia and trains in Europe offer a low-cost, low-stress way to see the local scenery.

Our advice: Always carry the address and telephone number of your hotel or any other place you may be traveling to, as taxi drivers don't always know every location by name, and if you don't speak the same language, they may have difficulty understanding you.

What about trip cancelation and traveler's health insurance? If you are at all concerned that you may need to cancel your trip, then buying travel insurance is a wise idea. You'll often be offered the option to purchase a trip cancelation policy when you book your airfare or a package tour. Before you do that, be sure to read all the fine print to be sure you understand what's covered and what's not. And note that some credit card companies provide this type of coverage, so be sure to check with your card provider about its policies.

And while we don't recommend traveling with expensive jewelry, you may want to contact your homeowners or home rental insurance policy provider to see if it covers you or offers a rider for overseas travel to cover your electronics and/or expensive sporting equipment.

As for health insurance, your regular health plan probably won't cover you while abroad, so check into purchasing a policy that offers coverage for treatment at any licensed medical or emergency facility, rather than a complex web of preselected affiliated hospitals.

Experts suggest purchasing a policy from a company that's licensed in your home state and unaffiliated with any tour operator or other travel-related business. Two comparison sites to check out are InsureMyTrip.com and SquareMouth.com. Both offer several different types of coverage, including trip cancelation, medical insurance, and evacuation policies.

―――――――

THE SOLOIST: RETIRING OVERSEAS AS A SINGLE

The expat lifestyle is not for couples only. We know many single expats living overseas—and truth be told, many of them are women. They've fearlessly decided to move forward with their retirement dreams, partner or not.

Going solo has special challenges, though, that couples don't face. After all, singles have no life partner close at hand for companionship, conversation, or commiserating. You'll need to make friends and a new social circle in your new community for that.

But with a little strategizing—and soul-searching—you can make an easy transition to life as a single expat. Here are some tips that can help.

Be honest with yourself: Again, it's about ruthless self-profiling. If you prefer having lots of social engagements, you probably shouldn't move full-time to a remote beach village with no cable TV and a bunch of fishermen. Instead, recognize that you need a city that offers plenty of people and distractions. On the other hand, if you're okay with just a few good friends, a smaller location where you can easily meet people may suit you fine.

Go where the expats are: Realistically, as a single you're better off moving to an expat haven than to a destination with few or no expats. After all, you've made a life-changing move, and your best bet for finding kindred spirits is among others who have done the same.

Rent before you buy: This advice is especially important for singles. Renting for even a few months allows you to see if the destination you've chosen is really right for you. If it's not, you can move on with no regrets.

Have a strategy for meeting people: The biggest pitfalls for single expats are loneliness and boredom. If you've picked an expat haven, you'll have expats around you. But how do you meet them? It's important to have a proactive strategy; don't depend on anyone seeking *you* out. Take the initiative.

Start a project before you leave home: Maybe it's a hobby you've never had time to pursue, or taking up a sport you enjoy. It can even be a business you plan to ramp up. Ideally, it should be something that gets you out of the house and meeting people. Your project not only will keep you busy; it can also help you make friends and integrate into the community.

Learn the language: Learning the local language is one of the best investments you can make as a single expat. (It can even be that initial project to keep you busy while you settle in.) As a single person, *you're* the one who will have to deal with the plumber, the carpenter, and the telephone repairman, all of whom rarely speak English. Don't depend (for long, at least) on more language-savvy expat friends to translate for you—or you'll quickly outlast your welcome among them.

And finally, enjoy the adventure: Living overseas is fun. And, with just a little planning, your new life can exceed your expectations.

17

You Found Your Paradise. Now What?

Should You Rent or Buy? And How to Know When Halfway Isn't the Wrong Way

---

MOVING OVERSEAS MEANS FINDING A PLACE TO LIVE. And that's hard to do unless your feet are firmly planted on the ground in the overseas community where you'll be living. That's not to say that you can't find a property to buy or rent online . . . but why would you? Too much can go wrong.

From photos, for instance, you might be able to get a general idea of what the place looks like. But you have no idea when those photos were taken or what has transpired since that time. Is there a 24-hour construction site next door? Or a disco or barking dogs or crowing roosters? Is there reliable cell phone and Internet coverage? (Reliable to *you* and *not* the owner.)

And you can't tell from photos what the neighborhood looks like. Is it safe? Is it conveniently located to bus or taxi stops or grocery stores? That's why we recommend that you search for real estate only in person . . . when you can see and feel, touch and contemplate for yourself. Only you know what you can tolerate and what you can't when it comes to your living and sleeping arrangements.

TRY BEFORE YOU BUY: HOW TO FIND A RENTAL, AND WHEN YOU MIGHT WANT TO BITE THE BULLET AND BUY

Our mantra at *International Living* has always been "Try before you buy." As we've said, too much can go wrong if you don't know exactly what you're doing. Too many real estate agents overseas (especially the gringo agents just off the boat from the United States or Canada) don't really know what they're doing. They may give you bad advice in order to make a sale—and probably not maliciously, but because they just don't know any better. Believe us, we've seen it all. And we've even been victims ourselves of overzealous salespeople. But that's another book . . .

Still, despite taking *International Living*'s advice and renting for the first part of our overseas adventure, we're inveterate homeowners. We like a place we can make our own, with our comfy furnishings and our own sheets, towels, and mattress.

It helps, of course, to make a buying decision in a market that's on an upward spiral. For that, you'll need some expert advice.

One place to start is at PathfinderInternational.net. Pathfinder is a group *International Living* relies on to scout for the hottest international real estate opportunities. Check out the website to learn more about how they do this, and consider signing up for their free e-alert to learn, in real time, about the opportunities they uncover. They can also point you to individual real estate companies and real estate attorneys in the country of interest to you.

How can you best find decent rentals in the destination you've determined is right for you? Do a good bit of research. Get on expat forums and local Facebook pages and ask advice from expats who already live there. Once you're on the ground, pound the pavement. Go to expat hangouts and check out the bulletin boards. Check out the local newspapers and Craigslist. If need be, hire a local translator or facilitator to help you with your search.

When it comes time to sign a rental contract, exercise the same due diligence you would back home. Get the contract translated into English if you have to and read the fine print. If you need advice, contact a local attorney. This is something the experts at Pathfinder may be able to help you with. Just send them an e-mail at info@pathfinderinternational.net and ask if they can suggest a local attorney. Or, again, check with online expat forums and with local U.S. or Canadian embassies. You'll find their information online and they often offer a list of local legal resources.

DECIDED TO BUY? DON'T SUCCUMB TO MARGARITA MADNESS

Sitting on the beach at sunset, without a care in the world and nursing an ice-cold cocktail, it can be very easy to give into your emotions . . . even if you also have all the common sense in the world. So our advice is: Don't succumb to margarita madness. Don't make an impulsive decision to buy a piece of real estate.

Instead, take a few days—or even a few months or more—to think about it. There are many great real estate opportunities in the world, and new ones present themselves every day.

There is one major difference when buying overseas that you should know about, and that's the legal system. In Canada and the United States, the legal system is common law. But in most of the rest of the world (and especially in Latin America) the legal system is civil law. And the two are very different.

In common-law systems, there are many gray areas. For instance, if you agree to purchase a pre-construction condo and, on delivery, don't get what you thought you would (no ocean view, a cheaper kitchen, less floor space), you'll probably withhold a portion of the purchase price and go to court. You'll plead your case, argue for forgiveness ("I didn't close on my condo because the developer didn't deliver the kitchen he promised."), and reach a compromise.

Not so in a civil-law country. Civil law is very black and white. You're either right or you're wrong. If you don't close on your condo, you're automatically in default, and the developer can keep the condo and any monies you have paid to date. Your reasons don't matter. Instead, you'll need to close on the condo and then take the developer to court . . . which is likely to be a long, difficult process.

So if you buy property in a civil-law country, you'll need to make sure that your purchase or sales contract is watertight and covers all the possible worst-case scenarios *before* you sign on the dotted line. It's incredibly difficult to rectify problems afterward.

Also understand that legal terms don't automatically translate from common to civil law. A classic example is buying as "joint tenants with rights of survivorship" in a common-law country. This means, of course, that if something happens to one of you, the remaining partner will inherit the property without the need to go to court.

If, though, you direct your attorney in a civil-law country to add a joint tenancy clause, he may assume you mean "tenants in common," as there is no definition of "joint tenants" in civil law. "Tenants in common" is very similar—but there is one big difference: A remaining partner will need to go to court to inherit. It doesn't just happen automatically.

So be sure to explain your intent clearly to your civil law attorney. Instead of using legal terms from back home and assuming he will understand what that means, tell him specifically: We are buying as partners, and want to ensure that if one of us dies, the surviving partner inherits the property automatically without the need to go to court.

And by all means, hire an independent attorney and do not use the same attorney as the seller, developer, or real estate agent. You want one who represents your interests only.

WHEN HALFWAY ISN'T THE WRONG WAY: WHY LIVING OVERSEAS PART-TIME MAY MAKE SENSE FOR YOU

Maybe you're not ready to give up everything you have going on in your life right now, but you're intrigued by the idea of retiring overseas?

Don't feel alone. There are plenty of people who have learned that the adventure and great benefits of life overseas can be had without selling everything and making a "forever" move to get them.

One of the biggest concerns we hear from potential expats is about leaving children and grandkids behind. And that's understandable, although with today's advanced technology, it's easy to keep in touch from just about anywhere in the world.

Another concern, of course, is health care and health insurance. If you have worrisome health issues, or if you have Medicare or a good private insurance policy in the United States, you may be understandably reluctant to venture abroad full-time.

So rather than take the plunge, you may be better off with a part-time paddle to test the waters someplace new. We see plenty of retirees doing exactly that. They're taking a month or three to explore a new destination, sometimes with an eye to finding a new home. And sometimes it's just a short-term escape—a flexible alternative to an "all or nothing" move.

With this part-time approach, you'll also skirt the need for a residence visa. Perhaps you can rent your home while you're gone and help offset your travel costs. You may, in fact, find that it can cost you less to rent an apartment a month or two in a good-value escape than it will to pay your utility bills back home.

So how to start? Just pick one place and stay as long as you can. Rent an apartment or home to see what daily living is like. If you find it's not for you, head someplace else next year.

The point is: There are no rules. Do what works for you. You can keep a foothold back home and find out firsthand, and with little risk, if retiring overseas is for you.

Tip: With a little perseverance, you may be able to get a housesitting gig that will allow you a free stay in exchange for caring for a home and/or pets while the owners are away. We know a man who has traveled the world this way, paying only for his airfare. He stayed in our home, in fact, and tells us he manages to keep his monthly expenses to less than $500 this way. There are many online resources you can use to get started; our friend uses TrustedHousesitters.com.

Note: One of the most knowledgeable experts we know when it comes to buying property overseas is our friend, Turalu (Tuey) Brady Murdock. Not long ago, she retired after 34 years as vice president/counsel of the Latin America/Caribbean Division for First American Title Insurance Company. Her years of experience give her a unique perspective on what to watch out for when buying property outside of your home country.

She now runs an independent consulting business for individuals and companies buying property in Latin America and the Caribbean. By the way, where does an international title insurance attorney choose to live? Tuey lives with her family on the Pacific Coast of Nicaragua. We asked her to share some of her experience and tips with you. . . .

━━━━━

HOW TO ENSURE A PROBLEM-FREE REAL ESTATE PURCHASE
By Turalu Brady Murdock, JD

The partially renovated colonial house was just what we were looking for back then—a base in Granada, Nicaragua, to avoid staying in hotels every time we came to visit. Plus, we could have fun decorating it with the beautiful and inexpensive locally made furniture and folk art found throughout the country. We signed the contract to purchase, arranged for funds to be wired, discussed with the builder how we wanted the renovations to be completed, and left for home.

Fast forward a few months later, and we soon discovered that the dry cleaning business next door caused the adjoining wall to be in a continuous state of disrepair, that the toilets emptied into a 200-year-old septic tank that was located in the middle of the patio, and that no hot water was being piped into the kitchen. We thought since this was our second overseas purchase that we knew what we were doing, but that purchase taught us that due diligence is often "discovering what you don't know."

Due diligence can be easy if you know what questions to ask and what to look for. This checklist will help with the unknown.

1. *An attorney is worth the cost.* When you are buying property in an overseas location it is likely that you will be dealing with a

different legal system and possibly a different language. Even if it's an English-speaking country, you may not be able to understand the terminology—such as dower, curtsey, gazump, title certificate, and unregistered land. When the official language is not English, the legal terminology becomes even more difficult to decipher, even with translation—*título supletorio* (supplemental title), *usufructo* (usufruct), *relazione tecnica* (technical report), 2F (two faces), *bon de visite* (good visit) and *impuesto de sellos* (stamp tax).

An attorney who speaks English, understands how his legal system differs from yours, and is an advocate for you is invaluable. The attorney should be retained before you sign any documents or pay any money, even a good-faith deposit.

2. *Pay for a complete and thorough chain-of-title report.* Often, if the seller shows the buyer a registered deed, the buyer will feel comfortable that the seller owns the land. A good attorney will start with the seller's deed but then conduct full research to determine the validity of the title. In some countries, the chain of title should be researched back 30 years or more. In other countries, checking to see if the title is registered may be enough. Even with a thorough search, the attorney should explain any gaps or missing links in the chain.

Here's a true story: A home was bought from the heirs of a recently deceased man, but the attorney failed to tell the clients that only some of the heirs had signed the deed. The buyer discovered the error when the missing heirs knocked on the door of his recently purchased home, demanding their rights to the property.

3. *Do you need a survey?* If you are buying a condo, apartment, or an attached home, you probably do not need a survey. But if you are buying a vacant lot or a detached home, you will need to get a survey. The surveyor should mark all corners of the lot, show all improvements, including sheds, fences, driveways, wells, and anything else constructed on the land. He or she should give the buyer an affidavit as to whether the legal description in the deed matches the land he or she surveyed. The surveyor should also tell the buyer if there is anyone living on or using the land, whether there is a public road that abuts the land, and whether the land is

affected by any use restrictions. Beachfront lots are often difficult to survey and overlapping boundary lines may exist.

Another true story: A buyer received a nicely prepared survey that looked good on paper, but when the architect tried to use the legal dimensions to draw out the lot, she realized that the survey did not indicate an enclosed space, but described an open-ended boundary line. Again, check the legal dimensions against the survey drawing.

4. *Don't assume you have utilities or that you can use the property for a residence*. Is the house hooked up to water and sewer systems? Is there a restriction on using the land that affects how you want to use it? Land along any bodies of water may allow public access and may prevent you from using the area near the water. In some countries, if you don't have a livability permit you won't be able to move in, or you may not even be able to register the land. What about phone lines, electric lines, cable, and Internet—are they connected and/or available? These are things we take for granted but in many countries, they could be extra. Ask the right questions.

5. *The builder*. If you are buying a construction package, you need to ask about the builder's reputation. Is this his first project? What type of financial backing does the builder have?

6. *Put your deposit into a trust account*. Trust or escrow accounts do not exist in every country. When you give your deposit to a real estate agent, it may be going into his general account to pay salaries, office rent, and more. Does he have a trust account to hold funds or are the funds put into a general law firm account? Is the deposit refundable and under what circumstances?

All important issues can be verified, checked, and resolved by a good and competent attorney working for you. Another protection available in some countries is title insurance. In some countries, U.S. title insurance companies offer international title insurance to insure the validity of your title. For a small percentage of the purchase price, title insurance will protect you against unknown liens or encumbrances on the title.

But back to our renovated colonial home in Nicaragua. Was it a good purchase, even with the later discovered flaws? Absolutely, and it helped us understand what to ask the next time we decided to invest in an overseas property.

18

Once You Know Where You're Going

Put Your Plan in Action

YOU DECIDED TO RETIRE OVERSEAS. You've chosen the community where you'll live. Now what? There are a few things yet to do before you leave home that will help put your plan in action and streamline your move.

HEALTH CARE

If you don't believe vaccinations are of benefit or that they're detrimental to your health, that's certainly your choice. But if you do, now is a good time to make sure you're current with routine immunizations like measles/mumps/rubella (MMR), diphtheria/pertussis/tetanus (DPT), poliovirus, and so forth. If you're of retirement age, chances are that you're already up to date on all of these. You may, though, want to consider getting vaccinations for hepatitis A and B, typhoid, and—depending what country you are moving to—yellow fever.

Do You Need a Yellow Fever Vaccination?

While your chances of getting yellow fever are very low unless you travel deep into jungle areas, some countries—such as Costa Rica, where there is no risk—require proof of yellow fever vaccination if you are traveling there directly from other countries where the disease can be found. People who get vaccinated should be given an International Certificate of Vaccination. And note that the vaccine is to be given 10 days before travel to an endemic area.

In some countries, some vaccinations, such as for shingles, aren't yet available. Do some research and consideration about your health care needs. One resource for health care recommendations for travelers and those planning an extended stay overseas is the website of the Centers for Disease Control and Prevention (CDC): www.cdc.gov/travel.

What about malaria? Malaria is endemic in the tropics, there's no doubt about that. But in most of the countries we suggest for retirement living, you'll find very little risk. Again, the CDC offers helpful information at its website: www.cdc.gov/malaria.

We personally have never taken any malaria treatment, nor ever felt the need to do so. A bigger risk in the tropics is dengue fever, another mosquito-borne disease for which there is no vaccination. Primarily prevalent during rainy seasons, your best prevention is to protect yourself from mosquito bites. Use repellant and take other precautions, such as having screens on windows. Learn more at www.cdc.gov/dengue.

We also recommend that you make decisions about how you will pay for your health care needs. Do you have health insurance that will cover you overseas or will you purchase local coverage in your new home base? (See Chapter 5 for more information.)

Although it will not pay for coverage overseas, some U.S. expat retirees choose to maintain Medicare Part A and/or Part B and travel back to the United States for care if needed. Learn more about your options here: www.travel.state.gov/travel/living/living_1234.html.

Canadians who wish to maintain their public health care benefits can find more information here: www.servicecanada.gc.ca/eng/subjects/travel/abroad.shtml.

If you do decide to maintain your current U.S. or Canadian health benefits, consider purchasing an evacuation policy. You'll find information at websites like InsureMyTrip.com and SquareMouth.com.

Our advice: Before you leave home, stock up on medications you may be taking . . . enough to get you through the first two or three months and give you time to find local equivalents. (A handy website to look up comparable medications available in various countries is Drugs.com.) And be sure you have an emergency plan. Tell family and friends how to access your health information and/or financial information if you should become incapacitated in any way. Once you move into your new home, be sure a trusted in-country friend or neighbor has this information as well.

FINANCES: CREDIT CARDS, BANKING, AND TAXES

As you're planning to move overseas, it's also a wise move to evaluate your financial situation. Without a credit history in the country you're moving to, it's doubtful you'll be able to obtain a credit card there. So you'll need to keep your current card(s) and/or get new ones that don't charge foreign currency exchange fees. Some that don't are American Express, Capital One, Discover, Chase, and some Citi cards. One source for information about credit card options is CreditCards.com.

FATCA/FBAR Requirements

The U.S. government has enacted the Foreign Account Tax Compliance Act, which requires its citizens to file Foreign Bank and Financial Account reports with the IRS if your foreign account ever has more than $10,000 in it during a calendar year. Failure to file can result in stiff fines of up to $10,000. (Canadians have similar reporting requirements for any foreign accounts, income, or holdings that exceed $100,000.)

You'll need to maintain a bank account back home to pay those credit card bills. You're probably already a whiz at online banking, but if not, now's the time to bone up. Make sure you can access and manage your bank account online and learn how to use its bill-paying functions. If your bank doesn't offer free or low-cost ATM transaction fees, now may be the time to move to one that does. (Your ATM card will become one of your best friends when you live overseas. Know your PINs.) And be sure to choose a bank that offers favorable foreign currency exchange rates. We've had good luck with Capital One.

The same goes for your brokerage and investment accounts. Be sure you understand how to use your online management functions. It's best to work out all these issues several months before you move. In case you need help, it's much easier to do it in person with your account manager than over the phone from a foreign country.

What about opening a local account in your new community? That's up to you. We've found that we don't really need a local account. By using our Capital One ATM card and withdrawing our limit a couple of times a month we get by perfectly fine. Cash transactions are the name of the game in Latin America, especially, and we pay all our utility and other bills in cash, as they are due.

In some countries, however, you will need a local bank account. As a requirement of residence, a certain amount must be deposited each month or be held in a local bank. There may be advantages to having a local bank account, including the ability to pay bills online. In many countries, this can be an easy way to show financial solvency when you renew your residence visa. Statements will already be in the local language and currency and you won't need to have them translated or apostilled (see the following "What Is an Apostille?" sidebar), saving you time and money in the process.

Many banks require a resident's visa to open a checking account but will open a savings account for nonresidents. To open a local account, you may need a letter of introduction from a local in-country attorney. Typically, most banks we've dealt with will also require some local references (these can be expat friends and, often, they'll only ask for a name and address), as well as a copy of your passport and a local utility bill (needn't be in your name) so they can verify your address.

Our advice: Find out if your local bank can accept direct deposits of U.S. Social Security payments, and find out if deposits are insured and for how much. And look for branches in cities/towns where you will live. It defeats the purpose to open a bank account at a large bank in Panama City if you'll live in Boquete and there's no local branch. Even if there is a local branch, don't expect the Panama City and Boquete branches to be one and the same administratively. Also, in our experience, if you have a local checking account, learn to sign your name on every check identically to the signature in your passport. Only use black or blue ink and make sure there are no strikeouts or misspellings on your check.

As for your tax obligations, U.S. and Canadian citizens are required to file taxes each year no matter where in the world they live. Moving overseas does not exempt you from this obligation. Ordinarily, filing your taxes while living overseas entails much the same process as it does if you are still living in your home country.

If, however, you purchase foreign real estate, have a foreign bank account, or earn an income overseas, you will have some additional reporting requirements. If your current tax advisor doesn't understand these issues, you may want to look for one who does.

There are many good advisors in this area. One is Nick Hodges, a U.S. tax advisor with expertise in expat tax issues. You can contact him at nick@nchwealth.com. A Canadian tax attorney/advisor is Doug Hendler. Contact him at DHendler@blaney.com.

Documents you'll need: Start a file folder with all the documents you'll need along the way. It's also a good idea to scan and save digital copies of all these so you can print them out as needed.

What Is an "Apostille"?

It's a form of authentication issued for documents by countries that participate in the Hague Convention of 1961. You can find a list of countries that participate here: hcch.net. If the country of intended use does not participate in the Hague Convention, documents sent to that country can be "authenticated" or "certified." In the United States, your state's Office of the Secretary of State can provide apostille and authentication services. Canada is not a signatory to the Hague Apostille Convention, so for Canadian documents to be recognized in a foreign country they must be authenticated and legalized.

Typically, in order to get a residence visa overseas, you'll be asked to produce copies of your passport as well as apostilled or certified copies of your birth certificate, marriage certificate, and in some countries, past divorce decrees. You may also be asked for a criminal record report, and for current financial or pension statements. Some countries require a blood test by a local clinic to ensure that you do not have any communicable diseases.

The best place to get information about the specific requirements of the country you may be considering is through that country's embassy or consulate. Their online websites usually offer detailed information, although we've found these websites sometimes aren't updated on a regular basis. Therefore, you may have better luck contacting the embassy or consulate nearest you.

You may also want to start a file of health records for each person in your family who will be moving overseas as well as your children's immunization and school records if you'll be moving with them.

Our advice: Be sure your passport is up to date. Most countries will not allow you to travel if your passport is due to expire within six months. Airlines are very strict about checking this and you will be denied boarding if your passport will soon expire. It's also a good idea to renew your driver's license before your move.

MOVING YOUR PETS OVERSEAS

It's easy to move your pets overseas these days, even if it's not inexpensive. Be prepared to pay about the same amount for their airfare as you do for your own.

Most any country you might be considering moving to will also accept your pets, especially cats and dogs. Some will not allow exotic birds and reptiles.

Very few countries these days require any kind of quarantine period. Panama does have a 40-day in-home quarantine requirement, which basically requires that the pet be in your care for the first 40 days you are in the country.

Again, your best source of information for moving your pet overseas will be the country's embassy or consulate. And most countries' requirements for importation are basically the same.

Have your veterinarian prepare a standard International Health Certificate, preferably no more than 10 days before travel. The certificate needs to indicate the pet's name, breed, owner's name, and current country of residence. It should state that the pet is healthy and free of parasites. It must contain a list of inoculations including type, manufacturer, and batch number. (Typically, it's required that rabies vaccinations be given at least six months ahead of travel.)

You'll need to make a reservation with the airline for your pet to travel with you, so be sure to do this at the same time you book your own ticket. Dogs and cats can fly in the cabin if their crate is small enough to fit under the seat, as checked baggage, or as cargo.

Crates must adhere to airline guidelines and all airlines have this information posted online. Airlines ban animals flying as checked baggage between May 15 and September 15 or when temperatures are extreme, and you're advised to call a day ahead if you're concerned about weather conditions.

It's not advised to sedate your pet while traveling, especially if they are traveling as cargo. Nor should you give them any food that they might choke on, as no one will be available in the cargo hold to assist them. Be sure, though, to feed them far enough in advance that they have time to "do their duty" before boarding the flight.

In some cases, it may be wise (or easier) to utilize professional pet relocation services. The Independent Pet and Animal Transportation Association provides a list of companies and offers guidelines on choosing the best one for your needs. Learn more at ipata.com.

Our advice: If your pets fly cargo, put a block of ice in a bowl inside their crate. It won't spill and as it thaws, they'll have something to quench their thirst. And in the months before travel, help them grow accustomed to the crate by leaving it in a familiar place with the door open so they can explore it, and by putting them in it for longer stretches of time each day.

SHEDDING OR SHIPPING: WHAT ABOUT YOUR "STUFF"?

Should you move your household belongings overseas with you? That depends on how much they mean to you and/or how much it will cost to replace these things in your new community. And maybe you're not sure you'll stick in the place you first land . . . or whether you'll rent a furnished home or apartment and just won't need all that stuff. . . .

Sometimes moving your stuff just isn't worth it. You may be ready to shed most of what you have anyway. Or you're moving to a home that's completely out of character with the furniture you have. And remember the climate. Overstuffed chairs and Oriental rugs will be great in the mountains of Ecuador, but they'll be forever moldy on a Costa Rican beach.

Also, moving your items, including vehicles, into certain countries may be just too difficult or expensive to put up with . . . or not even allowed.

So what goes along and what stays behind? Deciding what to take will be a balancing act between economics and sentimentality. The economics part is easy. If you're moving to a place where high-quality, custom-made furniture is very inexpensive (like Ecuador), then it may be cheaper to buy new furniture than to ship the old stuff.

One Thing to Pack: Electric Converters

If you've traveled to Europe you already know that you'll need electric converters to run your U.S. appliances, because Europe runs on a 220-volt system rather than the 110-volt system most of us are used to. It may just be too much for your appliances (even as small as hair dryers), so if you're moving to Europe, you'd be better off buying major appliances there. You'll also need convertors in most of Asia, as well as in Argentina and Uruguay. But in the rest of Latin America, your U.S.-standard equipment will be just fine, although you may want surge protectors in your home and in older buildings, and three-to-two-prong adaptors that you can buy for a couple of bucks at any hardware store.

The sentimentality is harder to deal with. If you have furniture that's been in the family for generations, then you may not want to leave it behind . . . regardless of the shipping costs.

Remember that you've got three ways of shipping things: in your luggage and things you can carry with you, in an airfreight container, and in a shipboard container. Anything you carry as luggage or ship as air freight will basically come with you, so you'll be in business right away. It costs more on a per-pound basis, but the convenience may be worth it.

If you can't get by with air freight or overweight luggage, then you're likely to need at least a 20-foot shipboard container. Then the decision-making process changes, because container shipping is charged by volume, not weight. You'll pay the same whether you fill the container or not, so you may as well pack it full.

And if you are shipping a container, be sure to bring your large, quality North American appliances. In some countries they'll be available at reasonable cost (such as Mexico). In others you can replace them . . . at twice the price. Sometimes you won't find them at all.

Finding a shipping company: There are companies that specialize in international transfers and that often have good prices. It's often best to use companies recommended by expats who have gone before you and are already living in the community you'll be moving to. There are a number of online forums and Facebook pages where you can find this information. (Just enter the name of the country and "expat forum" into your search engine.)

Whatever company you choose, make sure it provides a door-to-door contract, rather than referring you to someone on the destination end. That way you won't find yourself stranded on the dock while the guy you paid is safely in New York or Chicago.

Also, prepare a complete inventory of everything you own, with model and serial numbers and approximate value . . . then add the mover's box number as items are packed. Be sure to also list each item's name in the language of the country you're moving to, or hire a translator to do this for you once you've completed your document. Have the list reviewed by your mover's contact at the destination end. Some firms may have a specialist to do all this for you, and if not, it can be very worth your while to work with a local customs broker in your destination country.

You'll use this list for customs, insurance, or eventual claims. Virtually *every mover* will tell you this is not necessary, but having a specific list will get you through customs most easily.

Will you pay customs duties? Some countries allow duty-free imports and some don't. But don't get hung up on this until you know the fee. Duties on used furniture (for personal use) can be very low. You don't want to re-purchase $20,000 in furniture to save $600 in customs fees. This seems obvious. But many people give up once they learn that they're not eligible for duty-free import — without checking further to see what the actual fee would be.

A good source of information for shipping your household goods (and much more) can be found in the country-specific manuals you can browse at the *International Living* bookstore at ILBookstore.com.

PART THREE

Once You Get There
Adjusting to Your New Life

———

YOU'VE ARRIVED IN A FOREIGN COUNTRY with as many suitcases as the airline will allow . . . and maybe a pet or two. Now what? How can you, as easily as possible, go about settling into this new life you're making for yourself?

After all, this is not a small life event. It's a big deal. You'll be saying "so long" to the past—friends, family, familiar surroundings—and hello to a completely new set of challenges and opportunities.

The key is to recognize and act on those opportunities. In the following pages, we'll help you determine a strategy for staying connected with the most important things from home, and we'll offer some tips to help you readily adapt to your new environment.

If you're newly retired, adjusting to life without "work" can be daunting, no matter where you live. So we'll also offer up some ideas on what to do with your free time once you've settled in.

"What do you do all day?" is one of the most common questions asked of expats. While most will tell you that they have a more active social life than ever before, they're also finding new and rewarding interests to fill their time. If you're worried about being bored when you move overseas, don't be. This will be the most action-packed, fulfilling, and fun time of your life.

And much of it has to do with attitude. . . .

19

Changes in Latitudes, Changes in Attitude

Maintaining the Bridge between
Your Past and Present Lives

———

MOVING OVERSEAS, AS WE'VE SAID, is a great adventure . . . if you approach it as such. But to be sure, despite all the rewards, it takes a bit of emotional fortitude. After all, it's not easy to uproot your life and start over in a foreign country.

You'll have to say good-bye to family members and friends, you'll probably need to downsize and store some treasured possessions or pass them on to others, and you'll have what seems like a never-ending checklist of things to do in preparation for your move. Once you get where you're going, it will be a full-time job to learn the lay of the land in your new community.

So how can you make things easier?

The best advice we can give is to try not to put too much pressure on yourself. Everything will get done, although maybe not in the timeframe you expect. Try to relax and go with the flow.

SAYING "SEE YOU LATER" INSTEAD OF "GOOD-BYE"

People will think you're crazy for moving overseas, no doubt about it. Family members may react with anger or sadness. If you're close to your family, the hardest thing you may ever do is to say good-bye to them. But remember, most of the retirement destinations we've named in this book are just a short plane ride from the United States—sometimes less time than it takes to fly from the East Coast to the West Coast.

Everyone Says They'll Come Visit

We've had friends and family visit over the years, but not nearly as many who said they would. So we've ditched the big multi-bedroom home that rarely housed visitors in favor of a two-bedroom condo that better suits our needs. It's small and easy to care for, and we can lock it and leave it at will when we travel. When someone does come to visit, we find an inexpensive hotel or a friend's vacant home where they can stay.

Many of today's families are spread far and wide. As our friend Edd Staton, who retired to Cuenca, Ecuador, says, he and his wife, Cynthia, expect to see their grandkids *more* because they've lowered their monthly expenses and are no longer tied to jobs.

"If we were still working in the U.S.," he says, "we'd have three or four weeks of vacation time a year and hope we had enough money to visit. Plus, our two children live in different states, so there's no way we could live near both of them simultaneously. Therefore some form of travel would always be necessary."

And remember that depending where you live, you'll probably save money overall, allowing you to afford to go back and visit with some regularity.

THE INTERNET WILL BE YOUR NEW BEST FRIEND

Nothing takes the place of real human-to-human contact, of course, but the Internet can be the next best thing. You can get your newspapers, magazines, and TV and radio stations online. You can also buy books, rent or buy movies, and more with just a few simple mouse clicks.

You Can Do It! Learn to Improvise.

At first, you'll miss your convenience items, no doubt. Not everything on your grocer's shelf at home can be so easily had in other corners of the world. So learn to be a problem solver. Sour cream . . . ranch dressing . . . baked beans . . . dryer sheet fabric softeners . . . you can easily make all these things from scratch. Recipes for just about anything can be found on the Internet, and what a feeling of accomplishment and self-reliance!

How much will you pay for Internet overseas? You're likely to pay a little more in some parts of the world than you do in the United States or Canada . . . but not a lot. High-speed Internet in Ecuador, for example (comparable to a DSL connection in the States starts at about $35 a month. Be aware, though, that while you'll find Internet connections of acceptable speed almost everywhere now, high-speed Internet service may not be available in every corner of every country.

In most countries, Internet service will be available through the local telephone or cable television companies. Two options for expats who do find themselves off the Internet grid are a portable pay-as-you-go USB modem service offered by mobile phone providers or a satellite system. Satellite systems are faster and costs generally run $500 to $600 up front, with a monthly service fee thereafter.

We certainly can't live without the Internet—it's critically important for our work and for keeping in touch with family, friends, and anyone else anywhere in the world.

STAYING IN TOUCH: EASIER THAN YOU THINK

Telephone and video calls: For calling from country to country, VOIP services are the way to go. Skype is the most popular of these services. If you call from computer to computer, your calls are free, including video calls—the next best thing to visiting in person with friends and family back home. (One expat we know reads nightly bedtime stories to her grandkids this way.)

You can also get SkypeOut service, for a very small fee, that allows you to call landlines anywhere in the world from your computer. And SkypeIn allows you to get a phone number with the area code of your choice so your contacts back home can call you without extra charges, just as they would if you were across the street. You can even use Skype to text, send a fax, and on your mobile devices. And it offers many other must-have features for business users. Learn more at Skype.com.

Facebook and Blogs

There's no easier way to keep in touch with lots of people all the time than at Facebook.com. You can post photos and see those of your contacts and keep up with one another as much as you like.

Many expats have also started their own blogs, writing an online diary, complete with photos, about their experiences living overseas. If you'd like to do the same, one place to start is at WordPress.com.

There are other popular VOIP phone options such as Vonage and Magic Jack that allow you to plug a handheld phone receiver into your modem or via a USB port (as does Skype, by the way.) There are some one-time costs and subscription fees associated with these services. Check the details at Vonage.com and MagicJack.com.

Local cell phones: You can buy a local phone just about anywhere. In many international airports today you'll find phone kiosks where you can buy a cell phone and load it up with phone time. In fact, we have never signed up for local cell phone service, but have always relied on pay-as-you-go phones.

One thing to note: In many countries there is more than one service network. Be sure you choose the one that is the most popular—this is one area where getting the input of fellow expats is important. And of course, you can get a cell phone service plan just about anywhere, too. Be sure to read the fine print so you understand your contractual obligations.

Also: If you are traveling and wish to use your cell phone from home, you may already have a plan that allows you to make international calls. If you're not sure, call your service provider before you leave home to learn about your options so you aren't stuck with a hefty bill.

What about "snail" mail? This may sound impossible, but we no longer receive much snail mail sent through any regular postal services—except, of course, for credit card come-ons and other junk mail sent to us through the address attached to our credit cards and frequent flyer accounts. But most of our mail these days—especially anything of a critical nature—is delivered electronically via e-mail.

We also don't order anything via the Internet that has to be shipped to us overseas. (We're fortunate to be able to travel back to the States a couple of times each year and we stock up on everything we need then.) But we know expats, of course, who order items from online shopping services and/or who occasionally need something shipped from home.

Most of the cities or towns overseas where you might choose to live will offer some kind of postal service, although often in the form of a P.O. box rather than home delivery. While your mail may not arrive in the timeliest manner, this is typically a very inexpensive way to receive mail. (In Ecuador, for instance, the cost of annual box rental is less than $35.)

Due to the possibility of loss, we don't recommend mailing valuables via the postal system. Use a courier service like FedEx, UPS, or DHL—all of which ship worldwide. A word of caution: If you receive forwarded mail or other printed material by regular mail or courier, make sure the sender does not put a value on it, or it will be subject to duty. (We've asked our family not to send us gifts this way . . . the customs duties just aren't worth it. And by now, they're accustomed to gifting us electronically, with gift certificates we can use online.)

Another way to receive mail is through a mail forwarding service. Your mail can be sent to the address of the mail forwarding service and then on to you. Two mail forwarding services popular with expats are Executive Mail Drop (ExecutiveMailDropServices .com) and Earth Class Mail (EarthClassMail.com). Earth Class scans selected mail and sends it to your e-mail account, and you can decide whether you want it discarded, recycled, or forwarded.

And don't worry about missing your favorite television programs. Cable or satellite television service is widely available in the countries we recommend for overseas retirement. If you are a sports fan, pop culture devotee, or news junkie, this is probably something you won't want to do without. Depending on the service you sign up for, you will have access to U.S. and international news in English on CNN, Fox, or the BBC, as well as U.S. network television programs, international sports and movie channels such as HBO, Cinemax, The Learning Channel, and others (usually in English with subtitles in Spanish or another language). As a general rule of thumb, a typical television package—in Latin America at least—costs $40 to $70 per month. Basic cable usually costs about $25.

We no longer watch much television, but when we do, we rely once again on the Internet. Instead of subscribing to a program package, we watch television selectively via websites such as USTVnow.com that stream the major U.S. channels for free over the Internet. If a certain program we want to watch, such as a sports event, isn't on one of the channels offered for free, we can opt to pay a small fee to watch that particular event.

Since the company now offers service to Latin America, we're also big fans of Netflix.com. For just $8 a month we can watch as much Netflix programming as we can handle: movies, television series, documentaries, and more. And because we don't like to be slaves to a schedule, we buy our favorite television series from iTunes.com and then have a marathon night or weekend where we watch episode after episode.

Slingbox is another system used by lots of expats to satisfy their television habit. (Learn more at Slingbox.com.) Basically, it's a set-top box that connects to any TV or any other video-output device back home (this is where loyal friends and family come in handy) and streams the signal to your Internet-connected computer or cell phone anywhere in the world. It's pretty slick and, once you get it set up, it's easy to use.

So there you have it. Today's technology makes living overseas easier than it has ever been. It may not be a small world geographically, but in terms of staying connected and communicating with anyone anywhere and at any time, you can easily and affordably do just that.

20

When the Hammock Gets Boring

What to Do after You Retire and Move Overseas

WE HAVE TWO FAMILY MEMBERS WHO, up until a few years ago, were looking forward to retiring in the next few years to a small beach community. He's already retired, in fact, from his work as a police officer. She's a high-powered attorney for a multinational company, currently on assignment in China.

Before their posting to China, they'd never lived overseas or even traveled much beyond a few trips to Mexico to visit us. They wanted nothing more from their retirement than to hang in a hammock with a good book (her) and to drink beer on the terrace overlooking the water (him).

Today, though, their retirement wish list has changed a bit. Living overseas has been an eye-opener for them, especially for our now-retired male relative. It was a struggle for him to make friends at first, since most of the expats in China were still working, as was his wife. And most of the nonworking spouses were female. He soon learned that drinking beer and watching the world go by was fun for a while but wasn't what he wanted to do in his retirement years.

As we said, today this couple has a more realistic vision of what retirement will be for them. They still think they'd like to live on the beach, but in a bigger locale with more offerings for cultural and other activities. He'd like to play golf and she'd like to volunteer in a mentoring-type position. They've decided that instead of a small, isolated village, they'd like to be in a community that offers many activities that they can participate in.

So what will you do in retirement? This is a question that needs to be answered even if you never leave the United States or Canada. The most important thing, of course, is to follow your bliss. As mentioned in Chapter 3, if you've an interest in a certain hobby or sport, such as golf, diving, fishing, and so on, be sure that community supports your interests.

And if you want or need to work, or you have a burning desire to get involved in charitable activities and give back to your community, by all means, full speed ahead.

Here are some ideas to get you started.

WHAT THE WORLD NEEDS NOW: VOLUNTEERING

You'll no doubt find plenty of opportunities to "do good" and give back to your new community overseas. You can join already established volunteer organizations or form one of your own.

For example, a retired teacher friend moved to Mexico with her husband. He spends his days managing their investment accounts and working on a book he's writing. She plays bridge three days a week and also volunteers at a local orphanage, teaching English. A dedicated teacher, she has found a way to "repackage" her former career.

"I love it," she says. "It's a way I stay in touch with the old me, but in a brand-new, *better* way."

Learn More about Volunteering

Discover how to choose the volunteer opportunity that's right for you at wikiHow.com/Volunteer. To get some pointers on starting your own nonprofit organization, see wikiHow.com/Start-a-501c3-Nonprofit-Organization.

If you live in a city or town with an established foreign community, you're apt to find many established organizations to join. Start by asking other expats about volunteer activities in your new community. Find out if there are opportunities to work in areas you most enjoy: with children, the elderly, animals, the environment, the arts, and so forth.

If your community has a local embassy, it can be a good source of information about volunteer opportunities and expat organizations. In Quito, Ecuador, for instance, there is group called *Damas Norteamericanas y Británicas* (North American and British Ladies). Each country's embassy in Ecuador, in fact, has a branch, and the organization holds monthly luncheons and annual events such as a Christmas Bazaar and the *Damas* Ball, a grand black-tie event. Proceeds go to support local charities.

Many communities with large expat populations will have organizations you can join, like Lake Chapala's Friends of Chamber Music, Friends of Opera, and *Feria Maestros del Arte* (www .Mexicoartshow.com), which benefit the arts. To learn more about the many local charitable opportunities in this area, contact the Lake Chapala Society at LakeChapalaSociety.org.

There are similar organizations and opportunities for very worthwhile activities in every expat community where we've lived or visited. There are women's clubs, men's clubs, English libraries, and a host of organizations devoted to every type of interest. All you need to do is show up and be willing to lend a hand.

If you're not yet ready to move overseas, but you'd like to investigate some travel opportunities that fulfill your volunteer interests—some of which are even paid positions—consider becoming a "voluntourist."

Some helpful resources:

- *International Volunteer Programs Association*: You'll find activities for nearly every interest in almost any country in the world at Volunteerinternational.org.

- *Action without Borders*: This information-rich, searchable database serves as a clearinghouse for more than 46,000 nonprofit organizations worldwide. You'll find listings for internships, volunteering, jobs, nonprofit career fairs, and more. There's a section specifically for international volunteers at Idealist.org.

- *International Voluntary Service (SCI-IVS)*: You'll find volunteer-abroad program listings here. If you are looking for low-cost, short-term volunteer options in more than 50 countries, this is the place. Learn more at SCI-IVS.org.

- *Habitat for Humanity*: This organization works to provide safe, sturdy homes for low-income families and individuals: Habitat.org.

- *The Peace Corps*: Looking for a paying gig? The Peace Corps seeks individuals to serve as volunteers in overseas communities in the areas of education, small business development, the environment, health, youth development, and agriculture. A tour is 27 months, and you must be a U.S. citizen, over 18, in good health, and have education and/or experience relevant to programs. See Peacecorps.gov.

- *Travel for free*: WWOOF, an acronym for Worldwide Opportunities on Organic Farms, offers you a way to travel the world for next to nothing. (Typically, you pay only to get there and your room and board is free in exchange for helping out on a farm, orchard, vineyard, or eco-lodge.) At the website, Wwoof.org, you can search a database to see who's looking for someone to help out.

But I WANT (or NEED) to Keep Working!

Finding a traditional job overseas can be difficult, despite your education or skills. And if you do find a job, it may be one that barely covers your expenses.

Just as the United States and Canada do, governments of countries around the world want to be sure that their own citizens have access to employment. Unless you have an E.U. passport, it can be very difficult to find employment in Europe. It's equally difficult to obtain work permits in Latin America or Asia, and if you do, you'll find salaries offered by local employers to be very low. (Professionals such as entry-level attorneys and doctors in Latin America, for instance, typically earn less than $1,000 a month.)

In some countries, too, there are some jobs that foreigners are not allowed to hold, including quite often in the medical field. And if you don't speak the local language, you almost certainly will not find any type of traditional employment . . . with a few exceptions.

You may find a job "off the books," of course. We've know plenty of people who've found bartending jobs, for instance, especially in bars that cater to expats. You might find work managing a B&B, or helping out a local guide service or travel agency.

But if it's a traditional, pay-the-bills job you're looking for, you might try a search on a website like OverseasJobs.com or Monster.com. Your best options may be in the education field, teaching in an international elementary or secondary school or university, for instance, although keep in mind that the majority of these opportunities are to be found in large cities such as Quito, Panama City, Managua, Bangkok, Tokyo, and so on.

We'd suggest that if you're searching for a teaching job, you should decide where you want to live and then do an Internet search to see if any of the largest private schools are hiring. Start your search at IBO.org, the International Baccalaureate website. (It's important to note that you won't always need a teaching certificate to teach overseas, but you probably will need a college or university degree of some kind.)

Teaching English

If you're a native English speaker, you may be able to find a job teaching English. The best-paying positions for this kind of work will be in Asia and the Middle East. For instance, the Japanese government sponsors the Japan Exchange and Teaching

Programme (JET; jetprogramme.org), to improve its citizens' foreign-language skills.

No special training or certifications are required, although all teachers must speak English at a native level and must have graduated from a four-year university. Some additional training is provided during the course of time with the program. The average teacher in the JET Programme can make $25,000 to $30,000 annually after all deductions—money that is not taxed in either Japan or the United States when you qualify for the U.S. foreign-earned income exclusion.

According to Bridge TEFL, the largest U.S. provider of TEFL (teaching English as a foreign language) certification courses, salaries in select locations like Japan, Hong Kong, South Korea, Oman, Saudi Arabia, and the United Arab Emirates range from $1,700 to $4,000 per month, while estimated living expenses range from $600 to $1,700 per month. Employers in these countries also typically offer the most benefits, such as free or subsidized housing, language lessons, reimbursed airfare, and bonuses.

The lowest-paid opportunities are in Mexico, and Central and South America. In these places, you can possibly earn enough to get by, but not enough to live luxuriously, save money, or pay off debt. In fact, you'd probably want to have some savings or other financial buffer. However, it's possible to find a one-on-one position teaching English to business executives, and this can be far more lucrative. Learn more about teaching English overseas at BridgeTEFL.com.

Turn Your Passion into Profits

Most expats we know who are earning a living overseas are doing it by turning their passion into profits. If you have a hobby or an interest, and you're retiring overseas, this may be the perfect time to use that extra free time you'll have to parlay your interest into a moneymaking gig.

Teaching yoga, giving music lessons or concerts; pet sitting and grooming; massage; holding writer's workshops; making bread, cheese, or artisan chocolates . . . these are just some of the things we've seen expats do to earn extra income.

Social Entrepreneurship: Make a Living *and* Give Back

Patrice Wynne loves Mexico and Mexican style, and she has a creative flair and spirit. San Miguel de Allende, Mexico, where she lives, had a textile tradition that has been lost over time. Working with families of seamstresses, Patrice founded San Miguel Designs to create gorgeous Mexican art-themed products—clothing, handbags, housewares, and more. Her award-winning collections are sold in boutiques and museums from Mexico to Paris. Learn more at SanMiguelDesigns.com.

Similarly, Sandra Dayton wanted to help the Maya women of her community—Puerto Morelos, a small town on Mexico's Caribbean Riviera Maya—earn an income. So she created a community tourist center where the women make and sell all kinds of artisan products at a Sunday market, including lotions of natural local ingredients. At the Ixchel Jungle Spa, they offer treatments including full-body massages, aloe vera and banana-leaf wraps, chocolate scrubs, and so on. Learn more at MayaEcho.com.

In Mérida, Mexico, our neighbor, David Sterling, turned his love of Mexican food and culture into a very lucrative business. He opened a cooking school in his home (Los-Dos.com) and started offering classes to tourists and others with an interest in Mexican cuisine. On a typical class day, he gives tours of the local *mercado* to purchase ingredients, and then spends the day with his students preparing special Yucatecan dishes that this part of Mexico is famous for. (Followed by a fabulous feast, of course.)

Today, David has built a reputation as one of Mexico's best-known chefs and he's been featured on television programs with no less than Martha Stewart and PBS's Rick Bayless. His latest project is a cookbook called *Yucatán: Recipes from a Culinary Expedition*.

Another friend who also has a love of Mexican culture offers custom tours to off-the-track tourist destinations like the artisan villages of Oaxaca and Chiapas, and to see the monarch butterfly migration in Morélia.

More than a few people we know have parlayed their love of shopping into an income-producing lifestyle. They buy artisan items from around the world (Latin America and Asia are particularly resplendent with all kinds of arts and crafts) and take them home and resell them (with a markup, of course) at craft shows, parties, and to boutique shops. This import-export business can be very lucrative . . . and not only a way to pay for your travels, but also to put some extra money in your pocket.

Seeing the Niche and Filling It

Expat communities, especially, are rife with opportunity, and if you're the entrepreneurial sort, you can capitalize on this.

Just look for what's missing in the community. We've met expats who have opened traditional businesses like B&Bs, real estate companies, bookstores, coffee shops, and all kinds of restaurants, from American cuisine to the exotic fare that you just don't find yet in every international destination.

And we've seen others who've really thought outside the box and opened businesses such as a bakery in Luang Prabang, Laos; an art gallery and even an upscale hair salon in Mérida, Mexico; a spa and natural health center in Placencia, Belize; a fishing guide service on Lake Arenal, Costa Rica; a bagel shop in Quito, Ecuador; a chocolate shop in Mindo, Ecuador; a perfumery in Valladolid, Mexico; a Spanish school in Pedasí, Panama; and many more.

One of our favorite expat success stories is about our friends, Warren and Tuli Hardy, in San Miguel de Allende, Mexico. On their honeymoon to Mexico in 1989, they fell in love with charming San Miguel, in the Sierra Madre Mountains of Mexico, and decided to make it their home.

Having published his first Spanish textbook in 1972, Warren saw immediately that there was a growing number of expats moving to San Miguel and most were struggling with learning to speak Spanish. In 1990, he and Tuli opened the Warren Hardy Spanish school, which has been successful beyond their wildest dreams. More than 1,000 students pass through their doors every year. (We ourselves took classes there, and we give Warren's teaching and learning system our full endorsement.)

Today, along with running the school, Warren and Tuli produce and sell Spanish-learning books online and through Internet retailers like Amazon.com. In partnership with *International Living* they've developed an online learning course that's perfect for "mature" learners. Learn more at https://www.ilbookstore .com/Warren-Hardy-Spanish-the-Ultimate-Experience.html.

By the way, Warren's online course is something you can do anywhere, anytime—a perfect way to kick-start your retirement.

The Portable Career Option

Some careers know no borders. Writers, photographers, artists, yoga teachers, chefs, masseuses, and musicians, of course, can work from just about anywhere in the world. But you may be surprised to learn that just about any profession these days can be transitioned to a portable career.

We have a part-time neighbor in Ecuador who is a hair stylist back home. When he comes to Ecuador, he brings his shears with him and makes $10 or $20 a pop to trim up shaggy hairdos. Another expat we know is a handyman. He'll replace locks, fix the plumbing, hang curtain rods, do some electrical work . . . just about anything that needs doing. Neither of these fellows are tied to a particular destination. They could do what they do anywhere in the world.

And if you can use a computer your options expand exponentially . . . Winton Churchill of Barefoot Consultants, in fact, has made his own portable career of advising expats just how to do this. He offers advice about how to take the skills you already have—no matter if you're a butcher, a baker, or a candlestick maker . . . or a plumber, a welder, a knitter, or a gardener—and earn money with them as a freelancer or online consultant. Learn more at BarefootConsultants.com.

(One of the websites Winton points freelancers to is Elance.com. Take a look and see how many freelance projects you might qualify for. It's free to register and you can start earning immediately, as did a graphic artist friend of ours.)

And who doesn't want to be a travel writer? If it's a dream of yours to get paid to travel, moving overseas is the perfect opportunity to put that dream in motion. *International Living*, in fact,

---

Explore a World Rich with Opportunity

Due to popular demand, *International Living* has created *Incomes Abroad*, an online newsletter that will help you learn how to earn money overseas:

- Import/Export
- Travel Writing
- Copywriting
- Photography
- Income-Earning Blogs
- Freelancing
- Teaching English
- How (and Where) to Start a Bricks-and-Mortar Business Such as a B&B or Restaurant
- And Much More

Learn more at ILBookstore.com/IN or sign up for the free Fund Your Life Overseas e-letter at InternationalLiving.com/Fund-Your-Life.

---

is always looking for freelance submissions. And yes, if your article is accepted you will be paid for your work. Learn more at InternationalLiving.com/about-il/write-for-il.

Same goes for your travel photography. Stock photo houses are good places to submit your travel photos and then earn an income every time one is downloaded. Newspapers and newsletters, magazines, websites, advertising companies, and more are always looking for photos from around the world.

Our advice: Where there's a will, there's a way. Unless you've been offered a job overseas and have a signed contract of employment, you'll have to make your own path. Most expats we know who are earning an income overseas didn't really have a well-defined plan of attack in place before they left home. But once they settled into their new communities, they found opportunities and were able to act on those. In the meantime, they had a nest egg to tide them over. No matter how inexpensive it may be to live in the location where you'll relocate, if you need a source of income, don't move overseas without some way to support yourself.

For ideas and opportunities to earn an income overseas, sign up for the free Fund Your Life Overseas e-letter at InternationalLiving.com/Fund-Your-Life.

21

Moving On

This Is Not a One-Way Highway

DURING OUR SECOND MAJOR RELOCATION WITHIN LATIN AMERICA we discovered an important truth: There is really no such thing as your "last move." There is only your latest move. It *may* turn out to be the last one you ever make, but you simply can't know that for sure. As we love to say, life is what happens while you're busy making plans.

When we first moved to Quito, Ecuador in 2001, we thought for a while that we might possibly spend the rest of our lives there . . . until we moved to Ajijic, Mexico. We thought about settling there for good . . . until we moved to San Miguel de Allende.

By the time we moved from San Miguel to Panama City, we'd stopped looking at every place we lived as the last place we'd ever live—which turned out to be wise, because, after that, we went on to Nicaragua and back to Mexico and now on to Ecuador once again.

Moving abroad is not a trivial undertaking, and just entertaining the idea in the first place takes some real courage and a healthy sense of adventure. At that first critical point you'll concentrate on finding that perfect place to relocate—and it's very doubtful you'll be thinking about the next location *after that*.

But believe us, there could very well be a next one. And not just because the first place you try turns out not to be perfect. It could just as well be that you find another perfect place. And if you end up getting hooked on relocating like we have, another. And *another*.

THIS MAY NOT BE THE LAST MOVE YOU EVER MAKE

Everything gets easier with practice, and relocating is no different. The more you do it, the better you get at it, even if it's something you don't necessarily enjoy . . . and you may not enjoy packing up and leaving a place to which you've devoted lots of time, energy, and emotion.

But either way, if you fall out of love with one place or fall in love with another, that additional move won't be nearly as daunting.

The point is, there's no rule that says that once you make a decision to relocate, you're not allowed to move anywhere else ever again after that . . . even back home if you want.

Relocating and becoming an expat isn't a jump off a cliff or a drive down a one-way street. It's a journey, and most journeys include side trips, unexpected detours, even return trips and roads back home.

In fact, in our experience, those are the best journeys.

THE SERIAL RELOCATOR'S GUIDE TO STAYING LIGHT ON YOUR FEET

If your quest to find the perfect retirement location includes trying out lots of places, you've probably already considered these three Golden Rules:

I. Understand the Financial Issues

The first lesson a serial relocator learns is that relocating costs money. There is no way to sugarcoat it: If you pull up stakes and put them down somewhere else, cash will be involved, and the biggest expenses will be moving your stuff, finding accommodations, and jumping through the legal hoops of another international relocation (assuming you're not moving back home or from place to place within the same country).

The serial relocators we know handle this in two different ways. Most of them started their journey with a fixed amount of money, often what they got out of their property back home, any savings they've added to that, and any income they receive.

Then they either (1) rent in the location of their primary choice and nurse their nest egg, or (2) buy as soon as possible in their first choice of locations after doing all their research and due diligence (if they think prices are reasonable and the market is strong).

Those who stick with renting save money on the front end over buying property and have nothing much to leave behind if and when they choose to relocate. If their nest egg is big enough and rents are affordable enough, this strategy can go on indefinitely, especially if there is also an additional source of income such as a pension, Social Security, or ongoing work income.

Those who buy or build as soon as they feel comfortable with a market, assuming they buy or build wisely, then have an asset to sell if and when they relocate. This can help fund the next leg of the journey. This takes more time, attention, and involvement than the rental strategy, of course, and it requires you to view anything you buy or build with a certain amount of dispassion. If you end up buying or building the house of your dreams, not only might you become emotionally attached to it, but you might also have trouble finding someone else with exactly the same dream when you try to sell.

Of course, combining these strategies is ideal. Rent until you know the intricacies of the market well enough to buy or build well. And if that day never comes, so be it. If you aren't comfortable with the market or you hear the siren call of another location before you sink money into a property, you're that much better off.

With either of these strategies—saving money on the front end or making money on the back end—you may be able to afford a series of moves if that's what you want.

2. Shed the Baggage

We've known many expats who, after finding what they thought would be their retirement paradise for life, packed entire shipping containers full of their personal belongings to bring with them. And there is absolutely nothing wrong with that if you know you're never, ever going to move again.

Having your own furniture, appliances, cookware, bedding, electronics, books, artwork, rugs, tools, workout equipment, craft and hobby items, and car can certainly make life more comfortable, and a new, unfamiliar location feel more like home.

This works to your advantage, of course, until you get the urge to try another location. Then all the furniture, appliances, cookware, bedding, electronics, books, artwork, rugs, tools, workout equipment, craft and hobby items, and cars start to feel like anchors.

The trick is to learn the difference between what you really need and what you merely want. Keep in mind that in almost any community in the world where you might choose to retire, you can get what you need very easily: a bed to sleep in, a chair to sit in, a pot to cook in, and an Internet connection to play on. Everything else is icing on the cake for a serial relocator . . . and if it was sourced locally, it's probably relatively inexpensive icing that can readily be sold or left behind to brighten someone else's life.

3. Understand the Difference between a Serial Relocator and a Perpetual Traveler

Serial relocation and perpetual travel may sound similar, but they differ in a fundamental way.

As many times as we've relocated, it's always been to *live* in a new and interesting location for long enough to experience real, on-the-ground, day-to-day life there. Perpetual travelers sometimes do the same thing if they stay in one place long enough during their travels, but the object of perpetual travel is to *not* get tied down to a specific location for too long . . . to remain a gypsy and never let grass grow under your feet.

What a true serial relocator wants is precisely that: the contentment of watching the grass grow. It's just that sometimes, like a true gardener, it's time for a little variety and maybe a new landscape altogether.

―――――

GOING BACK HOME: NO HARM, NO FOUL

The world is full of people who wish they were in your shoes right now, taking the first step toward a life-changing move. As we've said so many times in these pages, retiring overseas is an adventure. In most cases, it's a *remarkable* adventure and one you will never regret.

As we've also pointed out, there will certainly be challenges. That's why doing as much research as you possibly can makes so much sense.

If, though, you move overseas and find it's not what you expected, don't fret. As we've said, there are hundreds—if not *thousands*—of wonderful destinations in the world worth exploring. And if the call of home grows strong, you can go back home— no harm, no foul.

In fact, that's exactly what happened to our friends Jack Moss and Debbie McClosky.

In 2008, after doing lots of research about the great weather in the Andes Mountains and the affordability of living there, they made their first trip to Ecuador.

Jack had just retired as a Broward County commissioner in southern Florida, and Debbie would soon be retiring from her 30-year career as a county prosecutor and general magistrate.

"Ecuador met a lot of our criteria," Jack says. So just a year later, Jack and Debbie arrived in Ecuador with 10 suitcases and their six-pound Pomeranian, Gizmo, to start their retirement.

But these two are some of the least "retiring" people you might meet. They both threw themselves into local activities. Jack played bridge and served as president of the homeowners association— and even as the local warden for the U.S. embassy in Quito. Debbie volunteered with a local animal rescue group and taught English to schoolkids. They entertained and socialized frequently.

They loved Ecuador—and especially the low cost of living. But they missed living by the ocean. Most of all, Debbie missed friends and family—especially her college-aged children and her elderly parents.

Fortunately, they were in the right place at the right time. "The downturn in the economy and the blowup of the real estate market in southern Florida meant our timing was just right," Debbie says. "We could easily sell our condo in Ecuador and buy something very nice back home."

And that's what they did.

"But we took far more home with us than we brought," Debbie says. "We wouldn't trade our experiences in Ecuador for anything . . . nor the friends and memories we made there. We have absolutely no regrets."

Jack agrees. "And to offset our increased costs in the U.S.," he says, "we plan to spend at least a few months every year back in the Andes . . . probably during the heat of the Florida summer. What we save on air conditioning will go far in Ecuador."

THE ONLY REGRET YOU MAY HAVE . . .

No matter what you're looking for in your overseas retirement—better weather, better scenery, a lower cost of living, an exotic culture, a slower pace—there's no doubt you'll find it.

As Debbie McClosky and Jack Moss say, even though they decided to return to Florida, they have no regrets about spending their first years of retirement overseas.

There is, however, one regret that most expats share . . . and that's not having made the move sooner. Yes, you can retire better for less overseas—in a place with better weather and where your quality of life will be improved. Yes, you can retire earlier by moving overseas. But unfortunately, you cannot turn back time.

EPILOGUE

If We Knew Then What We Know Now

AFTER MORE THAN A DOZEN YEARS of living and working abroad, we've learned a lot of lessons about expat life. And we've heard many, many stories from people who have learned their own lessons from hard-won experiences.

Hindsight is always 20/20, of course; it's easy to see the missteps and wrong assumptions and miscalculations *after* you've made them. But that doesn't make those insights any less valuable—especially to those who have yet to make a move overseas. Learning from experience and passing on that knowledge is what this book is about.

So we'll wrap things up with some of those insights. After all, when we get together with fellow expats, one of our favorite games is, "If I knew then what I know now," and it can be very instructive.

So, let's play. If we had known then what we know now . . .

WE'D HAVE PROFILED OURSELVES A BIT MORE RUTHLESSLY

So many things fall under this heading. In the excitement of researching exotic locations and dreaming about new lifestyles, it's easy to overlook some seemingly small things that take on huge significance later on.

For example, you may have always dreamed of living in the tropics. We certainly did. But before you make the move, ask yourself how much you like heat and humidity. Really, *really* like it. Because that's exactly what you'll get in most tropical locations, all day, every day, all year round . . . until rainy season, when it gets even hotter and more humid. If we'd been more honest with ourselves, there probably would have been one or two places we shouldn't have lived. If your heat and humidity answer is, "I can take it"—as ours was—instead of "I live for it," you may want to be a little more ruthless in your self-assessment of how much you'll like the tropics.

How much does efficiency mean to you? We know more than a few expats who thought they'd enjoy a more laid-back lifestyle, but who never dreamed that this would also apply to the store clerks, customer service personnel, electricians, telephone installers, and plumbers they'd deal with in their new home. You may think you're a patient, laid-back person . . . until you've stood in a slow-moving line at a government office for five hours, or waited two weeks for a technician to show up to fix the refrigerator. That's the way things are in much of the rest of the world. Be ruthless: How patient are you, really?

Extend this ruthless self-assessment to everything in your life, even things that seem silly to you now. How much do you like chicken? In many places, it's the standard protein source and may only be served one or two ways in every restaurant you go to. Same with fish. Want to live at the beach? Unless you live in a tourist resort with lots of different restaurants, you'd better be a *real* seafood fan—24/7/365. If you're not . . . well, there's usually chicken.

Does it bother you to see trash blowing in the wind? Stray dogs? Beggars? We know expats who have moved back to the

United States because they couldn't tolerate the blemishes of a developing nation.

Have an addiction to a particular sport or team? Think about finding yourself in a location with no U.S. or Canadian TV channels, no English-language newspaper with a sports page, and no Internet fast enough to satisfactorily stream online content. Ask yourself if you can get your fix by reading a texted play-by-play on game day on your team's website—if it's available.

Shine the light on every aspect of your life. Then ask yourself how much it really, really means to you and how adaptable you'd really, really be if it changed drastically.

The most successful expats we know—and we count ourselves among them—have found that moving overseas forced them to reassess who they are and what they want from life. They've learned that, in the scheme of things, the small stuff doesn't matter much. Friendships and family bonds, even if tested by distance apart, become stronger and richer. Small moments, like watching the local schoolkids picking up trash, attending the first meeting of a new animal rescue organization, or seeing a neighbor offer a hot meal to an elderly passerby (and doing the same yourself whenever you can), are what matter.

WE'D HAVE BEEN EASIER ON OURSELVES

We've told this story before: When we arrived in Ecuador back in 2001, we figured we'd hit the ground running. Get as much done as quickly as possible. Open a bank account. Have the phone and the cable TV installed. Get the electricity and water switched to our name. Start up the Internet service. Buy a decent printer somewhere. Find the right printer cartridges for the printer. Find a good doctor and dentist. Get some gas delivered. Find the local market. Find the right coffee filters for the coffee maker. Find those little screws with the plastic sleeves for hanging things on cement walls. Find a decent drill for drilling the holes for those little screws. Find the right-sized bit for the drill for drilling the holes for those little screws . . .

By the middle of the second week, one of us (not saying who) was in tears. We'd leave the house with a to-do list of eight or nine urgent and incredibly important things to get done *right now*, and crash at lunch somewhere without having crossed a single item off our list.

That was years ago and at the very beginning of our adventures abroad. We had no idea about the often glacial pace of Latin American bureaucracy and no way to prepare for it beforehand. We had to learn to adjust.

We cut our daily to-do list down to one item and took it easy on ourselves. Lo and behold, we began to successfully complete our daily to-do lists. What an improvement in our attitudes!

WE'D HAVE SPENT MORE TIME ON THE GROUND BEFORE WE BOUGHT

We've said it before and we'll say it again: Try before you buy. Close up your house or put your stuff in storage and go see what it's really like to have boots on the ground. It may initially be a bit of money out of your pocket, but it can save you in the long run.

It's easy to pull the trigger on a property that strikes your fancy on a two-week exploratory tour, only to find that it's too close to party central during fiesta time, or it's close, but not close enough, to the neighborhood where you'd really rather be living.

Along with trying before you buy, we always recommend making your exploratory visit during the season of the year when the weather is considered the worst. Go during the rainy season; it turned out that this is our favorite time of year, when streets are washed clean and hillsides turn green. But who knew?

The point is that the longer you can spend on the ground and the more firsthand research you can do there, the better off you'll be.

WE WOULDN'T HAVE TRUSTED THAT GUY JUST BECAUSE HE WAS FROM THE STATES

It can be frustrating and exhausting to deal with all the details of buying property or looking for a good investment in a country

where you don't speak the language. Finding a cheerful fellow
countryman or countrywoman who is bilingual and happy to help
can seem like a blessing from heaven. You may feel so grateful
and relieved that you simply put all your trust in them and follow
any advice (and buy anything) they offer.

Remember, just because someone hails from the same country
you do and knows how your ball team is doing this season doesn't
automatically make them trustworthy. Take the same precautions
and practice the same due diligence in your purchases and business and investment dealings that you would back home.

WE'D HAVE DONE IT SOONER

This is the one bit of hindsight we hear the most from expats,
hands down. "We wish we had retired overseas sooner."

Recently we were at an *International Living* conference in
Quito, Ecuador, and had just listened to a presentation by a friend
of ours. She and her husband moved from the United States to a
tiny mountain town in the middle of Ecuador's northern Andes—
with their two sons, aged 9 and 12. She talked about the challenges
and rewards of becoming expats, with school-age kids, and at an
age when most couples were just hitting their career strides back
in North America.

Afterward, an attendee just past retirement age came up to us
and said, "You know, 30 years ago I was in exactly the same place
she and her family was. I wish I'd known then that the expat life
was even an option. I'd have done it in a heartbeat."

That's something we hear at every conference and from many
of the expats we meet. For many, their biggest regret about starting their new lives overseas is that they didn't do it sooner.

Now, of course, no one should simply sell everything and hop
on a plane on a whim, hoping for the best. A certain amount of
research is essential in making the right choice . . . or even in finding out if this idea *isn't* right for you.

But at some point, if the expat life truly calls to you, you need
to take action. Because time is the most precious commodity

you have, and if you don't use it, you truly do lose it. You can get money back, you can even go back home if it comes to that. But the minutes, hours, days, weeks, years that tick by while you wait to get everything just right, to dig up the last bit of info, to read just one more economic report, to watch just one more how-to video . . . that's time you never get back.

When we first were offered the opportunity to move overseas to work for *International Living*, we were admittedly caught off guard. It was what we wanted . . . but then the opportunity actually presented itself. We sat together one evening, talking and trying to decide if it was really a good idea to leave our comfort zone, to shed our current life, to shock everyone we knew, and make the move.

Finally we decided, if we do it and fail, so be it. We will at least have followed our dreams. If we don't do it, we'll never know what could have been.

Thirteen years later, we have absolutely no regrets about taking the fork in life's road that led overseas. We know exactly what could have been, and we've lived it and enjoyed it. And we can pretty safely say that if we'd done it 10 years earlier, we'd have had 10 more years of a most wonderful adventure.

So do your research. Make some decisions about where you want to go. Write up your checklist. Consult family and friends. Put your plan in place. Spend as much time as necessary where you think you want to move. Then . . .

Live your adventure!

What now? Let *International Living* help. Sign up for a free e-letter that will put you on the direct path to living better, for less, in your dream spot overseas. Each day you'll find an intriguing story in your inbox from one of *International Living*'s more than 200 correspondents across the globe. They'll give you insider tips and tricks for living a more comfortable, more exciting, more profitable life for less than you ever thought possible. Learn more at InternationalLiving.com.

INDEX